# From Deedle to Dr. Judy:
## A Memoir of Metamorphosis

## Judith Oppenheimer

Typeset in Minion Pro and Myriad Pro

ISBN 9781938366130 Paper
ISBN 9781938355123 Hardcover

Library of Congress

*To Neal,*
*So you may get to know me better*

—Mom

"My life is a life put together from all these lives:
the lives of a poet."

—Pablo Neruda Memoirs

# Prologue

It was 4:00 a.m. on July 16, 1945, the fresh air was fragrant with the rosiny smell of piñon and sage mixed with the bracing, clean scent of the New Mexico desert after a night of thunderstorms. These storms, however, had not been welcome and made it questionable whether the experiment would proceed on schedule.

They were about to test the first atomic bomb.

The site of the experiment near Alamogordo, New Mexico was called Trinity. After some heated discussions between the scientists on site and General Groves, who was the military head of the Manhattan Project, they decided not to delay the test.

My father Frank, and his brother, my uncle J. Robert Oppenheimer, huddled that morning in a dimly lit bunker with Ken Bainbridge, Robert Wilson, Robert Serber, and a host of other intense young scientists. While they waited, they smoked cigarette after cigarette. My father—thin, six feet tall, with uncontrollable thick black hair—paced and periodically rubbed his blue eyes as he waited. All the men scanned the horizon to a tower six miles away that held the first atomic bomb, "the Gadget."

The countdown began. *Ten. Nine. Eight.*

The scientists fell to the ground for protection.

First came the light. Its intensity was so great everyone was forced to look away. Seconds after the explosion, a scorching heat blanketed the young men. From their positions on the ground, they watched as an unearthly red, purple, and lethal radioactive mushroom cloud rose from what remained of the tower in the desert. At last, a thunderous sound fell over them, bouncing on the rocks, continuing its echo seemingly into infinity. After an indefinable time, during which the men themselves were braced and prone, silence at last returned.

The two Oppenheimer brothers turned to each other, and the words they spoke were identical. "My god! It worked!"

At five years old, I had no clue about any of this. All I knew was we returned from Los Alamos to Berkeley soon after Trinity to once again resume the days in my safe, special world where life revolved around school, picnics, and playing with friends.

But in my thirties, I wanted to get my father to talk about this momentous piece of his past and to coax from him some of his deeper feelings about it.

And so my father and I sat in front of a fire blazing in the large stone fireplace in my San José home. We began to talk, but as one tactful remark followed the other, I felt as though I could not penetrate this seamless wall. My father spoke calmly and thoughtfully, but all he seemed to do was volunteer information I already knew, showing very little emotion. I hadn't asked him point-blank whether he felt guilty, or if he had nightmares about the estimated three hundred thousand humans lives obliterated or the people sentenced to die in protracted agony in Japan. At that time, God knew I felt guilty enough for the two of us. After half an hour of gentle prompting, I rose and went to the kitchen to help Mother.

Several years later, I found myself in front of the television screen watching *The Day After Trinity*, a documentary produced by Jon Else and televised on TV's Nova series. As I watched, a comprehension of my father's relationship to that infamous August day began to dawn on me. Throughout the interview, my father rubbed his blue eyes. They brimmed with sorrow. At times, tears surfaced.

> JON ELSE: What was your own reaction to the news of what had happened in Hiroshima?
>
> MY FATHER: The announcement of Hiroshima, I think I was in the hall right outside my brother's office, and it came over this sort of loudspeaker that was distributed throughout—that the bomb had been dropped and that it had devastated Hiroshima. So the first reaction was "Thank God it wasn't a dud." But before the whole sentence of the broadcast was finished, one suddenly got the horror of all the people that

had been killed. And I don't know why, up to then, I don't think I really thought about all those flattened people. We had talked often about having a demonstration where there weren't people, maybe on the mainland so that the military would see it, but where there weren't any people. And then came the thought that they'd actually dropped it on a place where all those people were and the image of those people, which came before any pictures of it—the devastation—was really pretty awful. But the first thing was, I'm sure, "Thank God it worked."

It's amazing how the technology and tools trap one. They're so powerful. I was impressed because most of the fervor for developing the bomb came as kind of an antifascist fervor against Germany. But when VE day came along, nobody slowed up one little bit. No one said, "Ah well, it doesn't matter now." We all kept working. And it wasn't because we understood the significance of using it against Japan. It was because the machinery had caught us in its trap, and we were anxious to get this thing developed.

# 1
## The Memorial

For a long time I could not face and accept the fact that I was a member of a historical family—that my last name would forever signify something monumental and play a key part in a vast and harrowing history. I didn't realize it as a child growing up in Berkeley or Minneapolis or even as an adolescent in the mountains of Colorado. I simply knew that my father and uncle had helped create the first atomic bomb. In fact, I was often so embarrassed by the fact that I would not use my last name when I first introduced myself to peers.

The enormity of my father's fame didn't compute until the cold, rainy morning of his death on February 3, 1985. It was only then that I fully appreciated how much he had figured in history at the dawn of the Nuclear age. The whole world seemed to converge by telephone on my parents' Sausalito home, desperately clamoring to know more about him.

My family and I were overwhelmed with phone calls from reporters of the major newspapers. Calls from the *New York Times,* the *Los Angeles Times,* the *Washington Post,* and the *San Francisco Chronicle* clogged our phone line, insisting on speaking with us. As the day wore on, reporters from the newsweeklies like Time and Newsweek called. Local and national radio and TV stations wanted information about my father. I hadn't been at all surprised when my uncle Robert's death in 1967 had provoked such a surge of attention—but my father's?

With little energy remaining that day, after staying up the entire night of my father's death, I was vulnerable. The family (my stepmother, Milly; my brother, Michael; his wife, Jeanne; their two-year-old daughter, Kate; and my two-year-old son, Neal, and I) had just spent two weeks together, taking turns shuffling back and forth to hold vigils in my father's study which had been converted into a hospital room. My father, now only a skeleton of himself, lay on his hospital bed, getting weaker and weaker. For two days before his death, he was essentially unresponsive. The day he died the reporters asked personal questions such as "How is it to be the daughter of such a brilliant man?"

I merely ignored these questions, and the reporter was forced to either stop the interview or ask another question. I knew that if I started to answer such personal, private questions while being in such a fragile, brittle state, I might say things that could potentially damage my family. I knew this when immediately after my father died, all I could think of was how he had hurt Michael, Mother, his present wife, Milly and me. The first words emitted from my own mouth after his death were "Thank God he can't hurt anyone anymore," and I found myself still mute with rage at him.

I didn't know what to do with this almost-subconscious vehemence. I didn't know where to take it.

Then one month later, in March 1985, driving home to San José from San Francisco's Exploratorium after attending my father's memorial, I thought hard about what I'd just witnessed.

People had flown in from all over the world to attend, and I was overwhelmed by the tremendous turnout. Entering the cavernous space of the Exploratorium—an enormous hall usually filled with families interacting with the hands-on exhibits—my brother Michael and I started to wend our way down to our front-row seats. With friends and acquaintances stopping us to talk, to reminisce, and to give us heartfelt hugs and weep, it felt like it took us forever to navigate the course.

We listened to my father's colleagues and friends eulogize him, among them Robert (Bob) Wilson and Ed Lofgren.

My brother and I held hands and, occasionally as a reality check, whispered to one another, "That is not the man I knew."

The staff at the Exploratorium organized the entire memorial, and I was hurt, angry, and, quite frankly, baffled that my brother and I had not been asked to speak. Nor were we asked about what kind of memorial we might like for our father. I still don't understand how this happened, but at least now Michael and I can laugh about it. We quipped that the Exploratorium staff considered themselves his real children and therefore were entitled to make all the plans. It was as if we two had been born from a shadowy first marriage and, thus, weren't really important.

Most of the speakers cited my father's contribution to physics and his founding of the Exploratorium. No one talked about the witch-hunts of the 1940s and 1950s or about his ranching and his sheer resilience.

One woman talked about his love of music and art, and Jon Else, an independent filmmaker, touched on his playfulness when he recalled our father's constant humming and gave funny examples of how he hated the microphone. Jon recounted how our father discovered that if he placed his cane over the microphone's antenna, he could pick up radio stations' broadcasts. Suddenly, from out of nowhere, the soundman for a documentary in progress about the Exploratorium was treated to a Mozart symphony from KKHI or to an Oakland A's baseball game from another station.

Driving home on I-280 from San Francisco to San José, I didn't admire the mist rising from the Crystal Springs Reservoir, the fog bank hanging over the coast range, or the cattle peacefully drowsing in green meadows. That afternoon, I was watching an internal film, a private home movie, unspooling memories of my father.

At forty-two and forty-five respectively, Michael and I had now become the elders of the Oppenheimer clan. From then on, we only had each other to depend upon, to corroborate memories, and to remind each other exactly how helping initiate the atomic age deeply affected our father.

Sometime after the memorial, it began to occur to me: *I had a story to tell.* The awareness had grown larger. It now included the uncharted impact that the horrors of the witch-hunts (and subsequent exile) had on my parents' self-concept, their ability to trust others, to parent, especially in facing the challenges of rearing a daughter who had a genetic abnormality.

I wasn't interested in rehashing the "Oppenheimer story." That one's been told too many times. My quest is more intimate and more personal: How my parents, together with a host of other circumstance, shaped my life.

This is MY story, not theirs.

# 2
## The Beginning

I was born in Berkeley, California, on May 25, 1940. My father was a post doctorate fellow then working on the Cyclotron at the University of California, Berkeley.

For the first seven years of my life, my family and I lived what anyone could call an ultra comfortable upper middle class life. The streets of Berkeley were peaceful, leaf strewn, weather softened. It was a university town filled with tolerant, smart people who were politically active. From there, we moved to Minneapolis where my father was an assistant professor of Physics at the University of Minnesota. Our life in Minneapolis was equally peaceful until 1948, when my parents were persecuted amid the tide of the anti-communist *witch-hunts* later known as "McCarthyism."

After just two years, my father was fired from the University of Minnesota. He was unable to find a position in academia, and so we moved to live on a ranch near Pagosa Springs, Colorado which my parents had bought the year before as a vacation place. It was there that I grew up and came of age. It was on that same ranch that I formed my earliest perceptions of how people lived and worked. Looking back at those years, from age nine until I went to college at the age of eighteen, I realized that although they were difficult, both physically and emotionally, the years on the ranch were also uniquely nurturing and productive. I spent much of my time smelling the high-altitude air (quick with the ammonia-like smell of manure), caring for my cattle, and participating in haying and branding amid the clouds of dust. The scenery was one of vast meadows surrounded by snow-capped mountains. Many times it was the majestic view of the area that sustained me. The ranch years were lonely but also formative. The silence, the time alone with nature, not to mention befriending ranchers, storekeepers, and old-timers provided me with a rich palette of narratives—a much richer exposure than if I had grown up sheltered and closeted in a college- dominated culture. It is striking to me now that my brother and I lived a rather unusual and rich life—an existence that most children, then and certainly now, would never have a chance to experience or truly comprehend.

# Oppenheimer Family Gallery

## Section A

Julius Oppenheimer and Ella Friedman Oppenheimer

Father (on left) and his brother, Robert Oppenheimer as children

Ella Friedman Oppenheimer as young woman

Mother (on the right) and her sister, Jean

Young Phoebe Quann Mundell  (Mother's mother)

Father's Passport Photo circa 1948

Father at Sausalito table in 1970's

Michael, my brother in Berkeley garden (age 2)

Mother, Michael, and our dog, Richard, in Minneapolis

Me on trike with Michael in Berkeley Garden

Me holding Lollipop sitting with Richard

Me in snow—Minneapolis

Berkeley House

Berkeley Garden

Front of our house at 4454 Edmund Blvd in Minneapolis

Back of 4454 Edmund Boulevard

Original Cabin on the ranch (1949)

Original Cabin-Winter

View of remodeled cabin and Flat Top Mountain

# 3
# Body Language

Much of my life's struggle centered on my body and my inability to successfully do many of the physical activities that my peers were able to.

My awareness that I was different from other children reaches back to around age four or five. It began with the search for clothes that fit.

During the years we lived in Berkeley, my mother and I would make ritual treks to San Francisco during which I hoisted myself up on my knees in the car or in the train seat to catch a better glimpse out the windows, looking at the view of the skyline of the City—as its long been fondly known. I tried to count the sailboats and freighters scattered across the glittering water of the bay. Part of the lure of the day was meeting mother's friend Martha for lunch and then going to I. Magnin to shop.

I. Magnin was a sedate, upscale store on Union Square. Going through the revolving doors placed me into the glitzy, adult world of luxury. Upon entering, the air smelled of cologne and perfume. A tall woman gracefully curving her fingers as she tried on a pair of long, white gloves fascinated me.

My mother pulled me along gleaming glass cases full of cosmetics and jewelry to the elevator. Once inside, I gawked at the well-dressed women and panned for the mirrors that lined the elevator's walls. The white-gloved attendant who manned the brass-colored lever also intrigued me. Her musical voice announced each floor. We stepped through the glossy elevator door to emerge on the fourth floor. Mother kept holding my hand as she glanced around, seeking Adele, our favorite saleslady. And if Adele weren't in view, my mother would stride over to whatever saleslady was in sight and ask for her.

Mother and Martha would commence their reconnaissance mission, sorting rapidly through racks and racks of clothing. There was a metallic sliding sound as they pushed hangers along. I stood patiently by, but invariably, my gaze wandered. I then spotted several girls my age also shopping with their mothers. These girls were wearing pretty dresses. Some of the dresses featured smocking; others had been tied like gift boxes with satin sashes in perfect bows.

I tugged my mother's sleeve as I stood on tiptoes to whisper to her,

"I want a dress just like the one that little girl over there is wearing." Mother smiled. "It is cute, isn't it? Let's see if they have it in your size."

Like a genie, Adele, a tall woman with salt-and-pepper hair pulled into a chignon wearing a tired but kind smile, appeared. She ushered us into a plush waiting room containing velvety upholstered chairs with round seats and curved legs. There were large brass hooks and a huge three-way mirror. She asked Martha and Mother what they were looking for. She vanished for a few minutes and returned, both arms filled with a stack of stiff, new dresses. One of the dresses for me was fashioned of yellow seersucker. "Mommy, I love this dress. I have to try it on first."

We tried. But it couldn't be zipped beyond my waist.

Gamely, Adele left to find the same dress one or two sizes larger. I tried on the largest. It could be zipped, but the waist was much too long, and the neck gaped. Mother and Martha yanked and pulled at the neck. Mother continued to fiddle with the baggy dress, trying to determine whether the waist could be shortened and the neck tightened. Finally, she gave up.

"Judy, this is a cute dress, but it doesn't fit you."

The hook on the wall of the fancy dressing room on which we hung my rejected dresses grew and grew—almost at the same pace as my interest in shopping shrank and shrank. I was tired and deflated. I longed to get out of there, to go outdoors. At length, a measly few selections found their way to my "keep" pile.

However, that didn't conclude the ordeal. The alteration lady, Ruth, a stocky, no-nonsense matron sporting a tight brass-colored permanent wave, arrived with her pincushions and wooden measuring stick. She commanded me to stand on a small wooden platform. The orders started one after another and seemed never to stop.

"Don't slouch. Stand straight."

I did my best to obey but soon forgot and slouched again.

"Turn to the right," I clumsily turned to the left. Ruth frowned and restated her request. This time I spun in the correct direction. Over and over again the drill sergeant repeated her slogan: "Stop moving." Mother ordered me to pay attention to Ruth.

After what felt like hours, the pins were in place. In haste, I peeled off the dress, and if for a final flourish of hostility, a pin clawed my neck.

Typically, Martha and Mother would exit I. Magnin with bags filled with new clothes for themselves. I, by contrast, would have to endure waiting many weeks before my wardrobe became shortened or altered. As we left, I caught sight of the other little girls I'd originally spied now toting armloads of packages. Envious and somewhat ashamed, I pictured them modeling their new clothes for their fathers as soon as they got home.

At five years old, I learned that Mother was concerned about my size. She and her friend Molly Essene were sitting outside in our portico, drinking coffee. Molly's two kids (Eric and Karen), my brother, and I were playing on the grass near them.

I overheard Mother tell Molly, "I'm somewhat worried. Karen and Eric are so much taller than Judy."

I hung my head and blushed as she continued, "God, even Michael is as tall as Judy, and he's three years younger." I was devastated. These words confirmed once again that I was not like other kids.

A few days later, she was once again talking to Molly when I heard her say. "Judy's pediatrician has ordered a BMR." Molly asked, "What in the hell is a BMR?"

Mother explained it was a test for my thyroid; for my *basal metabolic rate*. She told Molly that I would have to breathe into a large machine. Instantly I envisioned a torture involving unimaginable pain. Fear and imagination turned the pending event into a colorful, meticulously detailed nightmare.

I panicked on the day of the test. The sanitary medical smell, the alien white walls, and shiny-waxed floors of Oakland Children's Hospital all telegraphed utmost terror to me. I started screaming and turned to run out the door. Mother caught me and carried me down the stairs to the basement where the test was to be done.

In the basement room, I stared at the gigantic machine to which they were going to hook me up. I started shaking. The huge silvery apparatus had every manner of knobs, inert hoses of all shapes and sizes dangling from it.

The technician, a gentle young woman, was able to calm me down by having me hold and manipulate the hose and the black rubber mouthpiece I was to breathe into. I still remember the odd *"clang clang"* sound the machine made as I took a breath. The taste and smell of the mouthpiece—a combination of rubber and antiseptic—can still, after seventy-some years, penetrate my senses.

The test revealed that my thyroid was a little low, and I was placed on thyroid medication for a while, but to no effect. My weight and height remained unchanged. All I knew was that my tummy was too round, my legs too stocky. Thinking of myself as fat, I complained about this. Mother and her friends told me that I wasn't fat, only chubby.

I knew I was plump; I still wasn't aware of how short I was. All I knew was that shopping for clothes was frustrating. It wasn't until much later when I was a pediatrician and looked at a photo of myself when I was five or six standing on our front steps next to our sitting standard schnauzer, Richard.

Richard was almost as tall as I.

It was only then that I understood, retrospectively, the gravity of my pediatrician's concern. As a pediatrician, I, too would have ordered a series of tests to help diagnose my patient's short stature.

# 4
## Berkeley

Mother, smelling of cigarettes and coffee, often took me with her on one of her petition-signing jaunts. When I was four years old Mother and I would frequently stand in the warm sun on the bustling corner of Shattuck and University, passing out political leaflets. I was dressed in a frosting-pink dress with darker pink smocking, and people of all ages and backgrounds were stopping to tell her about what a cute little girl she had.

This provided her opening.

Smiling, she quickly handed them a pamphlet and a petition to sign, passionately launching into the reasoning behind the *cause du jour*.

She cultivated other approaches, of course, including simply stepping into people's paths and greeting them with a dazzling smile and the innocuous "Hello. Would you like to sign a petition? We are sending it to several of the steamship companies to try to get them to increase the wages of the longshoremen."

This was her element: out on the ragtag Berkeley street, campaigning for progressive humanist causes. Very often she and a passerby would strike up on long, sometimes heated conversations. If the target stopped but was not sympathetic, she would try everything in her power to convince him or her of the justice of her cause.

"You realize that in spite of working forty-or sixty-hour weeks, the dock workers barely can make a living wage." She might begin briskly in a tone that seemed to assume the listener's intelligent, automatic, even conspiratorial agreement with this reasoning. "Many of them have children and are barely able to provide food for them."

One passerby would reply, rather huffily, "Ma'am, they should have gone to school. They don't deserve any more than they are making. You're nothing but a stinking Communist." The people who argued with her scared me, and I tried to hide behind her.

Many people agreed with her. Longing to feel important and to participate with people as smartly and confidently as she did, I asked my mother if I could give out some leaflets. She placed one in my hand. But when the next person stopped to talk, shyness intervened, and I made no attempt to give a leaflet to them.

Nonetheless, one of the letters I later found among those my mother had written to my father while he was doing research on the atomic bomb in Oak Ridge, Tennessee, made it obvious that my political training had begun:

> *Judy and I were playing house yesterday, and she was the mommy and I was the daddy. At one point she came in with a purse and said. "Come on, we're going out." I asked her where we were going. She said, "We're going to a union meeting. You see, we both work."*

Another important element of my upbringing was developing a love for classical music.

My parents' record collection contained a large repertoire of classical music, and if the strains of Mozart, Bach, Telemann, and others were not serenading us from the record player, my father would take up his flute and play for an hour or more. Several of his friends and colleagues also played instruments: piano, violas, oboes, and cellos. Many times after dinner, they played classical music. Sometimes I was up to see them play, but more often I was banished to bed by the time the soothing harmonies of their chamber pieces wafted up to my bedroom where they lulled me to sleep. Throughout my life at home, I often woke up to my father's flute music.

Not only was I surrounded by music in our home, but I was also treated to live ballets or children's concerts. One of the ballets that persists in my memories was a production of *Peter and the Wolf*. I remember that the chandeliers in the lobby of the San Francisco Opera House looked to me like lighted jewels.

The women wore impossibly dramatic gowns in rainbow hues, and they sparkled with diamonds and emeralds. The men, to me, looked a bit like penguins in their black suits or tuxedoes. I myself was dressed in a blue coat and beret. My hands were warm in a white rabbit- fur muff. Under my coat, I wore my best silk dress made of a soft cream- colored fabric decorated with abstract patterns of yellows, roses, blues, reds, and greens. It had white rickrack around the neck and puffed sleeves. The gathered skirt flowed gracefully from the waist where a broad sash was tied in a perfect bow in the back. With my white socks and shiny black Mary Janes, I felt like royalty.

Inside the lobby, I instantly spotted a novelty counter with small pet turtles and chameleons for sale. I begged my mother to buy me a chameleon. I was ecstatic when she did. The tiny creature was the first of many small pets: turtles, lizards, and other chameleons.

Once we entered the theater, I couldn't stop staring straight up at the dome with its burnished gold-and-red patterns. What a fairy-tale palace!

During the performance, which engrossed and delighted me all the way through, my newfound reptile friend changed colors as he rested on my shoulder. I sat on one of my parents' laps or on my knees in my seat so I could see better. And I stayed awake for the entire performance. Driving home tired, cozy, reverberating with all I'd seen and heard, I felt as though I'd been initiated into a magical, adult enchantment: that of the opera house.

Another of the wonders of my early childhood was the fact that my parents were irrepressibly social. There seemed no end, during all those Berkeley years, of a stream of friends flowing through the house or departing it for kid-oriented outings. They had many friends and acquaintances. Mother and I would often meet her friends and their children for lunch. Many times the kids would come over to play with Michael and me. Just as often, our parents would leave Michael and me with a sitter and sail off to dinners, parties, or to political meetings.

They had many enormous, boisterous parties.

I recall one in particular; I must have been five or six. In the sunny kitchen of our Berkeley home, Mother and her friends were cooking, gossiping, and laughing. They stood cutting, stuffing, and beating eggs for various dishes. They smashed avocados for guacamole. The kitchen became more raucous as everyone now and then would take a sip or two from strategically placed wine or brandy glasses. At five o'clock, wine was replaced with an Old Fashioned or martini. The kitchen smelled of cooking— pies or cakes, roasts, and other succulent prizes. At seven, the guests began to arrive. Coats and purses quickly made a wool mountain on my parents' bed. On occasion, Michael and I would crawl onto this soft fragrant pile and roll around and laugh. Before the guests arrived, Mother would give us our dinner and then shepherd Michael and me to bed. I knew there would be no bedtime stories.

From my room, I heard the music: a nonstop mélange of polkas, swing, waltzes, tangos, and rumbas. I crept out of bed to the top of the stairs, trying to keep out of sight while I spied on the adults. Ladies' shoes by now were scattered near the walls and at the bases of chairs and couches. Rugs were rolled up and pushed to the sides of the room. Record albums spun out every kind of dance music, and the whole party seemed to be on the dance floor at once. Mother loved to polka. I watched as she and my father would energetically canter across the room, laughing and talking. The sight made me breathless. I thought they were the best dancers there or anywhere. The records those days were all 78rpm. Most played only five to ten minutes of music on each side. The moment a record finished, someone would shout, "Change the record!"

Still later in the evening, my father and a group of his musician friends grabbed up their instruments and formed a circle of chairs to play classical music together—an instant chamber music ensemble. My father, the flute player, stood tapping his foot to the rhythm, his eyes open wide, his brow furrowed, nodding and conducting as he played. Guests listened thoughtfully with real pleasure in their eyes.

How sad I felt when I was discovered at my spy post and sent back to bed.

In Berkeley, life was gentle and secure. Even the usual stresses of early childhood didn't mar my general happiness. It was a time when my father was my hero. Often my mother would get Michael and me ready for bed and then the three of us would drive to collect my father at the radiation lab where he was a postdoctoral fellow working with E. O. Lawrence on one of the first cyclotrons. In a half-dream state, with the light of day fading, I would snuggle up to him or my mother, who was holding Michael, as we navigated the winding road that lead from the radiation lab to home.

In Berkeley, both my brother and I were indulged, showered by almost any toy we wanted.

On Christmas 1944, I found a brightly papered present under the tree. It was decorated with small sprigs of a fir boughs tied into the bow. Tiny sleigh bells fastened to the package jingled when I moved it. The tag read, "From Daddy to Judy—Merry Christmas."

I tore open the package to find a large clay piggy bank. Gaily colored flowers decorated its terra-cotta body. I was dazzled. It was one of the best presents in the world, certainly among the best that Christmas. Throughout the year to follow, my parents remembered to donate much of their loose change to me to drop into the bank.

Filling the bank became a wonderful ritual. It became heavier and heavier as the coins accumulated. I often shook it as the year progressed. As the vessel filled, leaving less and less room for the coins to slosh around, the sound became quieter and quieter.

One day, I was trying to figure out how to extract some money when my father walked into my room.

"Judy, leave the money in the bank. I've a plan for the money that's going to be a surprise."

I jumped up and down.

"What's the surprise?"

"If I told you, it wouldn't be a surprise," he said, smiling.

One morning at breakfast just before the next Christmas, my father said, "Judy, I thought you and I would take the ferry to San Francisco, have lunch, and use the money you have in your piggy bank to buy presents for Michael, Mommy, and your friends."

We arrived at Union Square, which was brilliantly festooned with bells, a giant tree, lights, oversized ribbons, and flocking everywhere—a child's Christmas dream. It was a gorgeous San Francisco December day. We had lunch in Chinatown and began our shopping spree. In the first store we entered, I selected some presents: a little toy car for Michael and a small doll for my friend Karen.

As we went to the counter, I asked, "Daddy, how're we going to get enough money out?"

He looked at me a little tentatively. "We have to break the piggy bank."

At this, my joyful spree was almost smashed to smithereens. My face must have first registered shock, and then began sliding down. I started to cry.

My father, who must have been ready for this tirade on my part, acted quickly. "Don't worry. I promise I'll buy you another almost exactly like this one. We'll do it all over again next Christmas."

I flinched as he broke the bank with a small hammer that he brought with him for the task. It made a horrendous noise.

The coins too, made plenty of racket, rolling out along the glass counter, many falling to the floor. I picked them all up as carefully as Easter eggs and counted them out to pay for my purchases. Carefully, I deposited what was left into my small purse, and my father and I left the saleslady with the job of cleaning up the remaining pieces of the broken piggy bank.

Before the day had ended, we stopped at one more store in Chinatown where I selected a scarf for my mother, and true to his promise, my father purchased a new piggy bank for me to start filling for next Christmas. This ritual continued until I was seven and we moved to Minneapolis.

Another bright memory of a charmed childhood occurred on my sixth birthday. I rushed downstairs to see what presents my mother and father had gathered for me.

The table in the breakfast nook was covered with flowers and presents.

I tore open the presents and was disappointed to find only books and clothes. Mother then led me into the living room. Michael and our father followed. On one of the tables was a brown phonograph with the word *CAPITAL* on the lid. With a sharp intake of breath, I rushed over to the magical box and gingerly opened its fragrant leather-covered lid. My father plugged it in and showed me how to start it. He'd already placed a record they had just bought for me on the spindle. My friend Karen had the same record, *Dumbo,* and I loved its humor and the dramatic background music.

My own phonograph! The magic machine also ran on a battery and with a hand crank. I could play it in my bedroom and even take it where there was no electricity. I dreamed of a picnic where I could take my new phonograph. The opportunity presented itself the very next weekend. We headed for the Berkeley hills for a picnic with my new phonograph. My father helped me through the barbed wire fence, into a rolling green field. Mother spread out our blanket and began to retrieve the food from the picnic basket. I had just begun to play my records in the pastoral atmosphere when, apparently out of nowhere, a tall, gangly, sour-looking man approached. He yelled at my father to get the hell off his property.

After a brief argument with the rancher, my father shook his head and shrugged his shoulders. He was clearly annoyed. We struggled back through the fence and set our picnic up just outside the rancher's fence line. Michael was crying and I was afraid.

"Daddy, are you sure that man won't come back? He seemed so mad."

"Don't worry. We're no longer on his land. He can't do anything to us."

My father knew everything. I relaxed. I wound up my phonograph and resumed listening. Besides my own children's records, *Babar* and *Dumbo,* I listened to two of my favorite singers: Burl Ives singing "The Foggy, Foggy Dew" and Paul Robeson singing "The Four Insurgent Generals." These, and many of songs in those two singers' repertoires, soon became my favorites. My brother and I tried to sing along with the music. The rancher's cattle wandered to the fence to watch us eat. They too seemed to enjoy the music. Their tails seemed to swish back and forth with the beat.

One day many years later, just before Christmas—long after my magical phonograph was gone—I drove up to my house in San José, California, and noticed a big box from my brother sitting at the front door. I opened the box, and the very first thing I spotted was the word *CAPITAL.* Hardly able to contain myself, I gave a loud shout of glee that reverberated throughout the house.

Somehow my bother had found the exact model of the very phonograph I had owned as a child. He had restored it to working condition and sent it to me as my Christmas present.

Many of my parents' old 78rpm records were still stored in my garage, buried in dust and cobwebs. Lovingly, I cleaned them and, with my heart racing, placed them each in turn on the little machine's turntable. I then telephoned my brother, put the receiver next to the phonograph, and played him the same Burl Ives and Paul Robeson records I had played in that field so long ago. Their scratchiness didn't dampen the excitement. We both laughed in delight.

In 1944, my father spent most of his time in Oak Ridge, Tennessee. There he was involved with others in purifying uranium into an isotope that could be used for the atomic bomb.

Before he left Berkeley, he had promised me that he would write to me often. He did.

Every day, one of my first activities was to scamper to our mailbox to scour its rusty interior for a special letter from my father.

The letters that arrived served as a kind of witty, expurgated journal of his day, clever and lively as a children's book, combining his own hand- sketched drawing with little snatches of writing and captions in between.

Whenever I received one, Mother read it aloud to me. Soon, though, I was almost able to read the letters on my own. I carried them around to show off to my friends, Karen Essene and Judy Shirek. They particularly loved the drawings.

Another memory from my Berkeley days was that of Mother, her friend Jane Wilson, and me sitting in a red leather booth at the famous St. Francis bar in San Francisco. They talked and drank their martinis or Old Fashioned. As was the manner of the times, each had mastered the art of speaking with a cigarette roguishly pasted to a lower corner of their mouths. The air in the St. Francis bar, like every bar in that era, was filled with cigarette smoke. At length, I noticed Jane and Mother had stopped talking.

Jane nudged Mother and whispered, "There are two FBI agents watching us."

Popping the shiny-sweet maraschino cherry from my Shirley Temple into my mouth, I tried to follow their gazes. *Who or what was an FBI agent? And why would they want to spy?* From the two women's voices, I could tell at once that these weren't friends.

As an adult, I have often wondered how they managed to recognize them. Did the men wear uniforms then, like young Mormon men on their missions? Were they the well-groomed types with immaculate blue suits, narrow ties, and white shirts, sitting nonchalantly with their cigarettes at the bar? Or did they masquerade as jocks with crew cuts in sports coats, huddled over their drinks in the booth next to ours?

Nothing was explained to me about it at the time. But once I was older, Mother told stories about the games that she and her friends played whenever they suspected their phones were being tapped or agents were tailing them. In the 1940s, technology had not yet been sufficiently advanced to permit noiseless spying. Each time the FBI listened on the phone, for example, a very audible click announced their presence. Whenever they heard this signal, Mother and her friends almost enjoyed it. They set about with dramatic energy to discuss the most mundane things: vacations, children's shoes, and the cute things their kids did that day.

I'd always assumed my mother had exaggerated. It was only many years later when I sat at my desk at home in San José reading my parents' FBI files, which I had obtained through the Freedom of Information Act, that the sledgehammer hit me. Her stories had in no way been exaggerations. The FBI surveillance of my parents began at least as early as 1941. Their snooping continued straight through until the late 1960s when my parents were living in Boulder, Colorado, where my father was a physics professor at the University of Colorado. Many of the entries had large portions redacted (blacked out). Most of the redacted portions appeared to be names. There are many pages I did not receive. In verbatim quotes from the FBI files, these pages were "deleted under exemptions B-1 with no segregable material available to you." I have no idea what B-1 means. I assume it is some security code indicating that the repressed information was so volatile that even after sixty or more years, the government still deemed it necessary to keep it secret. The following entries were made when my parents went on a vacation in Mexico. I've read and reread this data, uncertain whether to rage, laugh, or weep. The physical description of my parents suggests some sleazy fashion magazine reporter's scribbling on the sighting of a celebrity. Comments in the brackets are my own.

| | |
|---|---|
| Name: | Frank Oppenheimer |
| Nativity: | New York City |
| Birth date: | August 14, 1912 |
| Age: | 33 |
| Height: | 5'll" [in reality he was 6'0"] |
| Weight: | 145 |
| Build: | Slender |
| Eyes: | Blue, prominent, large |
| Hair: | Black, very long, stuck out all around his hat, is curly |
| Dress: | Light blue necktie, bluish suit with lighter blue stripes; pants appeared to be without cuffs and a little short; black homburg-type hat, which sits on top of his head with wider brim than ordinary |
| Characteristics: | Walks with a lope |
| | |
| Name: | Jacquenette Oppenheimer |

| | |
|---|---|
| Birthdate: | Nov. 15, 1911 |
| Nativity: | Vancouver, BC |
| Age: | 34 |
| Height: | 5'4" |
| Eyes: | Believed to be blue. Hair straight brownish- blonde , worn up over ears tacked back with bobby pins and curly only on ends, which rests over neck in back. |
| Characteristics: | Sloppy appearing, wears no makeup, very ordinary looking |
| Dress: | Dark navy blue suit made of natural material; red sweater used as blouse with V-neck; carried WAC-type bag hung over left shoulder; black shoes with 1" strap on back of heels; black tam-type hat, which her husband was carrying; flat tam-type with bright white and other colored beads on top. |

The files then go on to describe my parents' activities while at the airport.

3/21/46

Dr. Frank Oppenheimer and wife arrived Los Angeles, California, January 17, 1946 at 1:05 P.M. by Western Airlines Flight 105, and departed 9:50 P.M. same date by Pan- American Flight 81, en route to Mexico City. U.S. customs search resulted negatively. Observation failed to disclose any contacts by Oppenheimer in Los Angeles. On return trip from Mexico City, Feb. 5, 1946 the Oppenheimers arrived at Los Angeles 11:03 P.M. from El Paso, American Airlines, Flight 91, and immediately thereafter at 11:45 P.M. departed for San Francisco via United Airlines, Flight 579. San Francisco advised.

No contacts observed in Los Angeles. . . .

> A United States Customs search of the luggage and personal effects of the Oppenheimers was conducted with negative results; however, it was noted that the Oppenheimer luggage contained the following books:
>
> "Obras Completas de Miguel de Unamuno–Vol. Quatro
>
> "Una Historia Pasion"– Abel Sanchez "Women and Children First"–Sally Benson "A Practical Spanish Grammar"––Seymour and Smithers
>
> "The Student's Dictionary, Spanish-English and English-Spanish."
>
> "Life and Works of Abraham Lincoln, Early
>
> Speeches" ––Centenary Edition
>
> "Arc of Triumph" ––Erich Maria Remarque
>
> "Neuro-Anatomy"– Kuntz

I looked at this list of books, chuckled to myself, and thought, *What vacation reading material!*

At some point in my life, I came to realize that my parents were not the only ones selected for the FBI's surveillance. Many other families endured similar monitoring, often leading to ugly upheavals of their lives. In those years, raw fear filled the air, and a large portion of the population became civil liberties crisis.

In 1943, my life in Berkeley had in the meantime, encountered a different brand of fear and difficulty.

I was three. My parents were giving one of their parties in the apartment above our garage. The room was bustling with women helping set up for this event. I slowly walked up the stairs to the apartment carrying two long baguettes of French bread. Mother stayed behind me to make sure I didn't fall. I had just relearned to walk after my hospitalization for encephalitis, a serious viral infection of the brain. This proud ascent was the first time I had been able to climb stairs on my own. I reached the top and broke into a huge smile. I cried out, "I did it!" Everyone clapped and then hugged me. My accomplishment was important evidence of my recovery. I can imagine how relieved my parents must have been.

Full recuperation wouldn't prove so swift. Though I once again was able to climb steps, I continued to have frequent falls whenever descending. I solved that problem for the interim by learning how to slide down on my butt.

Looking back, I'm sure that my genetic abnormality played a large part in my clumsiness. However, an even more important event undoubtedly played a large part in my lack of coordination. Not too long before this triumphal event of climbing the stairs I had undergone a routine tonsillectomy and didn't waken from the anesthesia. My temperature soared to 104–105 degrees, and for ten days, I remained in a deep coma.

During their lives, my parents enjoyed telling the story of my waking from my coma, and they told it often. Apparently, I heard a dog bark in the distance and suddenly opened my eyes and said, "Bowwow." In fact, my illness was discussed so often that I'm not sure which portion of this period of my life is composed of real memories, which might be simply be a collection of stories imprinted on me at an early age. One thing is undeniable: every time my parents told the coma story, their joy and excitement surged in their faces and voices and their gestures. It was all my father could do to suppress the tears. Mother's hazel eyes would go wide and pained and then lapse into the softness of deep relief as she spoke of my awakening. From their reports, I have painted a child's mental picture:

> *From total darkness, my three-year-old eyes*
> *open. I am in a bright, sunny hospital room.*
> *Slowly, I look around. I am in a white crib with*
> *the side rail down. Mommy sits next to me,*
> *holding my hand. Daddy paces. I hear a dog*
> *bark in the distance, and I answer, "Bow Wow."*
> *Mommy jumps up and hugs me. Daddy rushes*
> *over. He also hugs me. Tears welled from their*
> *eyes. They are smiling, almost dancing.*

While telling the story my parents never mentioned the light hospital room. I believe this to be one of my earliest memories.

At first it wasn't clear what caused the coma, but after many tests, my doctors told my parents I had a form of encephalitis. Years later, after I became a pediatrician, I wondered in retrospect if I might not have contracted a mild case of paralytic polio.

In kindergarten and grade school, I frequently sat on the edge of the playground while my classmates played on the monkey bars or rings. I never could master them. Even the jungle gym presented a challenge for me. I never could run as fast as my friends or classmates either. In a letter my mother wrote to my father when he was in Oak Ridge, she noted,

> *I took Judy to UC today for an IQ test, but she didn't want to play games. Her teacher, Miss Gardiner sort of gave an analysis of Judy, too, which I thought was alright [sic], but also which I thought was inadequate, Miss Gardiner admitted as much, too. It seems Judy's greatest lack is in large motor activity and her greatest value is her social adaptedness. However, not many seek her out as a playmate but I claim she doesn't give a damn. She is a little too interested in her own activities to put out for others.*

Life in Berkeley as I knew it was about to end when, in 1945, we briefly moved to Los Alamos, New Mexico, where my father was involved in the final stages of developing the atomic bomb. After Trinity, we did return to Berkeley where my father continued his research fellowship at the cyclotron. However, nothing seemed the same. In 1947 when my father's research fellowship ended, he accepted an assistant professorship at the University of Minnesota.

As February 1947 drew to a close, I remember my mother sitting with me at the breakfast table. Her face and eyes wore a mournful expression as she told me that we were going to move far away to Minneapolis, Minnesota. I began to cry. I couldn't imagine being separated from my friends Karen and Eric Essene, Judy Shireck, and my cousin Janet.

"Why do we have to move? I don't want to."

Mother reached out to hold my hand as she said, "Daddy's job here is over, and he really wants to do something new. In Minneapolis he will be able to do the kind of research he is interested in, and he also will be teaching graduate students."

She paused to take a sip of coffee and puff on her cigarette. "I don't want to move either, but we'll all make new friends."

That night, I tossed and fretted. The next morning, convinced that if I pleaded long and hard enough I would prevail in convincing my father not to move, I confronted him. I told my father that we just couldn't move.

We just couldn't.

He tried to explain. "Judy, we have to. I'm not too interested in the work I'm doing here. In Minneapolis, I can do the kind of work I want to do and I can teach."

He smiled as he tried to reassure me the move would be an adventure, and I would make new friends. I didn't believe him.

With a gleam in his eye, he added, "There will be snow and ice in Minneapolis. We can sled and ice-skate and sit by the fire sipping hot chocolate."

I relaxed a little.

*It might be fun to learn to ice-skate.*

After what seemed an eternity of urgent preparation, moving day came.

My last childhood memory of our house at 148 Tunnel Road was making a final sweep through its empty rooms to make sure we hadn't left anything. Without our furniture and Michael's and my toys, the rooms' floors seemed weirdly naked, marked where heavy object had stood or worn grooves where foot traffic had concentrated. The house looked stripped, huge, foreboding. Our footsteps echoed throughout the entire house as we walked toward the door. After Mother locked the door, she said very quietly, "I loved this house." Her voice tightened. "One thing for sure, I'll never have another garden like this again."

I know now that it was best that none of us could foresee how right she'd prove to be.

We piled into our green DeSoto convertible where Richard, our Schnauzer, was waiting and headed for the Claremont Hotel, where we stayed while my father finished his work at the radiation lab.

From reading my parents' FBI files, I learned that the FBI knew about our route to Minneapolis even before we left Berkeley.

> (Redacted) Advised that Frank Oppenheimer and their two children moved from their 148 Tunnel Road home to the Claremont hotel where they stayed from Feb. 25, 1947 until March 1, 1947. They departed from Berkeley on March 1, 1947 en route to Minneapolis, Minnesota, by automobile. They planned to spend a week en route at Death Valley, California and were accompanied on the Death Valley trip by (redacted) probably the Robert Serbers).

By the time we reached Minneapolis, the FBI stooges were already on the scene.

> March 15, 1947
>
> To: Director, FBI Dear Sir,
>
> Reference is made to my teletyped message of March 6, 1947, concerning the scheduled arrival of the above-captioned in Minneapolis, Minnesota, March 15 instant. Please be advised that the subject arrived in Minneapolis on the evening of March 14, 1947. He is currently residing in Suite 122E, Curtis Hotel, Minneapolis, with his wife and two children.
>
> An attempt was made to cover subject's significant contacts by means of loose physical surveillance; however, because of the physical difficulties encountered by the hotel setup, this has not been feasible. Bureau authorization is therefore requested for this office to install a technical and microphone surveillance on the present residence of the subject. (FBI Files)

Authorization for the surveillance was soon granted. While waiting for our new house, we moved to an apartment in the King Cole Hotel. Two months later, we moved into our new house at 4454 Edmund Boulevard. The house was a stately four-story brick mansion situated across from the banks of the Mississippi. Before we moved into the house, the FBI had also tried to bug it.

Director, FBI

May 24, 1947

This is to advise that it is not feasible at this time to install instant technical surveillance and monitor same from our consolidated plant (blacked out) as originally planned at the time the authorization was requested.

For that reason it is believed at this time that instant technical installation should not be made.

It is my recommendation that this office for the time being continue to cover the activities of Oppenheimer by spot surveillance through our existing confidential coverage and by means of informants at the University of Minnesota who know Oppenheimer and are closely following his experimental activity in connection with nuclear energy. (FBI files)

The FBI was completely ignorant about what my father was doing. For starters, he no longer was working directly with nuclear energy. Instead, he was working on discovering the nature of the high-energy particles that came from outer space—cosmic rays. After reading the transcript, I wondered, with a strange mix of anger and curiosity, who the informants at the University of Minnesota were.

The move to Minneapolis proved an irrevocable turning point in all our lives—particularly for my mother. The Bay Area was her womb. She attended both high school and the University of California, where she earned an equivalent of an AA degree in social work. She had developed strong friendships in Berkeley. Berkeley and the San Francisco Bay Area were a vibrant ongoing hotbed of leftist progressive politics. She became deeply involved in this, active in supporting the unions, especially the ILWU (International Longshoremen and Warehousemen Union) and other progressive causes.

The Minneapolis political environment, of course, was much more conservative, and she found it difficult to locate others who felt as she did— those who were simpatico with her. Too soon, she learned she had little in common with the faculty wives or academia in any meaningful way. To increase her unhappiness, my father spent most of his time at work. Mother felt useless and lonely. Throughout our two-year stay in Minneapolis, she made no secret of yearning to return to the Bay Area. Her longing was a silent but perpetual condition among us, almost like a force field she projected. She spent more time at home and entertained only when my father insisted. She stopped her political activities and vented her frustration by arguing with my father.

In the beginning I didn't mind being in Minneapolis. I met new friends and fell in love with my first grade teacher, Mrs. Marshall. Somehow I learned where my teacher lived, and on several occasions, my new friend and neighbor, Susie Greenberg, and I made pilgrimages, crossing the bridge from Minneapolis to St. Paul to visit her. Mrs. Marshall was always welcoming and gave us snacks and juice. Today I marvel at the woman's hospitality and at our chutzpah.

It was in Minneapolis that we all became acutely aware of my physical limitations. Evidence was pointed. In the winter we drove to Nakomas Park with our sleds. My father and I also brought our ice skates. Whenever I found myself sledding too fast, I developed the method of either dragging a foot or simply rolling off. Michael, who was three years younger, of course, repeatedly won our brother-sister races. After a time, I'd stop sledding and ask my father to take me skating. He tightly laced my new white skates, and we'd head for one of the frozen streams that were in the park. This part of our winter outings never failed to thrill me. We laughed as we zigzagged around the heads of fish frozen in the ice. Holding my father's hand, I felt safe and graceful. But whenever I tried skating on my own, no matter how much concentration I poured into being successful, I fell. My father's strong hands hoisted me up, and I felt safe again.

I eventually was able to at least remain upright while I was skating, and one winter, my father flooded a portion of our backyard to create a skating rink. Friends arrived, and refreshments were produced—steaming cider, hot cocoa, and cookies. We skated for hours. I recall adoring the sight of the brilliant red cardinals silhouetted against the white snow.

During our neighborhood skating parties, my friends gained confidence and began performing figure eights and skating backward. Yet I wasn't able to.

Skating lost its fascination.

Gradually, I began to realize it was not only sledding and skating that I couldn't master.

I was excited when I received my first bicycle, a shiny blue Schwinn, for my eighth birthday. The pedals had extra blocks of wood on them so I could reach, and for days, my father valiantly ran beside me as I tried, heart pounding with increasing desperation, to learn how to balance and pedal at the same time. Every single time he let go, I fell. The bike was so heavy; my father had to help me pick it up. The scraped ego and knees didn't help. I was so frustrated with my inability. Every time I fell, tears would flow. The final blow to my learning to ride a bike at that time came when my father, in a spasm of exasperation with my crying and whining, yelled at me. Anguished, frustrated, and feeling I'd failed my father as much as myself, I wept. The bike was put away forever.

In no time at all, of course, Michael was zooming along on his new bike. How I envied him.

I kept feeling that only if I tried harder, everything would be okay. With a powerful sense of denial or blindness to my problems, we kept pushing forward to find something physical that I could do.

A new project was selected: ballet.

And another memory appears—that of a modern Degas scene in the ballet studio, where a palate of leotarded little girls and I, fidgeting and giggling, lined up at the barre. Every time I looked at myself in the mirror and compared myself with the others, it was almost comically obvious that I didn't fit. The other little girls in the room were thin and tall and had necks like those of a swan. Their hair was blond and straight, arranged in a bun in back. I was short and stocky with curly brown hair. When the piano music began (*was it a phrase from a Chopin waltz?*), the other girls moved away from the barre and glided across the polished floor in what I perceived to be perfect unison, each using the correct foot, placing their hands in a graceful arc.

I never knew what foot to use and instantly fell out of step with the music. When each lesson was over, my mother, who'd arrived to collect me, gently asked me what I learned. I couldn't remember a single step to demonstrate for her. I was dragged back to these lessons two or three more times, more and more sadly and reluctantly. Naturally enough, I began to dread going. My mother and the maestro finally agreed that ballet was not for me.

It seems fairly astounding when I consider the predicament now that neither of my parents could acknowledge the fact that their daughter's lack of coordination might suggest a significant problem. Apparently, no one was connecting the dots.

Initially, my father was extremely happy with the Minneapolis move. He truly reveled in teaching at the graduate level and enjoyed his gifted, earnest students. He felt tremendous enthusiasm and optimism about his cosmic ray research, which involved sending something called a cloud chamber that was attached to a huge balloon into the stratosphere. These terms and activities thrilled my a brother and me not least because my father did his best to describe them in ways we could grasp.

During the first year in Minneapolis, he would often take my brother and me to work with him. This too provided an enormous thrill, though all I now recall of the campus is that it had wide, clean, tree-lined pathways and large expanses of grassy areas. I do remember how exciting it felt to climb a flight of stairs then venture down a dark narrow hallway to my father's office—a secret lair. He loved showing us everything in his office and lab, proudly introducing us to each of his colleagues. We learned about oscilloscopes, Geiger counters, soldering guns, and other magic tools— exotic and powerful. Everything fascinated me, but the most marvelous thing was a three- or four-foot silver sphere—the cloud chamber. My father explained that inside the ball, the air was like a cloud. He produced some photos for us to examine, showing all kinds of white lines that seemed to float across them. He told us these paths were made by very tiny invisible specks (high-energy particles) that came from outside the earth and that the lines appeared in the same way we left footprints while walking in the sand. He called them cosmic rays. My father and his colleagues launched these balloons throughout northern Minnesota.

Michael and I stood agog at the pure magic and mystery of it. It was like glimpsing ghosts in photographs. We talked about these pictures for days.

I have since created a mental picture of my father and his fellow physicists dressed in suits and ties, speeding down some rural Minnesota road in our huge wood-sided Chrysler convertible, screeching into some farmer's driveway like a fire brigade rushing to put out a fire and trying to explain to the farmer or his wife that a balloon with important equipment had landed in their field and the scientists needed to retrieve it. Or maybe they merely drove to the field, and while they were gathered their material, the farmer came and asked them what the hell they were doing.

# 5
# Cataclysm

*Everything changed for us forever in the summer of 1947.*

It began as an innocuous country getaway. Trying escape the heat of Minneapolis, my family decided to spend three weeks on a lake in northern Minnesota with the family of one of my father's colleagues, John Williams. The Williamses and their kids had the cabin next to ours. The wives and kids were to drive up first, with John and my father to follow in a few days.

The place sounded, in description, like a summer paradise. I could scarcely contain my anticipation. After a few days packing, we left Minneapolis to head north.

The air was considerably cooler than that of Minneapolis. I loved the smell of the piney fresh air. The shimmering lake loomed—vast, pristine, and surrounded by deep woods. Small cabins dotted the shore. They looked like toys from a distance. Many, including our own, had small docks jutting out into the water. We were always busy. We spent countless hours swimming or running on the beach. There were pebbles to collect, sand forts and waterways to build, minnows to chase, and the sun's warmth to bake us when we lay on the softened old wood of the pier.

The days felt long, lazy, and utterly peaceful. Our only connection to the outside world was the phone in a cabin down the road.

When my father and John joined us after the second week, my world felt complete. Both parents were with me.

Then in the middle of the first night that my father was there, I heard knocking on the door. Mother bolted upright.

"Frank. What's that?"

The knocking grew louder.

"Oh. Damn it. Someone is at the door. Where in the hell are my pants?"

My father rummaged in the nest of clothes at the side of the bed.

The knocking grew impatient.

"Just a minute. I'm coming," he called out in an exasperated voice. He opened the door a crack and peered out. "What do you want? It's after midnight."

The man from the cabin with the phone was at the door. In a sleepy somewhat irritated voice he said, "Phone call for you. Somebody from Minneapolis."

My father's voice sounded worried as he turned to Mother and said, "Who in the hell could be calling at this hour? It must be important. I'd better go answer it."

"Here, take the flashlight."

My mother then followed him to the door.

She stood leaning against the door as the moon silhouetted my departing father.

"Mommy, what is it? What's the matter?" I had crawled out of my bed.

"Oh, nothing. Go back to sleep." She did her best to sound nonchalant.

I climbed into bed with her. She didn't complain.

I tried to stay awake waiting for my father's return but eventually fell asleep. I woke up when he lifted me out of their bed and tucked me into mine. I fought to hang on to the cozy sleep, but my parents began arguing. Their arguing scared me. Didn't they like each other anymore? They sounded worried. I closed my eyes and pretended to be asleep.

"Come outside, Jackie. No point in waking the kids."

The two of them went out on the porch and started talking loudly and angrily. I tiptoed to the door and hid. I peeped out to see Mother shaking. In a loud voice, she said, "For Christ's sake, Frank. What in the hell were you thinking? How could you have told him that we hadn't belonged to the Party?"

"I was so taken by surprise that I couldn't think."

"Frank, you know if you start lying to them, they've won. You should have told him 'No comment.'"

"I know. I know. I could kick myself."

I heard my father's footsteps reverberating on the wooden porch. He had a cigarette in one hand and rubbed his eyes and his forehead with the other. He was pacing back and forth, back and forth.

Mother continued talking, and my father continued pacing. I crawled in bed with Michael and fell asleep with visions of my father pacing, pacing.

The next morning, my father quietly told me that he had to drive back to Minneapolis. No further details were provided, and the tone of his voice indicated that he was not at all happy about leaving.

As he moved toward the car, I held on to his leg to stop him from leaving. I began to cry. "You can't leave. You just got here."

Mother came up and gently took my hand.

"You'll see him very soon. We're going back to Minneapolis in a couple of days."

My father drove off. Our parents told us nothing more.

For many years, I assumed that it was the FBI that had called that night. However, shortly before my parents' deaths, I learned that the midnight phone call was from a reporter from the Minneapolis Star who was following up on an article that had appeared in the Washington Times- Herald.

The next day, July 12, 1947, the *Minneapolis Star* featured an article quoting the *Washington Times Herald* of the same date.

> The subject (Frank Oppenheimer) was accused with prewar membership in the Communist Party.

Again quoting the *Times Herald* the *Minneapolis Star* article continued.

> The House Un-American Activities Committee headed by Representative J. Parnell Thomas, which previously supplied information concerning Frank Oppenheimer's alleged Communist Party membership to give official confirmation. But the Times-Herald then went on to say that Dr. Frank Oppenheimer, under the name of Frank Folsom, held Communist party membership in 1937–1940. It is asserted in the Washington newspaper story that Dr. Frank Oppenheimer retained Communist Party membership during the years between December 7, 1941 and August 1945.

Upon arriving back in Minneapolis, my father made what was to be a fatal mistake. He told university officials, who had naturally made a beeline for him to ascertain the facts, "I am not and never have been a member of the Communist Party."

For the rest of his life, my father would wring his hands and lament, "I wish I hadn't lied to the reporter and the university."

Perhaps my parents had some premonition of the future, but I had no notion at the time of the hurricane that was about to engulf my parents and our family. We had all started down the road to exile.

# 6
## Return to Minneapolis

Still deeply tucked inside the soft cocoon of a child's perceptions, I wasn't aware that anything had changed when we returned from the lake. My friends and I still clambered on the old stone wall in the median across from our house. We still raced off to the park to swim in Lake Nakomas. August days were filled with the dreaminess of summer and its immediate pleasures: lemonade to quench our thirst after play, the mechanical sounds of hand-driven lawn mowers and scents of cut grass, the way the light filled the heavy green leaves of the maples and oaks along the wide hot streets. But by the time school had started and the temperature dropped and those leaves had begun turning to pale yellow and bright orange, I'd begun to realize that nothing was the same. My parents seemed distant, sad, preoccupied. They didn't smile or laugh anymore. I detected a new strain in their voices whenever they were talking to each other. New words and terminology popped up in their conversations—words of acronyms I only half-understood or didn't understand at all: "HUAC," "lawyer," "Communist," "FBI," and "fired." My parents closeted themselves behind doors with strangers bearing briefcases. They had distracted, agitated expression on their faces. Mother no longer read bedtime stories to Michael and me as she had every night for years. Often our parents yelled at us for things that never had bothered them before. No longer did my father squire us on special visits to his office.

My isolation and confusion were augmented by the fact that the heavy drapes were always drawn. I remember a dark house, a house silent and still—a house no longer packed with visitors, lunches, and spontaneous outings. There was no more excited play with my father's colleague's children, no laughter, no parties, no sense of warmth and joy. Mother told me the curtains were drawn to keep out the summer heat. As I look back, I see the closed curtains so clearly— floor to ceiling, a deep beige linen with heavy white linings, dusty and not admitting a speck of light. The curtains now seem a perfect metaphor for the new funereal era of our lives. Mother could no longer face the outside world. The curtains acted both as a symbol and a reinforcement of her depression. The heaviness of my parents' worries so permeated the house that I, too, began to worry. Although my thoughts still had no name, all the easy, lively order and security of my childhood flew away like the color of the autumn leaves.

The country was under siege. The American witch-hunts were in full force. One favored ploy of the hunters was using the tactic of guilt by association, whereby anyone associated with a suspected or known Communist was deemed to be a Communist sympathizer. The news that the FBI was investigating my parents spread quickly, and in the paranoid atmosphere of the day, many of our acquaintances and former friends started avoiding us. Vera and John and their kids, frequent visitors to our house before we went to the lake, simply stopped visiting. Other families also shied away from us. They might say hello nervously in the grocery store or on the street, and then very quickly, with embarrassed faces, they'd disappear.

On occasion we still saw Ed and Lenore Lofgren and their kids, but otherwise the Oppenheimers' social calendar was a barren, dying tree.

One night I heard Mother talking to my father, "Frank, I'm so lonely. We've become real pariahs. God, I wish we could move."

Even though my mother did plant some bulbs and trimmed the lilacs, her garden no longer offered a place for solace and creativity. The house became a shadow house where no one was welcome. One of her most predictable responses to my asking friends over was "Oh, Judy, not today. I really don't want to see the *Williamses* or the *Lofgrens* (or anyone else I suggested). I just can't face them at this moment."

My father received the same response whenever he tried to have people over for drinks or dinner.

"Damn it, Frank. Why do you keep insisting that we entertain those phonies? They'll turn on us like everyone else when the heat is on."

I began to hear one of Mother's other mantras. "I don't think we should bother them. They're probably busy with friends." This mantra stayed with me for years, causing me to be afraid to reach out and to trust.

My father buried himself in his work even more deeply than normal. He would leave early in the morning and wouldn't return home until long after Michael and I had gone to bed. We rarely saw him, and when we did— to our surprise and bewilderment—he basically ignored us or yelled at us. The patience and joy that he used to show with our childish enthusiasms— the gentle jokes, the twinkle—all were gone. Instead, he gave us a constant sense that we cluttered his path. Before the possibility of a subpoena to appear before the House of Un-American Activities Committee (HUAC) presented itself, casting its heavy ghost over the routines or our days, my father tolerated many of our childish pranks. If Michael and I attempted to blow through a straw into milk or water, he used to laugh and join us. After the subpoena, he would invariably get extremely angry and send us to our rooms.

At other times he admonished us with unkind words. "Quit whining. I've told you a thousand times that you can't come to work with me today." Or "Judy and Michael, calm down—be quiet. Can't you see I'm busy?"

The summer of 1948 was the first time I remember being afraid of my father's anger. We were spending our summer vacation in Nambé, New Mexico, with two other couples, Jane and Bob Morrison and Phil and Emily Morrison.

At times, we four Oppenheimers ventured off on our own, leaving the rest of the group behind. I loved these interludes. During these forays we spent time looking for horses for my parents and scouting for property we might possibly buy as a summer retreat.

One day I remember my father asking, "Would you like it if just you and I went looking for horses this weekend?"

Two days alone with my father! The day he and I left to drive to the Red River valley near the New Mexico-Colorado border, I skipped with elation to the car. Had the laws of gravity permitted, I would have floated.

We spent the day traveling through countryside filled with roiling streams and lush meadows, looking at horses and ranches. We talked and laughed. That night we stopped at a 1940s-type motel. I stayed in the car while my father registered.

Our room was compact, clean, and had one double bed.

"Daddy, there's only one bed!"

"I know. We can both sleep in it."

"I don't want to sleep in the bed with you without Mommy."

"Don't be ridiculous. You're going to sleep in the bed with me. It's Ok."

"Let's get a room with two beds."

"They don't have a room with two beds."

"Let's find another motel with a room with two beds."

With each minute of each exchange, my anxiety increased. I started to cry.

"Judy, what in the hell is wrong with you? Stop crying. Get ready for bed. I'm tired and want to sleep."

My father's face became contorted as he glared at me. He kept shouting. I had never seen him so angry. I huddled in a corner sobbing and thinking, *I'm not going to sleep in the same bed with him.* He came toward me, picked me up, and placed me under the covers. Once in bed, I continued sobbing silently, all the time thinking about how much I hated my father. I had wanted him to listen to me. I wanted to go home to my mother.

My father fell asleep, and I moved from under the covers to spend the rest of the night at the foot of the bed.

What I recall about the night, what seems most disturbing, was the supreme power struggle involved, concluding with my defeat. At the age of eight, I could have no insight into why I panicked. Reflecting now, probably missing my mother and some gesture or word on the part of my father initiated the fear and my reluctance to sleep in the bed with him. I now realize that although there were never any overt sexual advances, my relationship with my father was psychologically incestuous. And though I was only eight, I think that I must have intuitively sensed some of this.

When I was four or five, my father would gently pass his fingers through my hair. I didn't mind. It was a sign of his love. But as I approached adolescence, his stroking my hair began to make me uncomfortable and fearful. From that point on, I continued to cringe, to move away whenever he tried to touch me or stroke my hair. My father's hands, stroking my hair, my neck, became a symbol of his seductiveness, his power over me. I began to see my father as a cruel fisherman whose siren song—eerie, dangerous, yet demanding to be heeded—needed to be avoided.

When I was in my thirties, my father continued to try to stroke my hair. As usual, I moved away.

"Why don't you like me to stroke your hair? It's not as if I want to have intercourse with you."

These words stunned me. I was speechless, angry, and frightened. I couldn't believe what he had just expressed. Here was my father, a man who usually kept his deepest secrets and wounds hidden away, suddenly allowing his personal monsters to come to the surface.

I remember realizing that I hadn't really been crazy for all these years. I had been right to take evasive action.

# 7
# The Wallace Campaign

In the fall of 1948, my mother found a cause that would allow her to once again feel useful and hopeful. She became furiously active in the local Henry Wallace campaign committee. Henry Wallace had been vice president of the United States during Roosevelt's third term (1941–'45). In 1948, he mounted a campaign for president running against President Truman and the Republican candidate, Thomas Dewey. My parents were elected as delegates to the state convention of the Democratic-Farmer Labor Party that had endorsed Wallace for president over Truman.

I was eight years old.

As I shuffled through drying leaves on my way home from school with a group of classmates, one of them asked, "Who are your parents voting for?"

"Henry Wallace," I answered. "Who are yours voting for?"

"For Truman," she said.

"For Dewey," piped another.

The kids must have heard that my parents had been Communists and begin to taunt me.

"Traitor!" "Communist!"

"Why don't your parents just move to Russia?"

I tried hard not to cry and started to run as fast I could to get away from them. When I arrived home, tears were streaming down my cheeks.

I ran into the kitchen where Mother was preparing dinner. She saw my tears and came over. She bent over to put her arm around me and looked into my face. "Judy, what's the matter?"

"Some kids were really mean to me today. They told me we should go to Russia because you and Daddy are voting for Henry Wallace."

Mother's face turned red; she started trembling with fury. I could see her fighting for control as she walked over to the counter and began to assemble my favorite sandwich—peanut butter and mayonnaise.

Once composed, she began. "Judy, don't let the other kids bully you. They're just copying their parents who are ignorant bastards." She once again hugged me and handed me my sandwich. She then sat down beside me, cross-legged, cradling her cup of coffee and a cigarette drooping from her lips.

For an eight-year-old, this reasoning didn't offer much consolation.

"Why can't you just vote for Truman or Dewey like everyone else's parents? Then the other kids would like me, and I'd have friends. Why do you and Daddy have to vote for Wallace?"

"We're voting for Wallace because he believes in letting workers get together in groups called unions. Unions help workers be treated more fairly by their bosses."

"Don't Truman and Dewey believe the same thing?"

"Truman claims he is for unions and workers' rights, but some of the things he's done makes me think that he really doesn't care about them. Dewey thinks that there shouldn't be unions. Wallace in the only one who will help the workers."

"Is that the only reason you and Daddy are voting for Wallace?" "No."

She spoke gently, carefully, "I don't know if you've noticed that people we used to have as friends are avoiding us. This is because from 1936 to 1940, Daddy and I belonged to the Communist Party. We quit because it wasn't achieving what we had hoped." She paused to take a sip of her coffee. "People are so damned afraid of Russia that anyone who was ever a Communist is now considered dangerous to be around. Just being friends with someone who was a Communist is like being near a person who has a cold. It's contagious. They worry that just because we were their friends, the FBI and others would consider them communists too. It's called a witch-hunt. Truman and Dewey think this is okay."

"Why is being a communist so bad?"

"I don't think it is, but some people think that they want to take over our government."

"If you knew that some people thought it was a bad thing to do, why did you join the Communist Party anyway?"

"Because in many ways we agreed with the party's ideas of helping the poor, and they were the only ones who were helping fight against Francisco Franco, a bad man who rules Spain."

I tried to absorb this.

Mother stood up to get another cigarette for herself and some milk for me.

"Are there any other reasons why Wallace is better than Truman?" "Truman allowed the military to drop the A-bomb on Japan, not just once but twice. Daddy and I were angry that the bomb killed so many mothers, children, and others not involved in fighting."

"Didn't Daddy and Robert help make the bomb?" "You're right. They did."

"How could Daddy help build something that killed so many people?"

"He and many of the others who built the bomb ask themselves the same question every day. Now he's trying to make sure it is never used again."

Mother had given me a lot to think about. At some vague level, I sensed what sat most heavily on my shoulders was the fact that I had to face my classmates the next day. I was eight and wanted to belong. If only my parents could be like other kids' parents.

# 8
## Hearings

My parents were subpoenaed to testify before HUAC (the House of Un-American Activities Committee) in June 1949. When they began talking about going to Washington, DC, I remembered our trip there the year before. My father was going to a meeting of the American Physical Society, and Michael, Mother, and I traveled with him. While my father was at the meeting, We wandered the city, taking in the most famous sights. I thought the city completely magical. Pink blossoms had blanketed the cherry trees like frilly tutus. And at the Mall, the reflecting pond was crystal clear, the water still. Shimmering in the water were perfect mirror images of the Lincoln Memorial and the Washington Monument. I held my mother's hand as we walked up the broad steps to the Lincoln Memorial.

I had desperately wanted to return, but this time Michael and I weren't invited. I cornered my mother and asked, "Mommy, why can't I come with you on this trip? Mike and I went with you last time, and we all had fun."

Her face was taut, and though she struggled for an even tone, her voice too was grim. "Judy, this trip will be very different. We have to spend a lot of time with some men answering questions. We won't have any time to spend with you. It's best that you stay home. We'll only be away for three days."

I cried. I stamped my foot. I pleaded. I sulked. Nothing worked to get my parents to take me with them. Our housekeeper and friend, Electra (we called her E) stayed at our house to take care of Michael and me.

Years later, I went to the Bancroft Library at the University of California, Berkeley, where my father's papers were archived. Browsing through his papers, I came across his opening statement to the committee.

I believe that we have to win our security and our permanence by the way we live and by the strict adherence to our national principles. War is a poor gamble for us today....Wherever such a conflict exists, I favor the course that will increase the respect and not the fear with which the world views us....Even in the face of international tensions which are growing today, it is my active hope that the scientific and technical developments which have lead to the release of atomic energy will materially facilitate the solution of the social problems of war.

In the transcriptions of those sessions that I've been able to obtain, the committee never once asked my parents to talk about their reason for joining the party or their loyalty to America. Instead, the committee members kept looking for connecting ties, trying to implicate other people who may or may not have been members of the party. Louis J. Russell, senior investigator, did much of the questioning. Another member of the committee was Richard Nixon.

| Mr. Russell: | Are you acquainted with Frank J. Malina? |
| --- | --- |
| Dr. Oppenheimer: | Yes, I remember that name. |
| Mr. Russell: | Do you recall in what connection you were acquainted with him? |
| Dr. Oppenheimer: | I do not wish to talk about the political ideas of affiliations of any of my friends, but I knew him in Pasadena. |
| Mr. Wood: | I can't hear you |
| Dr. Oppenheimer: | I knew Mr. Malina in Pasadena. |
| Mr. Harrison: | He said he did not want to talk about the political affiliations of any of his friends. Is that what you said, Doctor? |
| Mr. Russell: | Mr. Chairman, Frank Malina is a very important subject to the committee, and perhaps I can refresh Dr. Oppenheimer's memory in some respects on his association with Frank Malina, after |

|  |  |
|---|---|
|  | which I would again like to ask if Frank Malina was known to him as a member of the Communist Party. Mr. Wood: It is a simple question, Doctor, whether you knew him as a member of the Communist Party. |
| Dr. Oppenheimer: | It is a very simple question, but I feel I know nothing evil of Mr. Malina. I know of no evil act of Mr. Malina and do not want to discuss his political opinions or affiliations. |
| Mr. Wood: | That is not an answer to the question. |
| Dr. Oppenheimer: | I can assure you that if there were there any acts of Mr. Malina of which I knew were inimical to any laws of the United States, I would have reported them. |
| Mr. Wood: | If you know if he was a member of the Communist Party, or not or was known to you as a member of the Communist Party at any time, can you answer that? |
| Dr. Oppenheimer: | I do not want to discuss that. |
| Mr. Russell: | Your preference is not an answer. Do you refuse to answer? |
| Dr. Oppenheimer: | I cannot answer that question |
| Mr. Wood: | But we must have an answer to it one way or the other. The question is very simple. Do you know or did you know him as a member of the Communist Party? |
| Dr. Oppenheimer: | I cannot answer that question about him. |
| Mr. Wood: | You mean you don't have the necessary information to answer it, or do you decline to answer for the reasons you have stated? |

| Dr. Oppenheimer: | I must decline to answer because of the reasons I have given. |
| --- | --- |
| Mr. Wood: | Because of your preference not to discuss the political affiliations of him or anybody else. Is that right? |
| Dr. Oppenheimer: | Of any people I know who have not committed any illegal act. |

While my father testified, Mother sat in the witness waiting room, forced to deal with her own thoughts alone. I can envision her smoking one cigarette after another as she waited for her time before the committee. After the hearings, she told my father of a phone conversation she had with one of her friends.

> They kept me waiting and stewing for hours in the outer office while they questioned Frank. It was an open hearing, but even so, they wouldn't let me go in. They said, "Madam, you are a witness." So I just sat in the outer office and listened to all the scuttlebutt and reading their literature: *100 Ways to Tell a Communist in Education, 100 Ways to Tell a Communist in the Church, 100 Ways to Tell a Communist in Labor.*
>
> The house committee is in a wonderful building with marble walls. It is surrounded by beautiful parks, carefully kept grounds, and is quite lovely. But as I sat there in the office, I looked out the window across the street and saw the rows of tumbledown houses. The little kids, most of them Negroes, were running around in the street barefoot. They looked ricketic [sic] and undernourished. All they had to play with was junk they found in the street. As I sat there reading and looking

out the window, I found myself alternately worrying about what the committee was going to try to do to me and getting madder and madder at the fact that I had been called down there so some fellow could question ME about being un-American. How do they stand it day after day to go on with their questioning and sit there looking out the window?

Once she entered the hearing room, her ordeal was the same as my father's:

| | |
|---|---|
| Mr. Russell: | Are you acquainted with Brownlee Shireck? |
| Mrs. Oppenheimer: | Yes |
| Mr. Russell: | Was he known to you as a member of the Communist Party? |
| Mrs. Oppenheimer: | I would rather not testify as to his political beliefs. |
| Mr. Russell: | Have you ever been a member of the Communist Party of the United States? |
| Mrs. Oppenheimer: | Yes. |
| Mr. Russell: | For how long a period? |
| Mrs. Oppenheimer: | From 1937 until the spring of 1941. |

These interrogations went on and on.

At the time, I had no idea what my parents were enduring. All I knew is that for reasons that I didn't fully comprehend, they had not taken me with them.

I can now imagine my father sitting in the witness chair, trying to look strong and confident but at the same time rubbing his forehead, his eyes, and if allowed to, smoking one cigarette after another. If it had been possible for him to do so, he would have paced up and down the aisles. I can see my mother also smoking, shaking with anger and fear. I can see her looking at her lawyer, Cliff Durr, for reassurance and willing herself to become a rock, hard and unyielding in her answers, thinking, *I'm not going to let these sons of bitches get to me.*

On the day that my parents were scheduled to arrive home from Washington, I kept asking E, "What time is it? How long before Mommy and Daddy come home?"

"It's ten o'clock. I think they'll be arriving soon after lunch."

I must have asked her the same question every fifteen to twenty minutes.

The morning crawled. Lunchtime finally came. I was so excited that I barely ate my bologna sandwich and banana.

After lunch, I began my vigil. I sat on the steps in the front of the house with Michael and my dog, Richard. There I waited, scanning both ends of the streets looking for my parents' cab to appear. I spent what felt like hours counting the cracks in the sidewalk, watching busy ants, listening to the distant bark of a dog. When the yellow cab finally came into view I was excited and with my heart pounding, Michael and I raced down the brick steps to the sidewalk. Mother emerged looking for the most part as she usually did, but tired and drained.

Opening her arms, she hugged and kissed us.

I looked back at the cab, expecting my father to materialize as well.

He didn't.

I didn't understand.

"Where's Daddy?"

"Daddy had to stay to talk more with some of the people."

"Why?"

"Because when they asked us questions about other people, he and I didn't answer them. They wanted him to stay so they could ask him more questions."

Mother and I trudged up the outdoor steps to our front door. I waited downstairs as she and E took my mother's suitcases up to my parents' room. That was when I heard her tell E that my father might have to go to jail.

The year before when we were visiting Washington, DC, I had overheard my parents talking to their lawyer, Clifford Durr. Although he was fully supportive of their decision only to talk about themselves and not answer any questions about anyone else, he told my parents that they could go to jail if they refused to talk about others. This time when my mother said that my father might end up in jail, I became frantic. I couldn't imagine it—my own father in jail. I had visions of him behind bars in a dungeon, his hands grasping the bars, his face sad and hopeless, not being able to talk to us.

My mind rocked and pitched.

*Will I ever see him again? How are we going to survive without him?*

"Mommy, I heard what you just told E. Will Daddy go to jail?"

Quickly, she knelt to hold me. She took me in her arms and cuddled me. After a moment, she murmured into my hair, "I don't think so. We will have to see."

Dazed, I asked, "Why doesn't he just answer the questions?"

"He can't. It would be like tattling on friends and other people. If he answered questions about other people, it could get them into trouble."

Silence descended on our fears like a gray cloud then, and there it sat—opaque, bursting with unreleased energy.

In time, to our inexpressible relief, we learned that Congress was not going to pursue the threat of citing my father for contempt of Congress. He came home two days later. I never learned why the contempt charges were not pursued. I'm not even sure that my parents ever knew.

Perhaps it was because the committee felt they had achieved what they had set out to do in the first place—destroy my father's career.

Even before the hearings, my father knew that his job had been irreversibly compromised. The chairman of the physics department, Dr. Buchta, had made it clear that depending on the outcome of the hearings, my father had two options: either resign or be fired. On June 14, 1949, the day of my parents' hearings before HUAC, the St. Paul Dispatch ran the following article.

> A local paper today [the St. Paul Dispatch] carries the story that the subject [my father] admitted before HUAC today his membership in the Communist Party while he was at CalTech. Attention is directed to an AP dispatch dated July 12, 1947 in which Oppenheimer categorically denied allegations of Communist Party membership. According to the news today, Oppenheimer stated that he and his wife, Jackie, joined the Communist Party in 1937 in his own words, "Seeking an answer to unemployment and want in the wealthiest country in the world." Oppenheimer and his wife dropped out of the Communist party three and a half

years later because the Party did not accomplish their objectives. He stated: "During the period of our membership neither I nor any of my friends did anything inconsistent with the welfare of our fellow man. Contrary to the belief that now has wide acceptance, we made no commitments and had no interests inconsistent with the complete loyalty to this country and its government." (FBI Files)

After the hearings, my father sent a handwritten note offering his resignation.

> *June 1949 [no day on note]*
> *Dear Professor Buchta,*
>
> *After a great deal of thought it seemed to me best to tender my resignation as a member of the University of Minnesota faculty.*
>
> *The events of the past years have placed both the university and myself in a position where my continued employment at the university might confine and endanger the strong stand it has persistently taken on all matters relating to academic freedom.*
>
> *I therefore tender my resignation not with any sense of guilt, but with a deep regret in order that the university may be free to avoid any embarrassment that the controversy of my appointment might cause.*
>
> *Sincerely*
> *F. Oppenheimer*

When my father lost his professorship at the University of Minnesota, he had no other job prospects. As an interim solution, my parents decided to spend the summer on our ranch near Pagosa Springs, Colorado. They had bought the 830-acre ranch the year before in 1948 while we were vacationing in Nambé, New Mexico, a small community just north of Santa FeeThey had already planned to spend many of our summers there, and my father felt that in addition to a vacation, he would be able to continue his job search..

On our way to Colorado, we detoured five hours to a site in northern Minnesota where my father was launching his last cosmic ray experiment. His colleagues had already done most of the preparations, and it was not long before the balloon was ready for launch. The one-hundred-foot-long balloon soared into the air, looking like a huge jellyfish with a silver sphere masquerading as it tentacles. The late afternoon sun hit the balloon's surface, creating colorful waves. After the balloon was aloft, my father's colleagues, Ed Lofgren, Ed Nye, and others rushed to their cars to follow their payload.

As my father's final balloon disappeared over the horizon, he looked at Mother. "I wonder if I'll ever be able to do such meaningful experiments again."

I noticed tears beginning to fall from his eyes as he turned and slowly walked to the car. The car doors slammed, and we headed west to our new ranch and an uncertain future.

# 9
## First Summer on the Ranch

It took us two and a half days to drive to Colorado. Our entourage consisted of Mother, Michael, and me driving in our wood-sided Chrysler convertible. My father was in our Studebaker pickup hauling a horse trailer with the two horses we had bought the year before when we were in Nambé, New Mexico. We stopped at Pagosa Springs to buy necessary supplies. Pagosa was a small town with a population of 1,500. With one main street that was also the main highway from Santa Fe, New Mexico, and Durango, Colorado, there wasn't too much to explore. The buildings fascinated me. Pagosa looked like a frontier town in the Westerns Nana (my great-grandmother) used to take me to in Minneapolis. It even had some hitching posts. The exploration of the town only took a few minutes: one or two cafés, several bars, a small hotel (Hotel Pagosa), a drugstore (Jakish Drugs), an old-fashioned general store (Hirsch's), and a clothing store (Goodman's). Most of the vehicles were Chevy pickups or sedans. Small groups of people stood on the sidewalks or leaned into car windows, talking. Whenever a car drove by, friendly greetings were exchanged among those in other cars or on the street.

With our goods purchased, we drove for a while when we came to a sign proclaiming **Blanco Basin Road—National Forest Access.** We turned off onto a gravel road, and because of the dust we all instantly began to cough and have burning eyes. We slowly inched our way up Harman Hill. From the top I saw vast expanses of meadow below. Beyond the meadow, the Blanco River could be seen shimmering between the cottonwoods and willows.

Carefully, we made our way down the road into the basin where snow-capped peaks that reached fourteen thousand feet above sea level surrounded a lush green valley floor on three sides forming a majestic open-air cathedral.

I was entranced. We all were. During our time on the ranch, I would often be looking out the window or walking through the meadow only to catch my breath at the majesty of the scenery. The scenery helped all of us survive for the entire time we lived on the ranch.

By the time my parents, six-year-old brother, Michael and I finally arrived at the ranch, we were sweaty and covered with dust.

What stood before us was a small shingled structure with a wood walkway connecting to an even smaller building. Both were situated at the edge of a large meadow that was framed on one side by cottonwoods and willows lining the river. The cabins looked like playhouses. I felt a bit deflated. How were we going to survive in such a small house?

In Berkeley where I lived until I was seven, our home was a large Spanish-style house surrounded by my mother's yard filled with flowers and fruit trees. A high white stucco fence protected what I thought of as my magical secret garden.

In Minneapolis, we lived in a literal mansion, a large four-story turn-of-the-century brick house on the banks of the Mississippi river. The Minneapolis garden wasn't as special as the one in Berkeley, but it did have lilacs in the spring, and my father made wonderful leaf houses for us to play in every fall.

Today, I look at pictures of those Colorado cabins and realize our new home was a metaphor for the drastic change our lives were about to undergo.

We unloaded our horses, Paint and Alamosa, into the small pasture between the house and the barn. They ran off, releasing large clouds of dust and a lot of pent-up energy.

After watching the horses for a minute or two, I was anxious to explore our new home.

While my parents began to unload the furniture, Michael and I ran through the cabin. With only one room and a lean-to, which served as the kitchen, it didn't take long to investigate. In the kitchen there was a small sink but no running water. I was puzzled. There wasn't a light switch or plug to be found in the entire house. A mystery had been solved. Suddenly, I understood why my parents had bought kerosene lanterns and candles. *There was no electricity*! I couldn't imagine being without electricity. Even in Berkeley during the wartime blackouts, my parents merely closed the drapes and kept the lights on.

Stopping at the large black wood-burning cook stove, I opened and shut the oven while Michael discovered the lever that opened the compartment in which the wood was placed. There was a thick layer of ashes and I wondered why no one had cleaned them out.

As we scampered around, we saw our parents take the beds into the smaller cabin, the bunkhouse. It became obvious we were all going to sleep in this miniscule shelter. When I first heard it called the bunkhouse, I fantasized we were cowboys in a Western movie.

Michael and I both had to go to the bathroom. We looked around and saw no evidence of such a room. We ran to our mother and explained our dilemma. She took us by the hand to a shack even smaller than my closet in Minneapolis. As I looked inside, I saw a ledge with two holes. Looking down one of the openings, all I could see was darkness. The size of the hole made me certain that if I sat over it, I would fall into the dark abyss. Mother saw my terror and reassured me no one had ever fallen through an outhouse hole.

Another mystery needed solving: I had seen no shower or bath. Mother explained that we would bathe using a galvanized tub or swim in the river.

That night, Mother walked to a spring five hundred yards or so away and returned with two buckets of water. After heating some of the water on the stove, she gave us a cursory sponge bath.

Until October 1949, when REA (Rural Electric Association) brought power lines into the Basin, we lived without electricity.

Going to bed by candlelight and exhausted by our trip and all the information I had to sort out, I fell into a deep sleep.

The next morning, I woke to the trills of redwing blackbirds. From the small window, a stream of light danced on the floor. Our parents were still asleep, but Michael and I soon woke them. They seemed as excited as we were.

After a breakfast of eggs, toast, and fresh orange juice, Michael and I went outside to investigate our new universe. We ran through the field between the cabin and the barn to see Paint and Alamosa. I giggled when Alamosa's soft nose nuzzled me. Paint was cannier, not letting us come near him.

For the first part of the summer, we all relaxed. We were on vacation. We played in the river, went horseback riding, and enjoyed getting to know our neighbors. They were welcoming and didn't appear contaminated by the nightmare that had sent us into exile.

Best of all, I loved going to the river. During our first day on the ranch, we walked there, and I was smitten. But the meadow between the house and the river was mainly bog. My father tried to show me how to walk from one firm clod to another. My short legs weren't able to negotiate some of the stretches, and by the time we reached the river, my shoes were squeaky and squishy. I kept jumping to make the water in my shoes slosh and bubble.

I discovered the resonant sound of rocks being rolled as the water whirled and tossed them around. I loved the clank clank they made as they hit against one another.

This idyllic mood changed rather abruptly in the middle of August when my father realized that he had become unemployable. In spite of Herculean efforts on the part of his friends and colleagues as well as that of his brother, it became apparent that no one was going to offer him a job in physics anytime soon. My parents once again began to pay less and less attention to my brother and me during dinner. With flickering candlelight casting ghostly shadows on their faces, they often engaged in heated tirades about our government and the witch-hunts. Worse still, in addition to the pressure on my father to find a job in physics, the FBI began to visit the ranch in the summer of 1949.

The two FBI men arrived at the ranch, trailing a tall spume of dust. They braked by the side of our garage, about two hundred yards from the house. Both emerged from the car and briskly strode toward the house. Every step denoted confidence and resolve. I was astonished that they looked like two ordinary men dressed in suits and ties. The tall one ignored me. He probably would have paid more attention to a dog. The shorter one asked me my name and how old I was. He seemed friendly enough.

During their visit, Michael and I were sent outside to play. I tried to keep busy playing with my brother while our parents talked to the two strangers. I felt like crying but did my best to hold it in because of Michael. Nonetheless, the terrifying question "Will they take Mommy and Daddy to jail this time?" reverberated in my consciousness. I felt better when the FBI agents left without either of my parents. Years later, while looking at my parents' FBI files I learned that my concerns about them facing jail sentences weren't too far-fetched. As late as 1951, Congress was still considering pursuing contempt charges.

I returned to the house to find my parents angry. Mother was red- faced and shaking. I heard her say, "I hope the bastards are satisfied. Maybe they will leave us alone when they realize that they didn't get any more information."

My father was pacing and smoking one cigarette after another. "I have the feeling that they will return."

His prediction was right on. The FBI visited the ranch twice a year for the ten years we lived there. It didn't take long for us to begin to view their visits as an annoyance and a joke.

The next day, our neighbors, the Sissons, told us the FBI had questioned them. One of the questions had been "Are you sure they don't have any transmitting equipment in the barn?" Both my parents and the Sissons laughed.

Like the Sissons, most of our neighbors basically told the FBI, "All we know is the Oppenheimers are good neighbors."

As I read my parents' FBI files, I was grieved to learn that not everyone in Pagosa was as honest or nonjudgmental as we had assumed. I was saddened to see that the postmaster had furnished the FBI with a list of my parents' mail. It wasn't clear from the files that I have whether the FBI actually read the letters.

Jan. 13, 1951

(Name Redacted) Postmaster, Pagosa Springs, Colorado furnished results of a mail cover of subject and the following were noted to corresponded with Oppenheimer.

Oct. 15, 1950 The Dispatcher [the newspaper of the ILWU]

Nov. 5, 1950 (Name Redacted) Los Angeles, California

Nov. 8, 1950 (Name Redacted) Santa Fe, New Mexico

Nov. 21,1950 (Name Redacted)—[probably the Greenbergs] Phoenix, Arizona

Nov. 26, 1950 (Name Redacted)—[probably the Robert Wilsons] Ithaca, New York

Several years later the phone rang again, and my father answered. "Yes, we're going to be here." He hung up the phone, his face showing contempt and annoyance.

"The FBI are in Pagosa. They're on their way out."

Mother looked at the clock. It was 11:00 a.m. "It'll be lunchtime by the time they get here," she declared. "I'm not going to feed those bastards lunch."

The agents did arrive before any of us had time to eat. At three o'clock they were still at the house, and we were all starving. When Michael and I wandered into the kitchen to ask for something to eat, my father started to boil eggs.

"Would you like some hard-boiled eggs?" he asked the agents tongue in cheek. This was sufficient, it seemed, to cause the agents to decide it was a good time to leave. This sequence somehow struck us as funny and vindictive. After the agents left, we all burst out laughing.

# 10
## Personal Cataclysm

Looking back on these first years on the ranch, I realized that although my parents appeared to be enjoying ranching, there was always a tension that was present. I now understand clearly that my parents, particularly my father, were depressed. He longed to get back into physics. My mother felt terribly lonely, and her trust in her fellow human beings had sunk to an all-time low. For my part, I still felt like an outsider.

At fourteen, my own life began to unravel even more. Shopping for clothes was still an ordeal. Mother had found a tailor in Santa Fe to make some of my clothes. She had a discerning eye and found clothes that minimized my weight and accentuated my height. In spite of this, I was rarely satisfied. I continued to hate the fact that I could never go into a store and find dresses that fit. I was relegated to wearing skirts and blouses and often had to wear suspenders to keep my skirts from sagging. My blouses seemed to be always sliding up, and I found myself forever trying to neaten them and tuck them in. I began to see myself as a waistless wonder. Even today, whenever I see a little girl or shapely teenager in an airy-looking sundress, I remember my longing to be able to wear such cute clothes.

At fourteen, I still looked like a ten-year-old. I was about 4'4" with a square body and showed no signs of puberty. My cousin Janet started her menses when she was nine. Janet became the subject of many conversations between Mother and her sister Jean. They were somewhat taken aback that Janet had had her first period at such a young age. I remember feeling curious and embarrassed whenever the topic came up. Later on when my best friend, Karen, had her first period at the age of thirteen, it was essentially treated as a nonevent, so at the time, the fact I hadn't started to develop didn't worry me too much.

But by this time, both my parents and my pediatrician, Valerie McNown, had become concerned. On one of my visits to her office in Nambé just outside Santa Fe, I was escorted into an airy exam room.

Val was a statuesque woman who wore her hair in a chignon. She knocked on the exam room door and entered. Her smile and gentle voice reassured me. I needed a stool to climb up on her tall exam table. I was relaxed as she examined my ears, eyes, heart, and lungs and felt my abdomen. When she began to examine my vagina, my breathing became more rapid. My muscles tightened. At first, she was gentle, but soon she said, "Judy, I'm going to have to do something that's going to hurt." A knifelike pain shot up from my pelvis. I had tears of pain and embarrassment. I was sure there was something very wrong with me. Years later as a pediatrician, I understood that Val had broken some vaginal adhesions.

While Val talked to my parents, I sat in the waiting room trying to read. I was too embarrassed and sore to be able to concentrate.

When they came out, Mother told me quietly, "Val wants you to go into the hospital for some tests."

"What for? I'm not sick."

"She wants to see why you aren't growing or developing."

I remembered that the last time I had had an appointment with Val she had told my parents that if I hadn't grown or begun to develop in the next six months, she would like to do some tests. I remembered how in Minneapolis I couldn't ride a bicycle in part because I couldn't reach the pedals. For a moment, it seemed okay to find out why I was so small.

"Can't they be done outside the hospital?"

My father turned to me and scowled. His voice boomed as he shouted, "No!" I turned to Mother. "Can you at least stay down in Santa Fe so you can visit me?"

"You know I can't. It's haying season. We can't have two missing from our crew. Think about it. You won't have to sit on the back of the baler tying knots."

I glared at her and yelled, "Big deal!"

She waited a beat, looked at me pointedly and asked, "Don't you want to find out what's wrong?"

"Nothing's wrong with me. I don't care why I'm not developing." She busied herself, steering me out of the door. "Let's at least go to the bookstore to get some new books for you to read while you're in the hospital."

The small hospital in Española turned out to be a pleasant place. The nurses were kind and supportive, and because I was not sick, I spent a lot of time with them. The worst part of the hospitalization was having my blood drawn.

Between reading, collecting my urine in containers, and having blood drawn, the days were broken only by the short visits from Val. I soon began helping with a frail ten-year-old girl who was recovering from a severe bout of encephalitis. Hours were spent wheeling her up and down the corridors in a wheelchair and helping the nurses bathe and care for her. Although I didn't grasp it at the time, I believe that helping care for this young girl was the first indication that I enjoyed helping others—the first glimmer of my wanting to become a doctor.

My parents came to pick me up after a week of hospitalization. I was still short, fat, and not developing, and no one knew why.

At the time, I was happy to ignore the reason for my small size and lack of puberty. I still hated it when I couldn't find clothes that fit or couldn't reach something that others my age could. I knew that I was different from other girls my age but hoped, had assumed, that in time I would grow and enter puberty.

I soon found out that my parents and Val weren't so sanguine.

* * *

My family and I went to New York for Christmas when I was fifteen. We were going to New York City and then on to Ithaca to spend Christmas with my parents' friends, Bob and Jane Wilson. All of us were in a festive mood as we drove to Santa Fe to catch the train. This was our first real vacation in the six years that we had been on the ranch. The trip was even more special because my friend from my Berkeley days, Karen Essene, had accepted my offer to spend Christmas with us.

After the three-day train trip, I arrived in New York exhausted but excited. My fatigue temporarily dissipated as we picked up Karen at the Greyhound bus station. The magic of the day was increased when I saw the Christmas lights and the bustle of New York City on our way from the station to our hotel in the Upper East Side of Manhattan.

Once we arrived at our hotel, we all took naps. Afterward, we were refreshed and hungry. During dinner in the hotel dining room, I told everyone I wanted to go for a walk to Rockefeller Plaza to see the skaters. Mother nixed that idea.

"We'll have to do it some other time. We need to get up early tomorrow morning."

"Why? We're on vacation. We don't need to get up early."

My father said, "Yes, we do. You have an appointment with Dr. Sobel at eight thirty tomorrow morning."

"Who is Dr. Sobel?"

"She's an endocrinologist. We need to find out why you aren't developing."

My euphoria at being in New York vanished as quickly as a late spring snow. I didn't talk to my parents but glared at them instead. I even found it hard to talk to Michael or Karen.

The next morning I was so upset, I couldn't eat breakfast. I threw on my coat and slammed the hotel door as we left. My father turned to me and screamed, "You're being impossible. Calm down. We're only going to talk to Dr. Sobel."

As we walked down the dirty green hospital corridor of Montefiore hospital in the Bronx, the only thing I wanted to do was run away. The doctor's office was a small windowless room with one large desk, a few straight-backed chairs, and bookcases filled with medical books. Dr. Sobel was a stocky woman of medium height with short brown hair. To me, she had none of the reassuring warmth of Val. I was angry and afraid. I don't remember her saying a word as she examined me.

After the first visit to her office, I was given several white opaque gallon-sized containers into which I was expected to collect every drop of urine for the next forty-eight hours. The containers were to be ever present.

My face puckered, and I'm sure my eyes showed anger and disappointment. "I won't be able to go anywhere."

My father said, "Sure you can. We will just take the containers with us."

"Are you kidding? I won't be seen dead with the damned containers."

I thought: *This is sooo embarrassing.*

Mother tried to convince me that it really wasn't too awful to have to carry the containers around.

I countered with, "You're not the one who needs to pee in them."

My father went into an army surplus store and came out with a canteen. He agreed to carry this albatross during the day. The urine was transferred to the appropriate containers whenever we returned to our hotel room. This helped, but I still needed to take the canteen, a cup, and funnel with me into the stall whenever I needed to pee. I was always watching over my shoulder to see whether anyone noticed.

The entire visit continued on its dark surreal path when we took the train to Princeton to visit my uncle Robert. After the war, Robert had returned to Berkeley where he continued to teach. Robert and his family moved to Princeton so he could assume duties as director of the Institute for Advanced Studies. We arrived at his house after lunch, and he ushered us into the heavily draped living room where we spent the rest of the afternoon seated before a warm fire. Robert and my father talked physics and paid little or no attention to Mother, Michael, Karen, and me.

We finally moved to the formal dining room where a maid served us a miniscule filet mignon and a few green beans—a meal fit for an anorexic. As I listened to Robert's wife, Kitty, and Mother talk, I became painfully aware that Kitty couldn't stand her own son, Peter. Robert didn't come to Peter's defense. At that moment, I remembered my cousin Peter sneaking into the kitchen earlier in the afternoon and almost begging for something to eat. It was a relief when we left to return to our hotel.

Two days later, I had my last visit with Dr. Sobel. All the blood had been analyzed, the urine tested. A diagnosis had been made. Entering Dr. Sobel's office, I had no idea what to expect. Without windows, the office seemed like a prison cell. My parents sat in the chairs in front of her desk, and I sat in a chair some distance away from them. Dr. Sobel, judge and executioner, briefly talked to me. I was confused; my heart was racing, my head pounding. I wanted to run away. I don't remember a thing she said. I was escorted out of the room so she could talk to my parents alone. They came out grim faced and tense.

Walking down the broad steps of Albert Einstein Medical Center, Mother paused as she said, "You have Turner's syndrome. You won't ever be able to have children."

Then she kept on walking. Silence descended. I was blasted by the bitter winter wind. I shivered and tried to hold back my tears. No iceberg had a deeper hidden dimension. I was only aware of myself. The rest of the world was a whiteout. Confused, scared, and devastated, I was in my own world of adolescent angst and was unable to talk to my parents.

Even our hotel room felt dark and sinister. I was numb. At the Museum of Modern Art, I had just seen Picasso's Guernica that was on loan from Spain. Its images returned to haunt me. The grays and blacks, the fragmented bodies human and animal, the eyes that screamed terror or no longer saw, the mother holding her chopped-up child, the loose arms that thrashed endlessly, spoke to the war, the chaos within me.

I sat on my bed, a fat little girl who was seriously flawed. My despair became even deeper as I looked at Karen sitting on the other bed. She was a tall shapely teenager. With her thick blond hair plaited in a perfect French braid, I thought of her as the picture of exquisite adolescent beauty. How could she not hate me with my grotesque and misshapen body? Neither of us had any idea of how to start the conversation. I didn't understand what Turner's was but knew it was bad and abnormal. I knew it had something to do with not being a woman. After all, Mother had just told me I would never be able to have children.

At the time of my diagnosis, not much was known about the cause of Turner's except that it was a genetic abnormality. Girls with Turner's have no ovaries and, therefore, don't enter puberty and are infertile.

What I remember about that night is that I wanted Karen to hug me, to tell me I was okay. She didn't because I was unable to talk to her, much less ask for her support. I wanted my mother to come in to hug me, to tell me the same thing. She didn't.

We did go to Bob and Jane's. On Christmas morning, I could barely get out of bed. I was in no shape to face the merriment of the holiday. I descended the stairs with a sad, sullen face and noticed my parents gazing up at me. My father admonished, "Cheer up, it's Christmas. Don't ruin it for the rest of us."

\* \* \*

Once home, I stood naked in front of a mirror that reflected back my short thick neck, my broad undeveloped chest, short arms and legs, and square body. Even my hair seemed too dark, too curly. Who's the fairest of them all? I knew the mirror would never answer back "You." I couldn't hold back the tears as I said to myself, You're a freak!

Val started me on vaginal estrogen suppositories as replacement for the estrogen I couldn't make myself. At first, Mother helped me insert them. When I had the courage to do it myself, I felt a little better, but I still recoiled at the thought of using them. Not only were they messy and yucky, often staining my underwear, but also the entire process of having to place them into my vagina was very shameful and humiliating. Three years later, I was placed on oral estrogen. This was infinitely better than the suppositories; however, the revulsion persisted.

The estrogen did help. The summer after my diagnosis, I was walking up from the house to the garage and noticed my shadow. I turned sideways, and I saw images of breasts where none used to be. I experimented. I put my arms beside me and looked at my shadow again. I softly said to the empty universe, "Oh my god, I am getting breasts! I even have an indentation, a waist—not much, but enough to allow the sunlight to shine between the shadows of my arms and body!"

I tried my arms in different positions to be sure.

"It's true! My body is beginning to change!"

My joy was short-lived. No one commented on my breast development and the fact that I had started to slowly grow. I was unable to share my emotions or my elation. To me, the others' silence was a signal that I shouldn't talk about how happy I was. I began to believe the changes really weren't important. That summer progesterone was added to my treatment. I had my first period, yet I really never equated developing breasts, a waist, or having a period with being normal. I recalled seeing the Diary of Anne Frank the year before when we were in New York. In one scene, Anne talked about her "sweet secret." I knew I would never feel that way about my period. I was sure my development and my menstrual flow were bogus. They occurred only because of medications. I was no more a woman than before.

Sometime during the summer after my diagnosis, I was about to enter the kitchen when I heard my mother say, "Never let a boy make love to you in the back of a car. At least make him take you to a motel." I stopped without letting my presence be known. I knew she was talking to Karen and Janet, talking about things that she never talked to me about. I so wanted to be included. Listening to the three of them, I was hurt, confused, and feeling very ostracized. I vowed then and there to find the courage, time, and place to ask my mother about it all.

That time came several weeks later when she was bent over quietly nurturing her garden. The rest of the kids were out riding, and I knew my father never came to the garden except in the spring when he plowed and disked it. I made my way from the house to the garden. On my way, I formulated my questions and concerns: "Ma, why don't others choose me as their friend? Will I ever be able to have a boyfriend? Will I get married? How do you know when to make love?"

Once in the garden, I went over to her. My mouth became dry and stiff. In my mind, these words that I meant to speak aloud only reverberated in my brain. After what seemed like hours, the silence was broken only when my mother asked me to pick some cosmos.

She and I never did have that conversation. As an adult, I wondered whether she, as I did, saw me as an asexual being that was destined to never have sensual, sexual feelings or an intimate relationship.

When I was eighteen, I had my karyotype (chromosomal pattern) done. It had just been reported that Turner's was caused by a missing X chromosome. (Normal females have two X chromosome (XX); males have XY.) My karyotype was XO—the O representing the missing X chromosome. This finding confirmed the diagnosis.

Knowing my karyotype only added fuel to the fire of my self-loathing and confusion. I began to think of myself as neither male nor female. I thought of myself as an "it." On more than one occasion, I told myself, *Nature sure has an efficient way of operating. It knows you can't have children, so it isolates you as one of its freaks. It makes you repulsive and unable to attract anyone much less someone of the opposite sex.*

I never was able to talk to my parents about what an impact my diagnosis made on my life and that there wasn't a day I didn't think about it. While they were alive, I don't remember the subject coming up in any significant way. I don't recall any discussion about the emotional impact my diagnosis had on me or them. Looking back on their silence, I suspect part of reluctance to talk was partly because of the shame and guilt they must have felt about producing a daughter with a genetic abnormality. Another factor that inevitably shaped their silence was that it was an era when sexual matters were not freely discussed. It is also true my parents were not able to discuss emotions easily. However, not long ago, I could no longer bear the conspiracy of silence. My parents were dead, but I could talk to my brother. Although Michael and I had talked before about the huge impact my diagnosis had on my life, I now asked him about what he was feeling on that cold December day when I learned I had Turner's.

He told me he couldn't recall how or when he was told about my diagnosis but that while we were in New York, he was aware of how distressed our parents and I were.

"My most vivid recollection was that of being worried that I, too, might have the same or similar problem. I was so frightened that I was not normal and that I would not enter puberty. One day I was so worried, I went up to Ma, who was in the garden and asked, 'Am I ever going to grow up or am I going to be like Deedle? (His nickname for me). Ma reassured me that I was normal."

"Oh god, I never even thought about that! Of course you would be worried. You were twelve and just beginning to be aware of your own development."

"I guess you're right. I think I secretly wanted to have a similar problem, probably because of guilt and wanting to support you by being different too. Throughout my life I've felt guilty because I can do so many things, especially physical, better than you."

Tears came to my eyes. Michael understood. My brother saw and accepted me for who I was.

# 11
## Camp Oppenheimer

For me, summers on the ranch were not officially underway until the middle of June when I saw the dust from the Essenes' VW bus billow past the barn and knew my friend Karen had come to spend the summer. Loneliness was about to be lifted.

Each summer, the Oppenheimer ranch morphed into what, as an adult, I began to call Camp Oppenheimer. I still marvel at the fact that, until my father built a two-room addition between the main cabin and the bunkhouse, for the first two or three summers, we all survived living in a one-room cabin. Even after the building of the addition, we often kept three sets of bunk beds in our upstairs bedroom. If more people showed up than we had beds for, we slept in a tent. The tent was not my favorite place. I often was so cold there that I had no choice but to pick up my sleeping bag and trek to the cabin, spending the rest of the night on the living room floor. The small five-room house was filled with youthful chaos.

Karen and her family started visiting the ranch the first summer we lived there. Besides Eric and Karen, the house was filled with other kids: my cousin Janet, (friends from Minneapolis days-Susie, Michael, and Harold Greenberg and Robert's son, Peter—all of them typically arriving in staggered intervals to spend four to six weeks with us. Others came sporadically. For ten years, this summer flow of friends became a ritual that sustained all of us.

These busy summers partially made up for the long isolated and sterile winters. It thrilled me to have all my friends and family around, but my real soul mate was Karen. In May each year, aware her arrival date was closing in, I began counting the weeks and finally the days before she and her family would appear. Karen was tall and pretty with thoughtful brown eyes. Her long blond hair was often pulled back into a thick French braid. Michael and others declared she looked like Ingrid Bergman. Secretly, I wished I could let my dark curly hair grow as long as Karen's so I too could have a French braid, but my hair was too thick and unruly.

If we weren't busy with chores or haying, she and I and the others rode horses along the gravel road, through the meadows or up the forest service trails, or went to the river to swim and build sand cities. I enjoyed all these activities, but my special times were when Karen and I played dolls together. We grouped them into families and social networks and gave them elaborate personalities and daily routines.

The summers ended all too quickly. In late August, the Essenes returned to pick up Karen. My heart would sink when I heard the familiar engine and saw the VW bus pulling up. The Essenes would stay for several days before they headed home. The rear of the bus had been converted into one large bed for Eric and Karen to travel on. It struck me as an ideal place to play, nap, and watch the world go by. In the late summer sun, we all embraced, saying our good-byes.

Inevitably, their van would be gorged with belongings as they left to rumble down the long dirt road and disappear into the dust. For a few minutes after their departure, I would stand silently in our driveway then slowly turn to walk into a quiet, empty house and make a beeline to my room to grieve. Not only would I mourn the loss of my best friend's leaving, but it was also a signal that winter was about to begin. Winters—a frigid buttoned-down hibernation when my brother and I had only one another for companionship and play.

Each summer when I retreated to weep after losing Karen, I hoped my mother would hear my sobbing and that she'd appear in my room to comfort me. Instead, she would offer a nonchalant dismissal. "It's not so bad. Karen will be back next summer." Inevitably, my father yelled to me to be quiet, and to add further salt in the wound, he scolded me. "Judy, don't be so snarky. Cheer up."

Until school started, I dragged around—long-faced, unrelentingly miserable, and undoubtedly miserable to be around. What I couldn't express to my family was that I lived with a powerful secret fear—that Karen wouldn't return. Any day I expected her to write or call telling me she was so busy with her friends and life in Kentucky that she couldn't come the following summer.

Thus, every year, until Karen contacted me to confirm she was coming, I was in a state of perilous, suspended animation. I had convinced myself that my friend really didn't want to come, that she found me boring. I was sure I didn't mean as much to her as she did to me.

Karen and I had played dolls together since I could remember. In Berkeley, I would I hear the wooden gate to our garden creek as Karen, her mother Molly, and brother Eric entered. That small sound was a clear signal that I'd be transported to the peculiar contentedness of playing dolls with my best pal. The moment we two little girls laid eyes on each other, the ritual began. Karen and I immediately took off to play together. We always ended up staging ambitious doll play in the "mother-in-law" cottage in the back of the yard. The cottage gave us a perfect setting, replete with everything we needed: toy stove, sink, baby buggies, and bassinets. We made our dolls lunch, bathed them, told them elaborate stories, scolded them softly for minor transgressions, and put them to bed. Gently we pulled their blankets up and said, "Good night." Then we'd skip to our mothers chatting in the patio for lunch or snacks. The smell of coffee and cigarettes comforted us deeply—signals of a safe and affectionate world, routine and reassuring.

By the time we were on the ranch, Karen and I had evolved from being simple mommies to more like being omnipotent gods, creating intricate dramas for our dolls to enact. At that point in our lives, our stories for our dolls' lives still remained fairly conventional. Their intricacies revolved mainly around our dolls going to school or to the park to play.

As we neared adolescence, the playing fields of our imaginations grew larger and our plots still more complex. One story we concocted starred two teenagers who ran away from home. They ended up living in an apartment. With pink bedspreads and frilly curtains and potted plants, the imaginary apartment was totally froufrou. Both of our doll characters possessed extremely bold and assertive personalities. They didn't hesitate to light out on adventures neither Karen or I had yet experienced: dating, going to work, and running a household.

It's poignant for me now to comprehend that while immersed in the busy and complicated lives of our dolls, I was able to forget my own anxieties and enter a world where I enjoyed supreme control. Playing dolls allowed me to imagine living as the girl/adolescent I wanted to be. The young woman I felt I could never be.

# 12
## Adolescence

With the aid of hormone supplement, my adolescence did indeed arrive. However, it was not filled, as most girls' were, with the smells of boys' aftershave and their testosterone-produced sweat. It was not filled with the amateur hour of struggling to insert the whirling dervish of a diaphragm. (Mother was angry when I inadvertently found hers in her dresser drawer.) My adolescent dream world was not peopled with bronzed young men vying to become my boyfriend and making love to me. Instead, my adolescence was filled with confusion, loneliness, and self-hatred. It was filled with sounds and physical convulsions of weeping and rocking my bed so hard as I tried to go to sleep that it slid across the room. It was filled with the enraged noise of my father and me arguing about everything. A red-hot branding iron of anger and fear seared my growing up.

Every three or four months, our 4-H club had square dances. They were often held in an abandoned one-room schoolhouse in Chromo, a small community not far from the Colorado-New Mexico border. The schoolhouse had several small windows with dirty white walls.

Most of the time the dances had a caller who shouted directions over the music provided by scratchy records. Kids appeared from all over the area, and we were organized into couples and squares. First, we were walked through each of the steps. It generally took several tries before the caller was satisfied that we were ready to try the steps with the music. In the self-consciousness and awkwardness of childhood, we rarely made it through an entire dance without someone making a mistake. When that happened, the whole square erupted into laughter and teasing, and we were obliged to begin again. When we actually marched through the entire dance without a major error, parents yelled and clapped.

The joy of square dancing quite suddenly and unexpectedly changed for me when I was fourteen. I was attending a dance after a long summer hiatus. Walking into the derelict schoolhouse, I was struck by the amazing dramatic changes that had occurred in the other girls. Unlike me, they had been transformed into flawless, graceful beauties. They were tall, curvy, and walked with a proud self-assuredness that I had never seen before and certainly did not feel within myself. Talking with the girls, attempting to catch up on their summers, caused me to feel even stranger and more different. They were, it seemed, only interested in boys, and as they talked, their eyes roved the room hungrily, waiting to be noticed by the boys across the floor.

Suddenly, I was an outsider.

During the dance practice, I noticed that, unlike the last time we all were together, the dance itself seemed unimportant to the girls I'd once thought I knew. They learned the calls quickly and perfectly and acted as if the whole exercise presented a minor distraction. The caller's voice reverberated from the walls and the ceiling. "Allemande left, do-si-do. Gals to the center-circle left, meet your partner halfway round, allemande right." Orange, yellow, red, and blue multilayered skirts swayed to the music. To my dismay, I found myself turning in the wrong direction and quickly fell out of step with the others. It appeared I was the only one unable to follow the calls. I hated my dark-blue square dance skirt with its crinoline petticoats. I felt clumsy, fat, and short. After a couple of dances, I took myself out and sat at the sidelines, looking at the floor or staring into space. During one such dance, a horrific screeching sound suddenly broke my insular trance. The dancing stopped, and we all rushed outside. A huge semi had lost its brakes descending the steep hill and was careening out of control right in front of the schoolhouse. Its empty flatbed trailer had flipped over, creating fireworks as it scraped along the pavement. The air reeked of burning rubber. We were all horrified and huddled together in our animated disbelief, and for a brief deeply relieving moment, I felt as if we were all related and close. It was a strange bittersweet reprieve, but I would never square dance again.

The atmosphere at Camp Oppenheimer also began to change when I was fourteen. The line was drawn one warm summer day. Karen and I were sitting outside near the woodshed, playing with our dolls as we always had. I, as usual, was relishing my ever-expanding fantasy play, weaving complex, sophisticated scenarios for our brave dolls to play. As a rule, Karen jumped into these stories with both feet. She often embellished and enriched them with her own plot-lines and details. In this way, we'd play for hours. But on this peaceful summer afternoon, Karen was distracted and only half-heartedly into our two-person narrative. Suddenly she looked up and, looking straight into my eyes, spoke quietly and clearly. "Judy, I don't want to play dolls anymore. It's too boring and childish."

I stared at her, stunned. What she had uttered struck me as inconceivable. How could she find playing with our dolls boring? Before she'd always leapt in with excitement. In fact, only last year, it was Karen who often suggested we play. She had often taken the lead, set the scenes, given special instructions, suggested story line changes. Never anticipating our theatrical imaging would end, I stared at her, numb with shock. Karen quietly added, "Peter wants me to go horseback riding with him."

By her tone of voice, it was clear that I wasn't invited. They took off up the road on Paint and Alamosa. Distraught, I picked my way down to the barn to find solace with my cattle. There, amid acrid smells of hay and manure, I'd lean my head against the shoulder of one of my cows, usually Knuckle Head's. Looking into her all-knowing obsidian eyes and talking about my loneliness made me feel better.

My grief didn't end there. Not only did Karen not want to play dolls, but also it appeared as if she and Janet were entering adolescence with a vengeance, the all-too-typical surge of estrogen-produced confusion and angst. Peter—tall and thin with bright blue eyes, high cheekbones, and thick black hair—found himself now flooded with raging testosterone. Often I would be at the barn and see Karen and Peter holding hands and looking at each other with what I later learned were called bedroom eyes. Whenever we all went to the movies in Pagosa, the two of them sat together several rows behind the rest of us.

Janet also had a beau in the old-fashioned sense. Russell was the son of one of the ranchers in the next valley. Even though theirs was a much more sedate, less intrusive relationship than the one between Karen and Peter, it added to my unhappiness.

One evening, Janet and Russell were going to a dance, and Peter and Karen were going to a movie. I knew there would be no communal poker game this night. I would be home alone with my parents and brother. I listened and watched from afar to the endless banter and gentle teasing from Michael, Peter, Karen, and even Mother as Janet prepared for her date with Russell. I tried not to break into tears. But when Mother suggested that Janet should wear one of my favorite bracelets, something in me snapped like a chicken's dried wishbone.

I took my mother aside and whispered viciously, "Why are you letting Janet wear my bracelet? I haven't even had a chance to wear it much myself."

Janet wore it anyway. Afterward, I was ashamed of myself for being so selfish. Fleeing upstairs to my room, I resorted to my usual sobbing uncontrollably, hoping someone might come up to ask me what was wrong. This tactic usually didn't work, but that night, Mother actually came up and stayed. She hugged me and sat on my bed beside me. Even today, I can feel her hug and hear her gentle and caring voice.

"What's wrong?" "Oh, nothing."

"Is it about Peter and Karen? They've shut you out, ignored you, haven't they?"

"I guess."

I started to sob once more.

"I feel so lonely. Karen doesn't seem to like me anymore. She never wants to spend time with me."

"Karen and Peter are just being teenagers, but I know how hard it is for you."

It was a rare validation of my pain. Starved for human understanding, I wished she and I could keep talking like this forever.

Adolescence had arrived at Camp Oppenheimer, and I was not part of it.

Though I often felt inadequate because Karen and I could no longer communicate on a deeper level, some of my most tender memories of my last years on the ranch were those intervals when I sat reading on the couch while Karen played on our Baldwin spinet piano. Though each of us engaged in her own pastime, the music was soothing and somehow linked the two of us. Occasionally, I'd stop reading and give my entire attention to my friend's playing. Sometimes her music made me smile and want to dance; at other times the sensitivity and lyricism of what she was playing almost brought tears to my eyes. Even today if I hear Bach's *Inventions,* Debussy's *Golliwog's Cakewalk,* a Beethoven sonata, or Schubert's *Impromptus,* my mind floods with those lovely memories of Karen.

At school, I listened silently as other young women talked about their loves and what they did over the weekends. My weekends didn't shine with that breathless anticipation of a special date; they consisted of staying at home. Other teenagers' hormones raged; mine didn't exist. They gossiped about the rare couple that ventured into forbidden territory by "going *all the way.*"

Sometimes my acquaintances came to me for help with their homework or for personal advice. I tried the best I could to understand their passions, their sexuality, but my demons overpowered me. I couldn't fully sympathize with their sexual, sensual teenage world because I had no experience of it. How I longed to own a tall graceful body like theirs. I coveted a ponytail jauntily sprouting from the top of my head, a ponytail that I could swish like a proud vital animal, one that would stream out in back of me when I ran.

One of the features of Turner's—that of having a hairline that grew very low on my neck—dictated that all I could hope for were "buffy braids," which I was certain made me like a ten-year-old.

Now and then I was invited to join several young women—Jean Corrigan, Marilyn Breedlove, Judy Thiele, and Barbara Baker—for lunch or even an occasional sleepover. However, the small gestures of their trying to reach out didn't lift my sense of not belonging. I was sure they had included me just because I was an Oppenheimer. Even though everyone in Pagosa knew my parents had been Communists, I felt reluctant to talk politics or world affairs. I was petrified my classmates would loathe me even more if they knew about my own liberal politics.

I survived these tumultuous adolescent years because of my cattle. In 1951, I joined 4-H and quickly began to build my own herd of cattle. By the time I was in high school, I owned and tended my own beautiful herd of twelve tame, gentle Herefords. Each year, another of my animals would be prepared for show. Not only did caring for them take much of my time, but also they became my solace. They gave me confidence and a purpose for my life.

When the others at Camp Oppenheimer would go to the river or horseback riding and I didn't feel like joining them, I would wander to the barn to talk to my cows. After having arguments with my parents, I would escape to my bovine friends. After a bad day at school, there was only one place to be: sitting on the earth, my back to the wooden wall, hugging my knees, talking softly to those big red-and-white beasts, my only constant friends.

My parents bought their first cattle in 1950. I fell in love with the red-and-white Herefords the moment they rambled down the cattle chute and began to mill around our corral.

4-H rapidly became a very important part of my life. We had selected the calf I was going raise one day while we were inspecting our cattle. The little heifer calf was all over the place running, playing with the other calves, and looking cute. Our neighbor, Red, noticed her too and proclaimed that she had all the attributes of a champion. I named her Knuckle Head.

On Thanksgiving morning 1951, the Colorado winter was at its best. The sky was blue and the air fresh and invigorating. The landscape glistened from a dusting of new snow the night before. I was excited not only because it was Thanksgiving, but also because it was the day when the mother cows and their calves were to be separated from one another. It was the day Knuckle Head would officially become mine. I traipsed down to the corral to help.

The cows circled the enclosure endlessly in hope of finding a way to be reunited with their babies. It was bedlam with calves and their mothers bellowing across the fence that separated them.

My father and Red isolated Knuckle Head from the other calves and herded her into the barn.

I confidently stated, "I'm going to put a halter on her."

I had no idea how to accomplish this task. After trying to coax her to come to me with hay and various other maneuvers, my father laughed and said, "Judy, let us help you."

We finally cornered Knuckle Head, and while the two men held her against the barn wall, I put her halter on.

Knuckle Head and I were both new at this game. She despised the idea of the halter. I had no idea how to control her.

She was a four-hundred or five-hundred-pound Hereford heifer, and I, a small but determined eleven-year-old. She took off running across the snow-covered field, bucking and trying to rid herself of the hated halter. I fell but held on to the lead as she pulled me through the snow. I was laughing. No way was I going to let her win this battle. Only when it became apparent neither she nor I were going to give up did my parents intervene.

Knuckle Head and I became great friends and spent hours together. I fed her, groomed her, led her around, and taught her how to set up for show. In the spring I washed her, bleached her white socks, and polished her hooves. She was transformed into a sleek red-and-white heifer and became so tame, my brother and I were able to ride her around the corral. I showed her at the fair in the fall, and she was grand champion.

Although I was fond of all my cattle, Knuckle Head remained my favorite.

# 13
## Wildflowers

Wildflowers, during our years at the ranch, were mythical. We all loved their dainty colorful flowers that appeared each spring, signifying the end of winter.

Wildflowers also dictated what portion of the meadow could be mowed. Each year my father, wearing his usual ranching uniform of a long- sleeved blue or khaki shirt and jeans, carefully circled around a patch of fringed gentians, leaving their delicate purple flowers intermingled with timothy, clover, and brome to reseed so they'd reappear the next summer.

My birthday is in May. It was time when yellow and purple lupine, fringed gentians, mariposa lilies, columbine, and other flowers transformed the meadows and hillsides into a pointillist painting.

Every year, my father woke up early on my birthday to pick wildflowers. When I walked into the sunny kitchen for breakfast, my place was decorated with a blue mat and orange juice surrounded by a profusion of dew-speckled yellow, pink, purple, and white wildflowers. Gaily wrapped presents surrounded my place.

This birthday tradition lasted the rest of my father's life. When my parents moved to Boulder where I was attending the University of Colorado and later when I was in medical school in Denver, my father combed the hills surrounding Boulder for these wildflowers. When they lived in Sausalito and I was living in San José, he searched the hills of Marin. Except for six years when I was too far away and he sent me bouquets from the florist instead, I received wildflowers on every birthday until the year before he died.

I was forty-four.

With colors of spring, these wildflowers radiated warmth and love. Ultimately, I learned the colors quickly faded, the petals dropped, the water turned into smelly primordial ooze. I found myself confused about my relationship with my father. I could not define, with any real certainty, what these flowers meant to him.

Growing older, my joy of this yearly ritual was overshadowed by my fear of being pulled into the whirlpool of my father's power. Until Michael reminded me, I didn't remember that he too had received wildflowers. However, for him the ritual stopped when he was ten or eleven.

Thus, the arrival of these flowers and my acceptance of them became, paradoxically, a dark event, its complexity compounded by guilt—the guilt of being singled out as a favorite child in my father's eyes to the exclusion of my brother.

# 14
# Anger

The spring I was sixteen found me often in the living room bent over books and papers writing furiously, determined to master piles of homework in history or literature. One afternoon I was totally immersed in reading and doing my history homework.

Struggling to remember the dates and events leading to the Norman conquest of Britain, I looked up, startled. My father, in a suit and tie, had suddenly appeared before me.

"Hurry up. You need to get ready."

I was puzzled as I said, "Ready for what?"

"To babysit. Mrs. Catchpole and I are going to perform a flute and piano recital at the Methodist church. I told the McGuires you would babysit so they could come to the recital. Hurry up or we'll be late."

I started to protest.

"But, Pa, I can't do it. I've never babysat in my life. Besides, I have a history test on Monday that I need to study for."

"Damn it, get your coat. You can study there."

"Why didn't you tell me before?"

Terror, like a dark blanket, covered every inch of my body. It suffocated and entrapped me. I had never been alone or played the role of a responsible adult. I had no idea how to keep kids occupied and quiet. I panicked at the thought that something might happen to them. I knew speaking these thoughts wouldn't change my father's mind.

"No more procrastinating. Bring your history books with you. You'll be able to study while the kids are asleep."

"Pa, I can't do it. I won't go."

As soon as I said these words, my father morphed into a giant red creature. He tried to haul me to the kitchen and then to the car. I broke away, ran to the woodshed, and barricaded the door. My father, like a bull out of control, kicked in the door, grabbed me, and started dragging me to the car five hundred feet away. He yanked my arms, screamed at me, and then grabbed my hair. I was catapulted through the snow and mud.

The pain was so great that for a moment, I entered another universe where time and pain no longer existed. My vision was blurred with tears, and spots like lightning raced across my vision.

Was it the freezing snow or my fear of his anger that made me shake? I was powerless against his rage. Michael and Mother were at the kitchen window watching my father drag me through the snow. Mother rushed outside. Once she did, I glimpsed at her face. It was locked, betraying no feeling at all. Would she help me? At that moment, there was simply no way to tell. I looked at her with wild pleading eyes that begged, "Do something! Help me!"

She looked away and in a tremulous voice told my father to stop. Her words had no effect. As he continued to drag me toward the car, she resorted to pleading.

"At least take Michael."

To this my father agreed. Michael emerged, angrily pulling on his jacket. Getting into the car, he didn't look up at our father or me and stared out the window, silent. None of us uttered a word for the entire hour's drive to Pagosa. During the drive, I trembled with all kinds of feelings: angry and horrified at my father, ashamed and disappointed with myself. Realizing that at sixteen I shouldn't be so afraid of something as ordinary as babysitting, I pictured myself as a bona fide brat. However, I felt stunned at my father's actions and nursed a slow-burning fury. I was furious at my father and knew he had no right to treat me as he had. Today, I realize no matter how immaturely I might have behaved, my father's actions were wrong. He'd been totally out of control. Incapable of understanding my fear, he'd simply mown over it with a grown man's physical strength to hasten himself to his goal. I can't forget or forgive his actions but can, at least emotionally, put them aside so they no longer hold me hostage.

The rest of the afternoon must have proceeded without serious incident for I remember little else of it. But another incident that sticks in memory occurred not long thereafter.

Upstairs in my bedroom, I'd spent hours bent over my desk trying to make sense of my math homework. The problems were beyond me however hard I tried to make sense of them. At last, in tears of frustration, I, with trepidation, walked down the stairs to seek my father's help. Mother was in the living room vacuuming. She looked up.

"What's wrong?"

"I can't finish my math because I don't understand the basic concept. I need Pa's help."

She scowled.

"Well, it's not a good time to go to him. He's been a bastard all day. All he's done is argue. As you know, I certainly can't help you. Sit down and relax a minute. Maybe if you go in there calmly, it will be okay."

"I need to turn in the assignment tomorrow."

In the background, the radio was on. Suddenly I started laughing.

Mother smiled. "What's so funny?"

"I was thinking about listening to *Our Miss Brooks* last night. It was hilarious."

She agreed. "It certainly was one of the funnier episodes."

Remembering the radio comedy that both she and I enjoyed helped. We laughed together so that by the time we finished talking, I felt more at ease and was determined to remain calm while talking to my father.

He sat at his desk writing an article.

"Pa, can you explain factoring to me? I can't figure it out and can't do the problems."

He stopped, nodded, and then began to explain the concept to me in a reasonable, calm manner. I watched his face and listened carefully, but his words did not create the click in my thinking that would lead me to comprehend. He backed up and tried several different approaches. Listening as hard as I knew how, I still could not fathom it.

Both of us grew frustrated. At long last I broke into tears, and that lit the match to the dynamite. My father's control evaporated. He jumped from his chair and slapped me so hard, I was thrown across the room. He moved toward me. I ran out of the room and back upstairs where I threw myself on the bed and cried myself to sleep. During the night his explanations gelled, and the next day, I finally understood the assignment.

Although my mother had warned me about my father's mood, she never appeared to comfort or support me.

Fifty years later, when she was dying of cancer, Mother apologized for not coming to my rescue during each of these episodes. My father never spoke to me with any remorse.

# 15
## Education on the Ranch

Time had arrived to think about applying for college. I realized that my education while on the ranch was far from stellar. In fact, Michael's and my education had been one of the first dilemmas my parents faced when we first moved to the ranch in 1949.

The nearest school was twenty miles away in Pagosa. To get there, we would have to travel eight miles on a gravel road in the winter just to reach the highway where the school bus would carry us the additional twelve miles into town.

I recall a night in the middle of August during our first summer on the ranch. My parents had just gone to bed. Michael and I were tucked in across the room in our bunk beds. I listened as my father whispered to Mother that since he hadn't found a job, they needed to make a decision about whether they should stay on the ranch during the winter or move. They then began to consider the question of our schooling if we did stay. Mother lit a cigarette and reminded my father that although moving would certainly solve the problem of our education, our family really had no place to go. At least on the ranch we had a roof over our heads.

My father then said something that caused my heart to freeze. He had seen an ad in the *New Yorker* for a boarding school in Arizona; maybe they should send us there. My eyes popped open and my heart pounded in horror as I listened to them consider this possibility. I saw the glow of my father's cigarette; it moved around when he gestured like a shining baton that orchestrated his thinking. Though I was not entirely clear about what boarding school was, I knew Arizona was far away from the ranch. If I were sent to a school in Arizona, I would see my parents only during vacations and summer. The prospect sounded like jail. Would I even be allowed to take my toys or books? And the larger question floated in the miasma. Were our parents willing to send us so far away because they didn't like us anymore?

Upon hearing Mother say, "I can't see it. I can't imagine not having Mike and Judy here. They're so young, and I'd miss them too much. Also, Frank, think of the crap they might be taught, and we wouldn't be there to counteract it." I smiled and went limp with relief.

I heard more whispering. Finally my father mentioned correspondence schools. My mother rejected that idea, telling him he didn't have the patience it would take to teach us.

As I listened to my parents, I became more and more concerned about school and what was going to happen to me. I'd been extremely bored ever since my friends had left for home and their schools. The vision of spending a winter without going to school disturbed me more and more. I loved school and couldn't imagine not going. What would I do instead? Michael and I could play with each other only so much. But by the middle of September, a solution to the riddle of our education had been found. The one-room schoolhouse a mile from us would be reopened. It had been closed for a year or two because of the lack of a teacher and the small numbers of children in the Basin. Our neighbor Red Sisson's wife, Ruby, used to teach at the school but was now teaching math in the high school in Pagosa and therefore was not available. At first, no one thought reopening the school was a possibility.

However, four other potential students, the Bramwells, lived in the valley, and with Ruby's lobbying, the school board finally agreed to find a teacher for the school. A young woman named Phyllis was hired, so Michael, the four Bramwells and I were able to start school in the middle of October 1949. On the first day of school I was so excited my breakfast remained half eaten. I was dressed and ready to go long before I needed to be. That day Mother drove us. For the rest of the five years that we attended the Blanco Basin School, we usually walked or rode horseback.

At that time, the concept of school to me meant a big building housing many kids in different rooms. In this case, however, there were only going to be six of us. Strangest of all, no one was going to be in fourth grade with me. I was a class of one.

The tiny school stood at the edge of a small meadow that was divided by the road. In back of the school was an even tinier one-room building called the teacherage where Phyllis lived. Across the road were a barn and two outhouses. The aspen and fir forests surrounding this meadow were dense and filled with ferns and chokecherries.

Until that first day of school, I had gone past the small white clapboard building many times but had never been inside. As Mother, Michael, and I walked up the steps of the building, I was curious about what the school would look like inside.

The room we entered proved to be a miniature of all my other classrooms, complete with a blackboard and teacher's desk in front. Only the desks were different. They struck me as weird. The desks had slanted surfaces that opened like a hinged lid to hold our school supplies. In the back of each desk was a hole with a covered glass pot. My mother called them inkwells. Ballpoint pens didn't exist, and fountain pens were for high school students. I felt very grown up when, in the fifth grade, I was the first one in school to dip the straight pen into the ink.

To one side of the room was an old black potbellied wood-burning stove that was the only heat. When REA (Rural Electric Association), a New Deal program that helped rural areas get electricity, came to the Basin in late October, Red and my father wired the schoolhouse and teacherage. Until then, the only light was from two small windows on each side of the room.

I don't recall much about Phyllis or her teaching except that she was kind and pretty. She left after one year, and Ruby returned to teach. Ruby was our teacher until I entered high school. One year, Michael and I were the only students in school.

Ruby was a small wiry lady with gray hair that made her look older than she was. She was a strict disciplinarian, and I held no doubts she was capable of smacking my hand with a wooden ruler or making me sit on the edge of a wastepaper basket if I misbehaved. She never had to resort to either, but I was afraid of her. I think the only reason she didn't overpower me and seem to be more of an ogre at school was because she also happened to be a generous and gracious neighbor.

One day, I remember Ruby walked purposefully over to my desk. I had just finished writing my multiplication tables. She asked me to go up to the blackboard to write all the 8x. I knew most of them but couldn't, for the life of me, remember 8 × 7. In a loud, shrill voice she asked, "Didn't you study?" Everyone in the room stared at me. It was one of those moments that etched itself on my brain. I wanted to run and hide in the forest, but instead I went back to my desk and practiced, practiced, practiced.

A week later, Ruby and Red were at our house for dinner.

Red turned to me and said, "Ruby tells me you don't know 8 × 7."

By then I had memorized the answer, but when I tried to tell him, I couldn't. He kept taunting me. I wanted my parents to tell him to shut up. They didn't. Red teased me for months after even though I had long ago convinced him I knew the answer.

I also remember having a terrible time with the Palmer method of writing, whereby one had to copy out perfectly formed shapes within the prescribed lines. My swirls were never even, nor would they behave well and stay within the lines. Ruby was forever pointing out how bad my handwriting was. However, when Ruby was busy helping another student, she often let me sit at a small table in the corner helping a younger child with spelling and reading. I felt very grown-up and proud when she asked me to do this.

Everyone else played tag or hide-and-seek at recess or lunch. Because I was slower than the other kids, I was always it. I sat on the open steps of the schoolhouse, feeling sad and lonely. Often I felt angry with myself for having made a mistake on my assignment. Sometimes my sadness was caused by something Ruby had said or something that had happened at home. Sitting on those wide schoolhouse steps, watching the rustling of the aspen, and absorbing the sights and smells of the fir forest and the trills of the red-winged blackbirds helped my unhappiness evaporate.

It took Michael and me several years to realize that nothing we told Ruby remained secret. We told her about the fights the two of us had while walking to school. In the winter, this often involved throwing ice balls at one another. She gave us many lectures in which one or both of us was chastised unmercifully.

After such talks, we both felt guilty and inadequate. She told our parents, and the lectures and tirades continued at home.

One morning, I told Ruby that the night before Mother had been so mad at my father, she threw a potholder at him. When Ruby told them I had told her, they were hurt and angry.

The next morning, Michael and I were walking on top of the huge mountains of snow at the side of the road that had been formed by the snowplow when a reasonable solution hit me.

"Michael, let's make a pact. Let's not tell Ruby about any of our fights or about anything that happens at home."

He agreed. We kept our pact and never regretted it.

When I started high school in Pagosa, the one-room schoolhouse closed forever. Our parents drove us the eight miles to the highway where a school bus picked us up for the rest of the trip. Ruby returned to teach math at Pagosa High where I had to endure her gruff teaching methods for another four years.

My senior year of high school, we no longer had to take the bus. My father had begun teaching science in Pagosa that year, and we rode with him. I actually took chemistry from him. I was concerned that he would either grade my papers too severely or automatically give me a high grade. It turned out that in the classroom setting, he was a clear and patient teacher. I earned my A+ honestly.

Pagosa didn't have any library or bookstore. The high school library was antiquated and only had a few reference books. The nearest bookstores were either in Durango 80 miles to the west or Santa Fe 150 miles to the south. Whenever I received a letter or phone call from Janet, Karen, or Susie, they'd tell me about a great book they had just read. I was jealous. I could hardly wait to go to the Santa Fe bookstore. My brother remembers receiving paperback books by mail. Recently he told me, "Whenever I opened the package, I sucked in the wonderful smell of newsprint."

It was while sitting around our six-foot round table that my brother's and my world blossomed. We began to understand more of the world than the small ranching community of Pagosa and the Blanco Basin. The table became our classroom in a way no formal education ever could.

The process of refurbishing the table was an education in itself. I watched as my parents sanded every part of this old table except for the pedestal with its four large feet. The layers of old stain disappeared, and the complex grain of golden oak developed. Many layers of hot linseed oil made the wood look even richer and warmer. Two of the four leaves were carefully sawed to make a round lazy susan. My father had found an antique ball bearing to attach the lazy susan to the table. He bought smooth stainless steel balls to replace the worn ones. I was fascinated as I watched him disassemble the racer[1] and insert the new balls.

"Damn it, I forgot to get spacers. I want to finish this tonight and don't want to drive the twenty miles into town." He rummaged around the house and found some used rifle shells. "These will work perfectly."

The lazy susan finished, we placed one of the remaining silver balls in the center and began spinning our new toy. The ball spiraled faster and faster and careened toward the outside of the lazy susan onto the table. It then deposited itself with a thump on the green linoleum floor. My father said, "Notice how when the ball circles outward, it goes faster and faster. That is because it has gained energy from the spinning lazy susan."

This was Michael's and my first practical lesson in momentum physics. From then on, anything was fair game: poker chips, paper clips, cards, paper, and even mustard jars. Mother would shake her head and shout, "Damn it, guys, stop!" as she dove to keep the mustard jar from hitting the floor. She was usually successful.

This table became a forum where I listened to my parents talk with Robert, their friends Jane and Bob Wilson and Phil and Emily Morrison and others. Politics, arts, and science were only some of the discussion subjects. I remember taking long walks with my father and Linus Pauling. His wispy white hair and gentle demeanor made me develop a childlike crush on him. I learned my parents' friend, David Hawkins, who had been Robert's assistant during the war, had also been caught up in the witch-hunts. Dave was a philosopher and was on the faculty of the University of Colorado in Boulder. He and his wife, Frances,

---

[1] Racers are the mechanism that allows the ball bearing to spin. It is comprised of two circular tracks with smooth metal balls between them.

were also called before HUAC because of his refusal to sign the loyalty oath that the university was forcing its employees to sign. Because of this and their involvement in leftist causes, he was threatened with dismissal, but he fought and was allowed to stay. When it became clear that the University of Colorado wasn't going to fire David, my father rubbed his eyes, turned to my mother, and said, "If I had been more honest and had fought harder, I might still have my job in Minnesota."

Mother countered, "Quit kicking yourself. The bastards in the FBI and the government were using you as a scapegoat to get to your brother and to perpetuate the hysteria."

The elections of 1952 and 1956 were discussed around this substantial table. I think that my parents really wanted to vote for Norman Thomas, the inveterate Socialist Party candidate, but ended up being enthusiastic Stevenson supporters. They discussed his pro-labor stance, his compassion for the working class. They were convinced that he would be able to stop the slaughter in Korea. They loved his intellectualism but also realized that this was a drawback.

My mother often said, "I can't believe how many people are put off by Stevenson's brain. They'd rather have Eisenhower's fame and mediocrity."

My mother most often held the post of chief raconteur at our table. I was awestruck as she told of leaving home at the age of sixteen because her mother had taken the first paycheck she earned from Safeway. Never learning where she went, I imagine that she probably stayed with some of her friends' families and later shared an apartment with friends. She never did return home but was able to finish high school at Oakland Tech and enrolled at the University of California, Berkeley. Even at seventeen or eighteen, I thought, I would never have had the courage to strike out on my own as she had.

I marveled at her chutzpah as she recounted how, during the height of the Depression, she and her coworkers at Safeway distributed any leftover produce to those in need in the alley in back of the store. This was totally contrary to the fact that the management demanded that all the produce be destroyed.

My father brought his intellect and interest in the arts to the table. His mother, Ella, was an artist. She and his father, Julius, collected many fine impressionist paintings.

On one of our visits to San Francisco while we were living on the ranch, I remember standing in the dusty basement of the old San Francisco Museum of Modern Art where a curator pulled out three original paintings for us to view.

They were part of my father's inheritance.

Even in the dim light, I gasped in awe of their beauty and the fact that they belonged to my family. Two of them were Picassos—*First Steps* and, from his blue period, *Mother and Child.* The third painting was van Gogh's *Portrait of Adeline Ravoux.* I was particularly impressed by it because I had seen it in an art book my parents had. The reproduction in the art book couldn't begin to compete with the vibrancy and complicated mixtures of paints that made up the portrait.

Looking at Picasso's *Mother and Child,* I fell in love with the soft blues, the serenity of the mother as she held her bigger-than-life child with her huge competent-looking hand.

My father developed a love for classical music, and even on the ranch, we often had it playing on the phonograph. As an adolescent, he studied flute with one of the foremost flutists of the time, George Barrere. He became a very good flutist and told stories of how when he was an undergraduate at Johns Hopkins, he would go to his professors' homes in Baltimore to play in small ensembles. He also played the piccolo but was discouraged in this by my mother, who disliked its high pitch. At one time he had an alto flute but had to give it away because every time he played it, the melancholy sounds brought tears to his eyes.

My father's flute playing became part of my life. Frequently I fell asleep to its melodies. At other times I sat on the couch in our living room reading as my father played. Today, whenever I hear a flute, I think of him.

Friends and neighbors came to lunch or dinner. I was fascinated as Tom and Veda Teeson and Joe and Mona Jones told stories about surviving the Depression. The only things they needed to buy were salt, flour, and sugar. They grew their own vegetables, slaughtered their meat, and had their own milk cows.

When we moved to the ranch, there was no electricity. In October, 1949, the REA came to the Basin, and my father wired our house. Once we had electricity, our lives changed dramatically. Not only did we have running water and an indoor bathroom, but also the radio, which we played nearly all day, providing us with news and entertainment. We were not able to get many stations, and when we did, the static often obliterated half the broadcast. Mother introduced me to Our Miss Brooks, The Shadow, Perry Mason, and many others. Michael and I discovered The Lone Ranger and other Westerns. We received most of our news by listening to the radio, which invariably evoked comments from Mother, often filled with swear words and cynicism.

On July 17, 1950, my mother was making bread as she listened to a Durango radio station.

> Today, the FBI arrested Julius Rosenberg. He has been
> accused of passing atomic secrets to the Soviets.

No more information was given. Mother began punching the beige lump of dough with all her strength.

When my father came into the house, she told him the news. He paced back and forth and rubbed his blue eyes, eyes that now emanated a profound sadness.

My parents could talk of nothing but the arrest at the dinner table that night.

"Jackie, we have to do something. This madness can't be allowed to continue."

In tones of combined resignation and anger Mother answered, "What in the hell can we do? We certainly are in no position to come to their defense."

On August 11, 1950, Ethyl Rosenberg was also arrested.

Michael and I listened too. Both of us had became frightened, especially about what was going to happen to their children. I thought about how scared, confused, and lonely these boys must have been. Unsurprisingly, the Rosenbergs' incarceration—later, their execution—awakened my concern that my parents too might suffer a similar fate.

Over the following weeks, I heard my parents talk about David Greenglass, Ethyl's brother. Greenglass had worked in Los Alamos as a machinist during the war and had allegedly passed the secrets on to the Soviets. When the government announced it intended to seek the death penalty for Julius and Ethyl, we watched Mother storm to the radio and turn it off. "God, I wish we could leave this Fascist country. I'm so sick and tired of the madness, the hysteria. There isn't a chance in hell that they can be saved."

Nonetheless, when the National Committee to Secure Justice in the

Rosenberg Case was formed, my parents circulated a petition that had been developed under the committee's auspices. They were actually able to get quite a few signatures from the small community of Pagosa. But all efforts to save the Rosenbergs were to no avail. On June 19, 1953, our radio blared the news:

President Eisenhower refused the Rosenbergs' appeal for clemency, and Ethyl and Julius Rosenberg were executed within minutes of each other.

My father had tears in his eyes. His body slumped, and his manner and face were those of a totally defeated man. The clop clop of his pacing reverberated throughout the room, pausing only when he stopped to confront my mother.

"Fuck. Jackie, do you think that if we'd tried harder, we could have saved their lives?"

My mother sat transfixed as she answered, her shocked eyes looking into nothingness.

Then she sat and held her head in her hands. Fury morphed into sorrow. "I doubt it. The government had to find some victims to show the world how tough, how efficient they are in dealing with alleged spies. I'm sure the government and the FBI manufactured evidence and insinuated relationships that didn't exist."

She drew a shaky breath. "It's cold-blooded murder."

The rest of the day, the house felt and sounded like a tomb. Mother occasionally broke the silence to rail against the American government and then she'd fall silent again. I spent the day obsessing in horror about the executions. Had there been pain? What was it like to die—and to die that way? How did their little boys feel? Who would take care of them now? At the dinner table as my parents resumed the same conversation that had gripped us around the clock, I grew still more anxious and sad.

Finally I blurted out, "How could our government murder two people? Even if they were spies, they didn't deserve to die."

Weary and sadder than I'd seen him in a long time, my father spoke quietly, "You're right. I don't have an answer."

At the time, my parents had neither the strength nor the certainty to reassure my brother and me that we'd be safe. I worried for weeks about what was going to happen to the Rosenberg children, Michael and Robert. Even when I learned later that Anne and Abel Meerpol had adopted them, I felt anguish.

On a cold winter's day, February 9, 1950, Michael and I sat around the table doing our homework while Mother was preparing dinner. The radio blared.

> The young junior senator from Wisconsin, Joseph McCarthy, gave a speech to the Republican Woman's Club in Wheeling, West Virginia, in which he said, "I have in my hands a list of 205 cases of individuals in the government who appear to be either card-caring members or certainly loyal to the Communist Party."

Mother stopped mashing the potatoes and said, "My god, when is this going to stop? Now we don't only have to worry about HUAC, the FBI, and Richard Nixon, but we have to deal with another demagogue in the Senate."

Over the next four years, her prediction of a demagogue emerging came true. In May 1954, McCarthy began to investigate communist activity in the army. These were the very first Senate hearings to be televised. Although we didn't have a TV, we were able to follow the hearings on the radio and in the *Denver Post*. McCarthy had manufactured evidence and was badgering witnesses. Initially, McCarthy intimidated even President Eisenhower, but as the hearings continued, Eisenhower finally intervened on behalf of some of the army personnel.

Over the radio, a reporter was saying,

> Today in the army hearings, Joseph McCarthy was relentlessly questioning and accusing a young soldier of being a Communist. Joseph Welch, the chief counsel for the army, had had enough. He issued a blistering condemnation of McCarthy's tactics.
>
> "Until this moment, Senator, I think I never really gauged your cruelty or recklessness. Let us not assassinate this lad further. You have done enough. Have you no sense of decency at long last? Have you no sense of decency?"

My parents looked at each other. Mother breathed, "It's about time some-one challenged the bastard."

On December 2, 1954, the evening news announced that the Senate had voted 65–22 to censure McCarthy for his abuse of legislative power. Around the table that night, my parents tried to analyze what the censure might mean. They wondered aloud if this might be a signal that our nation was finally coming to its senses—that the worst of the witch-hunts were over.

I asked my father, "Does this mean that you'll be able to get a job at an university?"

He started pacing and said, "I doubt it."

Michael chimed in, "Why not? If the witch-hunts are over, you should be able to."

Our father stopped pacing long enough to answer, "I doubt that they will be over for a while. But at least one of the people responsible for them has been found out."

Interspersed with the conversations about the Rosenbergs, McCarthy, and the general state of our country, my parents conducted many intense conversa-tions about my father's brother, Robert. This was especially true in 1954. At the time of Robert's hearings before the AEC (the Atomic Energy Commis-sion), he was director of the Institute for Advanced Studies at Princeton and also served as chairman of the AEC. Like many of the atomic scientists, he spent much of his time advocating for civilian control of atomic energy. He felt very strongly that there should be international dialogue and control of such a pow-erful weapon. On this issue, he vehemently disagreed with Edward Teller and a few other physicists who promoted the development of the hydrogen bomb. My father, and others who believed similarly, did not directly try to play the Washington political game but instead worked by publically speaking out or writing in public condemnation against the secrecy. By contrast, Robert tried to work within the Washington, DC power structure; talking to presidents Tru-man and Eisenhower, testifying before Congress, and working with Secretary of State Dean Acheson.

Both my parents had been upset about the way Robert and his lawyer handled his defense. Mother particularly—who was no great fan of Robert's—

felt that he wasn't being honest during the proceedings and that he too readily implicated others. She often called him a phony and power hungry. My father in turn would try to defend him. Their arguments often ended in an impasse.

Despite Mother's dislike of Robert, both parents fumed as Edward Teller told the hearing that he wouldn't feel comfortable with Robert having access to top secrets documents.

Robert lost his security clearance. After that, although he continued as director of the Institute of Advanced Studies, he was never the same.

My father went to visit Robert several times during this period. During each visit, he tried to get his brother to be more forthright and honest. After each visit, he would come back more distressed and worried.

"Jackie, I'm so worried about Robert. He has lost an extreme amount of weight and looks terrible. He thinks his life is over."

Dinner table conversations were not always an educational experience. Many times they simply erupted into violent verbal battles between my parents. Besides arguments about Robert, my parents would vent their anger toward each other.

I hated and feared these battles. I never knew when they would occur, and when they did, I wanted to shout, "Stop it!" Instead I would laugh nervously, avert my eyes, and begin fidgeting and then flee as soon as I could.

In spite of the battles, as a child and a young teenager, I soaked up all the information I was exposed to. However, the older I became, the more these dinner table conversations became loaded with negative energy. The game began to change when I was an adolescent. Wanting to engage with my parents and others and to develop my own ideas, I tried to enter the discussions. Whenever I did, my father turned his gaze—with cool, penetrating eyes—on me. Using his most authoritative voice, he'd calmly challenge me to debate. Being no match for his knowledge, his certitude, or his need to win, I went mute.

Many years later my parents, Phil Morrison, and his second wife, Phyllis, and I were sitting around the table in my parents' Sausalito home. I was in my late thirties, had my MD, and had been in private pediatric practice for four or five years. Phil and my father monopolized the conversation, pontificating on antibiotics and antibiotic resistance. It soon became apparent to me that these two men really didn't fully understand the mechanisms by which bacteria became resistant to antibiotics. I tried as they spoke to make my voice heard, to fill in the areas of knowledge they had missed—in short, to teach. Phil and my father acted as if I were on the dark side of a one-way mirror where they could neither see or hear me. It was as if I was not worthy of entering into their dialogue.

On my way home to San José that night, a revelation caused me to feel as if a great weight had been lifted.

*Those two Renaissance men aren't physicians. They're not gods. I know what I'm talking about! They don't really want to learn. They're so damned sure they have all the answers and know everything. And they don't. They simply don't!*

This was the beginning of the end of my silence, the beginning of the blending of the confident doctor and the (formerly) scared adolescent and woman. Still, it would take many years to gain the confidence I needed to enter into conversations—to let my ideas and my feelings soar.

# 16
## Applying to College

Summer was waning, and all the guests bunking with us at Camp Oppenheimer had gone home. My senior year in high school was about to begin, and looming over me was the project of applying to college.

My mother and I seated ourselves at the kitchen table in the best window light with stacks of college catalogues before us. For long periods we were silent as we turned pages, carefully scouring them, staring at photographs as if they were treasure maps. I felt proud and confident. All the long hours of studying had paid off. I graduated second in my class. My ambitions had already taken shape. I knew that I wanted to be either a veterinarian or a physician.

My interest in becoming a vet had, of course, taken root and been nourished by daily exposure on the ranch to the lives and trials of a steady population of animals, especially our cattle and horses. I'd lived each day as a close and affectionate friend to them, witnessing their births, deaths, and the numerous diseases they had experienced. The more time I spent around them, the more fascinated I became by their problems and the more I wanted to understand and help alleviate their sufferings. I'd already spent time in veterinarian boot camp.

Ranching is a risky business. Its success is vulnerable to all manner of attacking elements: the weather, the price of cattle, and last but not least, the health of the herd. The vagaries of ranching became apparent in 1950 with the heifers we had bought together with our neighbor, Fred Norton. Fred and my father had no idea at the time, that the heifers they'd bought carried *brucellosis* or *Bang's disease*.

The first sign that something was wrong with them surfaced later that summer when my father burst in the house from inspecting the cattle and the fences. He was clearly upset.

"Jackie, Fred and I saw a couple of dead fetuses. Fred has the idea the heifers might have brucellosis. He remembers hearing that there is an epidemic in cattle in this area."

My mother frowned.

"What in the hell is brucellosis?"

"Fred says it's a bacteria that can cause miscarriages in cattle."

With no further words, my parents began yanking every veterinary book we owned from our shelves. They sat paging fast through each manual until they found the sections discussing brucellosis. The only sounds in the room after that were unhappy murmurs or "Listen to this" followed by quoted passages that rang painfully familiar.

Blood tests confirmed the diagnosis of brucellosis. By the spring of 1951, all but twelve of the heifers had aborted. The only way to keep the disease from spreading was to isolate the infected animals and slaughter them. No way around it; the heifers that had already miscarried were sent to the slaughterhouse. Those that were still pregnant were isolated from all our other cattle and allowed to deliver. But after delivery, they too had to be killed. We were left with twelve orphaned calves to feed from buckets.

We called them our "banger babies." Each morning and evening, the corral was filled with bellowing calves. We poured the milk into galvanized buckets equipped with large rubber nipples. The calves raced over to the wooden fence where the buckets were hung. Every time they began to eat the little animals first butted the buckets with their cute rounded foreheads. Soon, our corral resounded with the *clank-clank* of the ball valves located at the attachment site of the nipple.

One day, I was inspecting my cattle herd and found Fern, one of my cows, lying on her side. She was breathing hard and coughing. I went to her at once and noticed that her white brisket, or dewlap, was swollen to almost twice its normal size. My fingers sank into the spongy tissue. I knew that something was terribly wrong and ran to get Mother. We raced back to the house once again pulling out every one of our veterinary books and sat at the kitchen table furiously poring over them. She bent the corners of the useful pages so she could find the information again.

At length, she looked up at me. "Judy, I think Fern has brisket disease." She sounded grim. "What's brisket disease?"

"According to the book, it's an accumulation of fluid due to heart failure." She scanned the page once more.

"Does it say what causes it?"

"The most common cause is a viral infection of the heart muscle."

The next day we loaded Fern into our horse trailer and took her to the vet in Durango. Fern stayed in Durango for several months where the lower elevation apparently helped her. We brought her home, and she did well for a time but eventually died of her disease. I was bereft but consoled myself by saying, "At least it wasn't Knuckle Head."

Then not long thereafter came the drama of Snowball, another one of my cows. She had gone into labor and delivered a healthy heifer calf, but once the placenta was delivered, her uterus prolapsed (turned inside out and protruded from her vagina). There was blood everywhere. The uterus was filthy. I was horrified. I ran to the house yelling, "Pa, come quickly! Snowball's in trouble!"

My father raced to the barn, took one look at Snowball, and went into action like a seasoned country vet. He gently but thoroughly cleaned the womb and skillfully pushed it back in. He then gave Snowball a penicillin shot. To his pride and my relief she survived, did well, and was even able to have several more successful pregnancies.

By this point, I had become deeply involved with all our cattle's diseases. I found that I wanted to know more and more about veterinary medicine and began to study our veterinary books more carefully. My interest in medicine, both veterinary and human, spiked when as a junior in high school, my parents bought me Gray's Anatomy. It was thrilling to unwrap and hold the heavy volume. I felt empowered by the collective knowledge in its pages. Since I myself suffered from a rare syndrome (Turner's) and had been forced, in turn, to deal with the myriad of medical problems associated with it, my curiosity and attention to biological science and medicine surged as I considered my various options in higher education.

Even though I had done very well in school, my education had been less-than- stellar. I was concerned about whether I would be accepted into any decent university. If I were accepted, could I fit in and be able to function in such an environment? Putting my doubts and fears below the surface, I applied to several top-ranked universities: Cornell, Stanford, Reed College, University of California, Berkeley, and Johns Hopkins. Reluctantly, I also applied to the University of Colorado. It would serve, I reasoned, as the safety net beneath those higher targets—my ace in the hole.

Filling out what seemed to be endless rounds of applications demanded constant attention to detail and a steady drive toward perfection, exerting intense pressure on me. Mother helped me edit and type my essays. We stuffed envelopes like a couple of campaign workers until at last we were ready to mail everything out.

During this time, I'd been daring to hope that my applications would make a sparkling splash when read by the admissions committees. In November, all the confidence I had been able to muster shriveled to dust when Jack Mallott summoned me into his office. Coach Mallott was a wizened character who served as our high school's counselor as well as the assistant coach. No sooner had I walked into his office he started grilling me as if I were a defendant in a trial.

"Judy, have you thought at all about what you're going to do after you graduate?"

"I've already applied to several universities."

"Which ones?"

Quietly, I told him. He looked at me with an incredulous scowl.

"Those are very hard schools to get into. What about Fort Lewis or Alamosa State?"[2]

His tone sapped whatever confidence I'd been able to generate.

I told him that I wanted to be either a vet or a physician and wanted somewhere challenging.

"Well, I think that you should become a vet. You're not too good at dealing with people."

[2] Fort Lewis was a junior college in Durango, and Alamosa State was a small four-year college in Alamosa.

This declaration stung as if he'd struck me. I looked at the ground, feeling my cheeks heat. His insensitive pronouncement confirmed what I felt about myself.

I was too shaken and too young to be able to contradict the impact of his statement. I didn't have the confidence to walk myself through the facts. For one, Jack Mallott really didn't know me. He had only observed me from afar. We had passed each other in the halls, and I'd seen him at the games. I had never had him as a teacher, and we had never sat down to have any kind of conversation. It's also possible he based his unkind opinion on the breathless gossip in the school yearbook. After all, I'd been voted "most shy" in its pages for three years running. And I knew the only reason for my not keeping the title for the fourth straight year was that I was serving as the yearbook's editor that year and had decreed that we would discontinue the practice of voting anybody the "most" anything.

Naturally, when I arrived home, I burst into tears as I told Mother about my encounter.

Her response was typical of the way she dealt with my brother's and my emotions. Instead of having us talk about our feelings or find strategies for helping us cope, she morphed into a lioness protecting her cubs, making the perpetrator the evil one. For better or for worse, she insisted on fighting most of our battles for us. This event was no exception. She was furious.

"That bastard. How can he be so insensitive? I'm going to talk to him and the principal."

Horrified, I begged her not to. Only reluctantly did she agree.

That spring, whenever we picked up the mail from the post office, I grabbed it hungrily, looking for responses from the universities.

Rejection after rejection trickled in. I felt sadder and more useless with each of them.

The single fat envelope, the single acceptance, came from the University of Colorado. It felt like salt in the wound. Maybe Jack Mallott was correct after all.

# 17
## Adios, Mi Rancho

From fifteen until I was eighteen, my life on the ranch was painted with a palate of dark colors.

During these intense, difficult years, my love of nature and for my cattle combined to form a comforting backdrop, a safety zone of rich bright textures that saturated my perception and that drew me out of myself, out of my then-unrecognized depression.

The forest, with its cathedral-like silence, also beckoned.

One day I sauntered across the gravel road, climbing through the barbed wire, and walking, singing through the meadow into the deep loamy-smelling forest of pines, firs, and aspen. The sound of a car engine was the only element that broke my reverie. I wanted so desperately to escape, to pretend no one else was around. I wanted to keep walking deeper into the forest until I no longer could see the road or hear the cars.

I couldn't push myself farther into the woods; I was too afraid.

At other times I wandered out to the meadow below the house where I would simply lie down on the warm earth to gaze into the sky. Scanning its vastness and clarity, I often spotted a hawk playing on the updrafts, swooping, gliding. As I lay on the dark spongy earth, the cattle came and formed a circle around me. Often, one brave red-and-white Hereford would cautiously approach me to investigate and to come close enough to lick my hair and face with her sandpaper tongue. The others moved in to form a tighter circle, ever curious. The silliness of their investigation would finally make me laugh, and the cows gently backed away to form their original circle. Soon they lost interest and wandered away.

I found special solace in walking to the barn with its smells of hay, old wood, and the pungent aroma of cattle. By the time I left for college, I had twelve bovine companions. Each one of them always listened patiently, never talked back, and their deep brown eyes seemed to convey perfect compassion. However Knuckle Head remained my "therapist in chief." The others were her co-therapists. I turned to her whenever my parents engaged in one of their yelling matches or whenever my father and I had our numerous confrontations. She was always there when I felt friendless or when something went awry at school.

During my blackest, most despairing moments, Knuckle Head licked my cheek and looked at me with her wise obsidian eyes while I talked to her and softly brushed her hair until it glistened. I would walk back to the house feeling settled, more thoughtful, and in better possession of myself, better able to deal with the day.

I remember the pungent smells of manure and pine that were unable to overcome the bittersweet red-hot-chili burning of loneliness.

The ranch provided other sensory stimuli as well. I remember the sounds of the aspens stirring and glittering in the wind, the red-winged blackbirds trilling as they sat on the fence, the rumble of river rocks being rolled and polished by the clear silver water. These sounds and sights as well as my cattle gave me a strengthened grip on life. They were my salvation during these chaotic times.

In 1959, my parents left the ranch. I remember my grief and anger when Knuckle Head and my other cattle were sold. I remember my helplessness of having no voice in the decision whether to sell them and the frustration of not being there to say good-bye.

For me it was the end of my childhood and of my life as a ranch girl. I was about to enter the world of academia.

# Oppenheimer Family Gallery

## Section B

Me hugging Knuckle Head

Mike on Knuckle Head

Mother, Mike Gomez (our hired hand) and me on baler

Meadow on our property on the Rito Blanco looking toward Square Top mountain

Snow Scene with Flattop from Potato Hill

Looking to head of valley from potato hill with house and our horses

Blanco Basin Schoolhouse

Haying upper meadow

Branding and dehorning

Going to Town: Janet, Mike, my father, and me

Barn and scale house

View from house with cattle in field

Karen with me standing on fence

Karen on Thunder

Karen (age 16 or 17)

Mother in her thirties on hill at Perro Caliente

Me at forty on same hill at Perro Caliente

# 18
## Onward to Boulder

Mother and I started off on our trip to Boulder early in the morning. On this, my first foray away from home, I was excited but also terrified. The car was packed with suitcases full of new clothes, boxes of books, my new Olympia typewriter, a blond phonograph with a record changer, and other necessities of college life.

On the trip to Boulder, my mother and I savored intervals of serious conversation that alternated with moments of comfortable silence. It was the first of many mother-daughter trips that drew us close, helping us bond in unprecedented ways. After this "maiden voyage" to Boulder together, whenever I moved—from Boulder to Palo Alto, Palo Alto to Denver, Denver to Madison, and from Madison to Houston—Mother was there to accompany me on my journey, allaying my fears and supporting me during these major changes in my life.

When we reached CU, I felt at once overwhelmed and charmed. The campus was landscaped with large expanses of lawns and old trees, among which stood many stately buildings of old stone and brick. To a new arrival, it looked distinguished and venerable, resembling the photographs in the catalogues we'd studied. Students walked along the tidy paths alone, in groups, or in pairs, or holding hands on shaded benches. They acted as if they'd been there all their lives. I envied their apparent serene confidence.

At first, I felt convinced that I'd never be able find my way around. It was weeks of map reading and asking directions before I felt comfortable navigating the campus.

When Mother and I arrived, all the dorms and the admissions building were hubbubs of activity. Standing in the doorway of the small room that was to be my home for the next nine months, I saw two single beds, two small desks with chairs, and two small dressers. Even though I had had to share a room with my brother, it was much larger. I felt very claustrophobic. In fairness, the room had been painted brightly, was filled with light, and looked out on an expanse of well-groomed lawn. My roommate, a young woman from a small town in Nebraska, was putting some of her clothes in her dresser. She was friendly and talkative. However, I couldn't help feeling apprehensive about living with anyone in such cramped quarters.

When we were alone, Mother's comment about my new roommate was perfunctory. "She seems like a nice enough young woman." To me, thoroughly schooled in the euphemistic code my mother spoke, the hidden message was clear: "I really don't think she's too bright or interesting.

I am sure some ancient computer—one that used punch cards—had matched us. I was from a small town. My roommate was too. I'd been active in 4-H. She had been also. I'd joined Rainbow Girls, a Masonic organization for teenaged girls; she'd done the same. The problem was that 4-H had occupied most of my life while Rainbow Girls had apparently dominated hers. In fact, I had only participated in Rainbow Girls for social acceptance. I soon tired of its secrecy and patriotism. I also was very uncomfortable whenever I went to any of their social occasions, especially the dances. I hated the religious aspect of the ritual, and I felt like such a hypocrite that I quit within a year.

Mother left me there in Boulder to return to Pagosa. I watched her car drive off, leaving me standing alone in the parking lot. I turned and walked toward the dorm. I was certain at that moment that I could not survive without my mother's support, both physical and mental. I was not even sure I would be able to wash and iron my clothes, much less master the myriad of other adult duties required for making it on my own.

Time took over, providing at least continuity. One day followed another, and I groped my way through new habits, courses, and the rules of the new setting.

During that first semester, several young women and I often met in one of our rooms to relive our day. Subjects ranged from who was rushing which sororities to dates, TV programs, and popular music.

In the course of these bull sessions, I sat and listened to others, seldom entering in these conversations. Unfortunately, as in high school, it seemed to be my fate that I would be unable to connect with their lives. Only on the rare occasions when we discussed ideas—our classes, philosophy, politics, or religion—did I become exhilarated and feel alive. We were all eighteen, and like most adolescents, our opinions were cast in concrete. We all tried to convince one another that our views were the only correct ones. I stood out as the sole atheist. At times I felt I was behaving like an insufferable snob. Many of the young women who participated in these sessions were ardent Christians and belonged to Campus Crusade for Christ. Their primary purpose appeared to be to convert as many other students as possible.

Even worse than that, my politics were also out of sync with the other students. At the time, I was styling myself as a strict pacifist, absolutely convinced that socialism was the way to end human misery. I joined the Young People's Socialist League (YPSL), but like my parents before, I became upset by their rigidity and their declared acceptance that violence was a legitimate means for achieving their goals. I quit within a few months. One day, the dorm resident advisor (probably a junior or senior girl) called me down to her office. She was wearing too much makeup, and her blond hair seemed splayed into a helmet that didn't have a strand out of place.

She motioned me to take a chair.

"Judy, how're things going?"

"Okay, I guess. My classes are hard, but I'm surviving."

She nodded as if not hearing. Then she lobbed her little grenade. "Judy, I've received some complaints from the girls about your religious beliefs and politics." She went on, "They feel you've been trying to convert them."

Taken totally by surprise, I was red-faced.

"What do you mean? I listened to their opinions, and they seemed to listen to mine. I thought everyone was encouraged to express their ideas equally here."

This didn't slow her or even cause her to blink.

"They tell me you're an atheist, and that upsets them."

"I'm sorry. What do you want me to do, lie?"

"No, but you must learn how, well, to round off your corners." I stared at her in bafflement.

"What do you mean by 'round off my corners'?"

She only shrugged and said nothing more about how I might best accomplish this enviable feat. I was dismissed.

Perplexed and angry, I phoned our family friend, Frances Hawkins. When I explained to Frances about the resident advisor's statements, she was naturally furious. To offer distraction and consolation, she invited me over. Walking the mile or so to the Hawkinses that brisk sunny afternoon and shuffling through the crunchy autumn leaves lifted my spirits. Frances and I talked awhile, had dinner, and by the time she drove me back to the dorm, we were even able to joke a bit about the situation.

Dave and Frances Hawkins had been friends of my parents in Berkeley since before I was born. Dave had been my uncle Robert's assistant at Los Alamos where he was in charge of writing the official history of the project. He was now a professor of philosophy at the University of Colorado. During that first year in Boulder, I found myself spending many Saturdays or Sundays at the Hawkins' home. At their dinner table, Dave, Frances, their daughter Julie (a senior in high school), and I sat and talked for hours. I amused them with stories and tasty information I had gleaned from my humanities course. We also talked about the politics of the day. By the end of such visits, I was able to cope with my loneliness and uncertainties.

Sadly, my roommate had no such support. Every time she talked to her parents on the phone, she wept. She told me how much she missed them and all her friends. She yearned to be with the young man back home with whom she was in love. Academically, her courses were difficult for her.

Initially, I tried to invent things to do together, to talk with her, and to help her with her schoolwork. I didn't make much headway. Midway through the semester, she became inconsolably homesick and dropped out of school. I had the little dorm room to myself for the remainder of the semester. I continued to have a single room for the rest of my time at the university. One might suppose that this rare luxury of space would have felt like a windfall. In sad truth, this only added to my sense of isolation—of being different, even dangerous.

On most Friday nights during my time in the dorm, I could be found sitting at my desk with a book or papers in front of me, periodically looking out my window, watching the setting sun paint the Flat Irons (landmark foothills that border Boulder) a deep amber. I could usually hear girls running up and down the hall, knocking on each other's doors. They yelled at each other, fretting about the choice of clothes for their upcoming date or asking if they could borrow a sweater. They talked about how they were going to Tulagi's or the Sink (popular local beer joints) and then to a fraternity party. Later, I watched from my window as swarms of young ladies trotted off with their dates.

At this juncture of the evening, the dorm became a tomb. When the silence became unbearable, I'd take a break in studying and wander to the lounge where one or two other girls joined me in watching *Route 66* and *Perry Mason*. Draped over couches and chairs, we watched television like zombies. None of us bothered to speak a word to each other. When the programs ended, I'd slowly return back to my room, finish my work, and curl up in bed. I was invariably awakened at around eleven by the excited chatter of girls' voices once again echoing through the halls. Many sounded jubilant. Others sounded slurred and boisterous, even caustic.

Every day I saw couples holding hands or kissing. I would turn away. Leaving class was an event I dreaded. At that point, two or three students usually went off together, and I'd later see them sitting studying and talking. I was so sure that my overtures would be rejected that I remained silent.

My companion, on the other hand, was Mozart. I often fell asleep to the strains of *Eine Kleine Nachtmusik* playing on my blond phonograph.

# 19
## Campus Crusade for Christ

One afternoon, I was in my room studying when there was a knock on the door. I opened it to face a group of four unsmiling young men and women. I recognized one as a young woman who had attended our dorm discussions earlier in the year.

"We're from the Campus Crusade for Christ. We'd like to talk with you."

I was somewhat surprised. I thought I had convinced them that I was intransient and wasn't worth their trying to convert me. I was cordial and polite, but guarded. "I need to work on a paper that's due tomorrow. I don't have time to talk."

Not waiting for an answer, they filed into the room, staring at me defiantly. Clearly they hadn't intended to leave until I'd listened to them. To be truthful, part of me was curious. How would I play their little game? How might I checkmate the lot of them?

Agreeing to talk to them for a short time, I ended up in one of their cars. I sat in the front seat, sandwiched between two of the young evangelists. Two others sat in the backseat, leaning forward to make sure I could hear.

The young missionaries kept quoting Bible passages that proved (to their satisfaction anyway) that unless I believed, I was most assuredly destined for hell. I tried to use my more intellectual arguments (e.g., If there is a god, who created him). In minutes, it became obvious that I couldn't argue successfully with them. The only part of the Bible I had read was Job, and that was in my humanities class. I tried using my more intellectual, rational reasoning to argue with them, but I was no match.

After what seemed liked hours, these young zealots were still pontificating, and I could not see any way to escape. I was beginning to sweat. Looking toward the car door, I realized that I could never overpower or climb over them. I began to think I was going to be spirited away to god knows where and either held for ransom or thoroughly brainwashed. Finally, after much pleading on my part, they let me go.

Disheartened and depressed, I trudged up to my room, wondering how I could have been so stupid as to even agree to talk with them. At least, though, this time, I had the consolation of having apparently convinced them I was hopeless. After this confrontation, the Campus Crusade for Christ contingent never bothered me again.

# 20
## Introduction to the Humanities

The screen in my Introduction to the Humanities class showed an image of a baroque cathedral, and the classroom was filled with the sound of a Bach cantata.

My eyes and ears drank the image and sound. I had probably heard the music and seen the picture before, but taken together, they touched something in me—a part I had not yet acknowledged. For that moment, my loneliness sprouted wings and vanished out the open window. I became immersed in the art, music, and literature of Western culture from the Greeks and Romans to the early twentieth century. It would prove to offer rich rewards.

But despite this comfort and stimulation from my courses and those warm accepting evenings with Dave and Frances, I found myself holing up in my room more and more. My life centered entirely on writing papers, reading, going to the library, and eating alone.

My pillow was often soggy. In the mirror I beheld a young woman with a drawn face, eyes cast downward. Suddenly, even keeping up with my schoolwork became a mountain I had difficulty climbing.

In desperation, I took myself to the university guidance center to speak with a counselor. She was a woman in her thirties, bland, and expressionless, who beckoned me to sit in a chair beside her desk. I talked about my loneliness and my sadness of not having a boyfriend. As I spoke of my deepest fears and longings, I wept. The counselor remained stone-faced.

At the time I had no sense, no suggestion that I might be exhibiting many of the classical symptoms of clinical depression: feeling life had no purpose, that I was a terrible human being, that when I wasn't in class or doing schoolwork all I did was sleep, and that at times I had suicidal thoughts.

The counselor didn't mention the d-word nor did she mention therapy. Her only recommendation was that I start using makeup. She proceeded to show me how to put on lipstick to make my thin lips look fuller. After that, I was dismissed.

# 21
## The Letter

In 1959, Karen, Julie Hawkins, and I spent two months touring Europe using Eurail passes and Arthur Frommer's first edition of *Europe on Five Dollars a Day*. At nineteen, I was the oldest. Julie and Karen were both eighteen. We had been to England, Denmark, France, Spain, Italy, and Yugoslavia. I was anxious to get home to spend a few weeks on the ranch with my cattle before I started my sophomore year at CU. We had arrived in Paris where we were to take the flight home the next day. At a sidewalk café on the Champs-Élysées, I sipped my orange pressé while Julie and Karen nursed their beers. We silently read the mail we had just picked up from the American Express. A thick envelope was addressed with my father's cramped handwriting.

He wrote that everyone would be moving to Boulder before I returned, and we wouldn't be returning to the ranch permanently. He had a very strong possibility of a professorship in the physics department at the University of Colorado. In the meantime, he had a job teaching high school physics in Wheatridge, a suburb of Denver.

Even though I was aware of how much my father continued to pine for academia, it seemed that it was only one of his unfulfilled dreams. I had never considered whether my parents would ever leave the ranch. I had assumed that it would be home forever. I was going to miss the ranch. I stopped reading his letter and was transported back to the summer of 1949 when we first moved to the ranch, when I first inhaled the magic of the sound of the river and the soaring peaks.

Although by 1959 my parents' physical exile ended, their emotional exile and their lack of trust of our government and people were never conquered.

Years later while in my parents' kitchen in Sausalito helping Mother cook dinner, I mentioned that I really missed the ranch. It was then that she told me how desperate my father had been to leave the ranch and once again enter the world of academia, to the stimulation a university atmosphere could provide. She then said, "Living on the ranch was actually one of the best times of our marriage."

I asked her how she could say that.

"On the ranch, our marriage was basically working. I was pleased Frank was doing something his brother would never have done: that he had finally begun to separate from Robert." She continued, "We were partners. He valued my ideas and help. I dreaded returning to university life with its pseudo sophistication. I hated the thought of being useless. I was also worried about your father having more affairs."

Mother then told me that when I was eighteen months old, she and I briefly left him because of his involvement with another woman. She never told me who the woman was or where we had gone or for how long. I suspect the woman was one of my father's old flames, Gloria. I had known about Gloria since I was a teenager. In fact, Gloria visited us one time when we were on the ranch. I don't remember much about that visit except that she waxed poetic about the beauty of the ranch. She had no interest in the day-to-day workings of the ranch and would sit around the house expecting to be waited on. I knew Mother never forgave my father for giving Gloria a small original lithograph. I had assumed his affair was over before he and my mother married. However, many years after my father died, I was looking through his correspondence at the Bancroft Library at the University of California, Berkeley, when my assumption was overturned. I found several love letters from Gloria dated in 1937, the year after he and Mother married. Mother's concerns that my father once again would begin his philandering were realized not long after they moved to Boulder. This time, it was not only my mother who was directly affected. Michael and I became deeply embroiled in the melodrama as it unfolded.

# 22
## Unwitting Accomplice

During my senior year at CU, my father invited me to go along with him to hear Louis Armstrong at the ballroom in the student union. I really didn't want to go with my father. All my instincts told me I shouldn't, but I wanted to hear the fabled "Satchmo" badly enough, and because of his persistence, I agreed.

When we arrived, we found the room transformed into a world of supper clubs and nightclubs. The lights were dimmed and around the dance floor the ballroom was strewn with cloth-covered tables featuring small low lamps and ashtrays. Pleasurable chatter of people anticipating a sophisticated evening filled the air. The room resounded with excited voices and clinking glasses. My father and I found a table in a quiet corner. For a few minutes, we talked and laughed. At first I didn't think one way or another about the fact this his eyes seemed to be scanning the scene periodically, looking out through the smoke-filled room toward the door. He often did that in public places, a sort of nervous reconnaissance. Soon, a woman walked through the door into the ballroom. It became apparent that she was the object of his search because his eyes became animated with delight once he spotted her. That was when the evening began to rapidly deteriorate for me.

She was Val, the wife of one of the psychology professors at the university. Val was certainly arresting to see—a petite vivacious woman with sparkling eyes and dark bouncing hair cut to shoulder length. No one could help but think her cute, including me. To me, she and her husband were merely close family friends.

Val commandeered a small table near the door. My father's eyes blazed like a chandelier as he announced he was going over to say hello to her. I watched as they sat and talked with each other warmly, animatedly. She gazed at him with fondness. They leaned toward one another, laughed often, and from time to time, I even glimpsed them holding hands. As he led her to the floor to dance a rag, I was hurt and angry.

During the entire evening, my father never returned to my table to talk to me or ask me for a dance. If I'd stopped breathing, he wouldn't have known. Feeling atrocious and abandoned, I crept out of the ballroom several times to weep. Returning to my lonely little table, I could hear the marvelous Satchmo's gravelly voice and witty rich horn, but the pain of being ignored muted any pleasure listening to this mighty musical legend might normally have given. Several hours later, I saw my father kiss Val good night—full and long on the lips. He escorted her out of the ballroom, a proud guiding hand at the small of her back. Then he trotted directly over to my table, happy and exuberant, to retrieve me. During our drive to my dorm, all he spoke of was how much fun he'd had. On and on he went about Val's superb dancing abilities, her vibrant intellect, and her wit.

He never uttered a single word about having left me alone all night.

Then, a year and a half after the Louis Armstrong episode, the confusion of that evening crystallized into cold slippery ice.

I was by then a first year medical student at the University of Colorado Medical School in Denver and had arrived home for the Christmas holidays. My father had departed the day after Christmas for a meeting in New York City and was due back New Year's Day. On New Year's Eve day, I began looking around the house for my mother and at last located her in my father's study. I came into the room to ask her what time we needed to leave that night for the New Year's Eve party at the home of my parents' friends, Phil and Milly Danielson.

As I entered, Mother was standing over an open drawer of my father's file cabinet. Papers were strewn everywhere. She looked anguished and flustered.

"Ma, what's going on?"

"I'm looking for Frank's passport." (My parents had at last, after being prohibited from doing so for many years, obtained passports.)

"But why?"

She answered, "Val's in New York, too."

My stomach served warning. It was about to drop. "So?"

"Judy, I know that he has been visiting Val when Howie isn't at home. Whenever we get together with Val and Howie, he ignores me and talks almost exclusively to Val. He must think I'm an idiot. I know the son of a bitch is with her. Now that I find he's taken his passport with him, I'm more convinced than ever something is going on between them."

I felt as if I were being tossed around by a giant wave. "Are you sure that the passport is not just misplaced?"

"Last time I saw it, it was here in the file cabinet with mine."

Eyes shining and angry, she held hers up for me to see.

I stood helpless, my heart beating heavily. My mother continued scouring through his desk and dresser, emptying his file cabinet for the third or fourth time. I flashed back to the evening with Louis Armstrong and all that I'd seen. At that instant, it all fell into place. My father had used me as a foil to allow him to be with Val. I knew Mother's suspicions were most probably dead accurate.

Telling her about the Satchmo evening and what I'd observed focused and increased my anger.

She listened, growing paler, and her face reconfigured briefly into one of sorrow before resuming to its momentum of fury.

Mother's suspicions about my father's motives for going to New York were no mystery. What I never quite clarified was the role of the passport—why she'd begun looking for it in the first place. Perhaps she'd seen a copy of a receipt for an airplane ticket to Paris, or maybe someone had told her that Val was going to Paris after visiting New York.

Until our exchange in my father's study, I had been looking forward to going to the Danielsons' New Year's party. I enjoyed the conversations there, especially the feeling of being accepted by the Hawkinses, the Danielsons, and others of my parents' friends.

When we got to the party that night, the Danielsons' living room was filled with friends, smoke, and conversation. And my expectations were happily fulfilled until after dinner, when the celebration quickly turned into something like a bad dream. Everyone had become terribly drunk. Mother spent the evening intermittently weeping and ranting about my father's betrayal. By turns,

Frances Hawkins and Milly Danielson hugged my mother, trying to calm her.

Then someone suggested that the Danielsons' living room needed rearranging, and Phil and Mother began shoving the piano into a different location.

At three or four in the morning, I was finally able to persuade her to go home. No one had enough sleep, and too much liquor had been consumed. When my father returned later that day, conditions were ripe for an ugly showdown. Greeting him icily, without approaching or touching him, Mother strode straight to his suitcase to "help" him unpack. This meant she began flinging his clothes to the floor as punctuation while she raged at him. Her back was rigid, her face gaunt and strained as she accused him of everything. I crept to my bedroom and closed the door. Their furious voices rose, pierced the walls. There was no avoiding hearing portions of their conversation.

Mother said, "I didn't know one needed a passport to go to New York. And what, may I ask, is the meaning of an airline ticket to Paris?" She gave him no time to reply and cut straight to it. "Were you with Val?"

I imagined my father pacing back and forth—his usual response to confrontation.

In a harsh voice, I heard him shout, "No! I wasn't in New York with Val."

A long pause followed. Then "I don't believe you, you lying son of a bitch. If you weren't with Val in New York, where in the hell did you take her? Why is this page torn out of your passport?"

His voice grew quieter. Perhaps at that point, he suddenly saw the futility of postponing the inevitable. Perhaps he felt that a clean swift amputation was better than sawing fruitlessly.

"I didn't think you'd even notice the passport was gone, but tore out the page with the French customs stamp just in case, hoping you wouldn't notice."

Mother's voice was low with fury.

"You stupid, stupid bastard! How could you not imagine I wouldn't notice this ragged torn page? You've just invalidated the passport that took you so long to get."

They continued to scream at one another. I couldn't bear it and ran to the kitchen to escape. Soon afterward, I heard the front door slam as my father left the house. Where he was going did not, at that point, matter a damn to me.

Mother appeared, vindicated and wrecked, tears streaming down her cheeks. Shaking and overwhelmed by what I'd just heard, I went to her and hugged her while she wept.

Half an hour later, she washed her face and was able to talk coherently. We sat at the kitchen table eating cheese and crackers and nursing drinks— Mother with her Old Fashioned, and I with my gin and tonic.

It's fortunate I had taken a few healthy swallows before she gave me one of the most disturbing aspect of the story.

Trembling, she explained to me that the baby Val had delivered the year before was in reality my half sister.

I gulped.

"What are you talking about?"

Until then, the little girl had simply been Howie and Val's daughter. I had held her and played with her and told them how cute she was.

Staring into her drink, her voice shaking, she went on. "Judy, I knew as soon as the baby was born that she was Frank's daughter."

My roaring mind obliterated all but the image of the child.

"But how?"

"She had the same high Oppenheimer cheekbones you and Michael had when you were born."

Pausing a moment, she angrily proclaimed, "You know what else the bastard did? He brought Val a spray of white orchids just like the ones he brought me when you were born."

Up until that moment, I'd thought situations like this only occurred in soap operas or B movies.

The two of us sank into a long silence, absorbing the incomprehensible. Some weeks later, I was sitting at my desk in my Denver apartment, giving my best effort to studying for a practical exam in anatomy, when my phone rang.

It was my father.

"Judy, I need to talk to you. I'm coming to take you to lunch."

Coldly, I told him I didn't have time and that I needed to study for the exam. He pooh-poohed this and even went so far as to insist that I'd ace the exam even without studying. There was no way to dissuade him from coming. I paced the apartment and stared out the window, racking my brain for a coping strategy. The last thing on earth I wanted to do was to see him, let alone listen to him. When he arrived, I could barely stand the sight of him. I wanted to shout, to strike him, to pummel him to the floor.

He waved my anger aside as though it were some minor teenage sulk.

Angrily, I threw on my coat and followed him to his car. When arrived at the restaurant, he began his defense.

"Judy, don't be so damned sullen. You're so important to me that I have to explain my version of the affair. I want you to understand and forgive me."

His voice took on a peeved, petulant tone, and in it, I could hear him speaking mainly to himself.

"I really don't know what this has to do with you anyway. It's between Jackie and me."

I suppressed the urge to scream. *Monster! You're nothing but a narcissistic bastard.* Tightly, I replied, "Oh really?"

Then the penitent took over. He stood before me head lowered, looking every inch the earnest, wronged petitioner. As he talked, he tried to look into my eyes. I averted my gaze knowing that his piercing blue eyes could make me feel sorry for him. I warned myself, *His eyes are the traps. Do not look into them. Above all, do not look into them.* Throughout the lunch, I was successful.

As we sat down at the table, he began his campaign. "Jackie and I just can't seem to communicate any longer." He paused. "All we seem to do is argue. She can't give me the love and support I need. Val does."

His words went on and on, all of them uttered in what sounded like passionate sincerity. I can't remember the precise words now. I must have blocked them out instantly. Instinctively, I knew that he was laboring to sway me to his side. I also knew if he succeeded in swaying my loyalities, I'd be performing a treasonous act. It took every ounce of will to remain silent. I couldn't locate the courage or language to point out how completely he had devastated another human being—my mother—or the fact that he was framing his entire argument from the point of view of himself as the center of the galaxy. Faced with his words today, I would have told him that that it was up to him to do some soul-searching to figure out why and how he could have hurt my mother so much.

I remained silent. I don't remember what food sat before me or where we ate. When the lunch was over, I exhaled with overpowering relief as we walked out the restaurant door.

We drove back to medical school in cold silence.

Looking back, the sadness of it all overwhelms me, and it begins to appear less like a soap opera or B movie than something Shakespearean and all-too human.

Years later while examining my father's archived papers, I found myself staring at a series of agonized ravings about the affair. These were written in his miniscule, almost undecipherable handwriting on differently shaped scraps: notebook paper, typing paper, or any small scrap of paper he could snatch up at the time. He recounted the saga in detail, first about visiting Val and Howie's initially for coffee and conversation and later as Val's lover. In these ramblings, which at times verged on incoherence, he tried to explain and justify his actions. No one's eyes but his own were meant to view these ramblings. Laboriously scanning his confessions, I was struck by how adolescent and chaotic his words were. He wanted what he wanted and was trying to make it all make sense to fit retroactively.

At the same time, I read a long straightforward letter Mother had written to him after the affair. In it, she told him she still loved him but that he needed to be honest with himself. She gave my father an ultimatum. He needed to make a once-and-for-all decision: whether he would stay with her or go with Val. She told him he could have a divorce if he wanted one. As I read this letter, I realized she had finally found a way to wrest some authority and strength from her long humiliation, dictating the terms on which she'd stay. I couldn't help smiling and murmured to myself, "Right on, Ma!"

My father opted to stay.

The rest of their marriage was lived out as an uneasy truce where Mother was never able to really trust him again.

Val, Howie, and their children moved to New York.

The drama didn't quite end there; it reprised until many years later when Michael and I sat in my kitchen in San José. Mother had talked to Michael about the affair, I think mainly because he was living at home at the time. However, she never told him about our half sister. Inevitably, many years later, someone outside of the family gave him this information.

That day in San José, he confronted me.

"Deedle, why didn't you ever tell me? Why did you exclude me?" I was chagrined to hear the anger and hurt in my brother's voice. Over the years, I vacillated between action and inaction, between telling my brother about our half sister and keeping her existence a secret. Reflecting on it now, I realize I had been brainwashed by the dynamics of the family. Perhaps because he was the youngest, in some clumsy effort to protect him, Michael was seldom included in many family discussions. The unspoken code of silence was so great, I'd become convinced my duty was to keep my secret—and my sorrow and outrage—to myself.

That day in San José, because we had to, we started talking. At first, his words were caustic and accusatory.

"So why have you kept this from me all our lives?"

I apologized to my brother. And then I began, in halting words, to describe my awkward, painful, lifelong position, which was some combination of family confessor and archivist.

It was a formidable task. How could I persuade Michael to understand my silence and duplicity if I could scarcely explain these to myself? I think that this conversation was one of the first times that Michael and I confronted our various demons. It paved the way for a much more honest and warm relationship between the two of us.

# 23
# Medical School

I graduated from college in 1962. I had succeeded in getting my BA in four years, in large part because I received credit for the work I did in T. T. Puck's cytogenetic lab in Denver.

I had received an NSF (National Science Foundation) fellowship to work in Puck's lab where I set up tissue cultures of human cells for cytogenetic studies. In a wondrous demonstration of serendipitous irony, this was the same lab that had confirmed my diagnosis of Turner's several years before. They had kept my skin cells from that research in living storage. They were still alive and well. When I looked at the petri dishes containing these cells, my mind raced wildly. I thought about immortality, about how part of me was living outside of my body. What an eerie feeling. Would these cells still be alive after I died? If so, what would this mean?

To satisfy what felt like an unappeased internal quest, I harvested some of my cells and did a karyotype—a process where each chromosome comes into distinct focus. There under the microscope were my abnormal cells. I snapped a picture of the chromosomes, cut them out, and organized them on a white piece of paper in what should have been twenty-three pairs.

However, there were only twenty-two pairs. At the end of the sequence was my lonely X chromosome. It had no partner. I stared at this solo chromosome and reflected on how the course of my life had been and would continue to be defined by this apparently simple omission of chromosomal material. Once again I felt alone and vulnerable.

In May of senior year of college, I still felt deeply uncertain about my life's direction. I had long decided that I didn't want to become a vet. If I had I knew that I wanted to treat both small and large animals. However, a vivid incident from the ranch years ago had stopped that aspiration.

Years before while at the vet's in Durango, I had witnessed a beautiful black stallion come out of anesthesia. The horse had gained consciousness in a violent frenzy. It took six strong men to subdue him. I watched in anguish, then sadness, understanding in that moment that because of my size, I would never be able to comfortably deal with such powerful animals.

I had taken all the prerequisites for medical school, but my still undiagnosed depression was so paralyzing that I couldn't imagine summoning enough energy to apply.

I was no longer sure I wanted to go or that, if I choose to do so, the schools would have accepted me. Anyway, applying was a mute point. It was too late to apply even if I had had the will and strength.

My favorite courses had been in humanities and history. I realized that by pursuing a career in either of those fields, I would need to start a series of undergraduate studies all over again. Worse, I had no idea how I could make a living in either of these endeavors.

I'd noticed myself growing keenly interested in embryology. Holding that fact close and in no small amount of desperation, I applied to graduate schools in zoology at Stanford and UC–Berkeley. During the summer, to my amazement, I was accepted into both graduate programs. I chose Stanford.

That fall, a familiar scene repeated itself. This time, instead of a dorm room, I was seated at my desk looking out at the pool of my apartment complex in Mountain View, California, laboring over my calculus homework. I watched while some of the other residents—younger people like me—laughed, chatted, and splashed around in the pool.

They seemed carefree and at ease in the world and with each other. Slamming my book close and standing up, I wondered yet again why in hell I was working so damned hard. Evidence had piled up like a mountain range surrounding me; there was so much more to life than studying and writing papers, and I seemed to be permanently barred from experiencing any of it. I closed my drapes and moved to my bed.

I dreamed of walking down to the river on our ranch, glimpsing at its silvery glitter, listening to the music of the water-tumbled rocks, lying in the meadow, watching the vast sky, brushing Knuckle Head once again until her red coat shone.

In the morning I felt calmer and able to carry on.

At Stanford, my life was even more barren, more devoid of friends and isolated than it had been in Boulder. At least in Boulder, I could always depend on my mother to check in, support me, and occasionally do things with me. At Stanford, though I tried from time to time to make contact with people, even becoming active in the civil rights and the antiwar movement, inevitably I felt shunted aside. Again I played the role of odd woman out. For me, going out to dinner or on a date were only unreachable dreams. I spent hours upon hours in the lab, gazing through a microscope. Occasionally I'd look up to see my classmates call one another over to show them some interesting bacteria. I heard them make plans to meet at the student union later to study together. No one asked me, and somehow Mother's mantra from Minneapolis days "I don't think I should bother them. They're busy with friends," reared it's ugly head and I could never muster the nerve to ask to join them.

It wasn't the wind that caused my tears as I rode my bike from Mountain View to the Stanford campus. (Yes, I eventually did manage the art of riding a bicycle.) Remembering my existential philosophy, my secret mantra became *je suis déspéré*.

Thinking about my father, his colleagues, and my professors at Stanford, I felt that they all seemed to lead lonely lives. Their days were spent in their labs. Their contact with colleagues seemed superficial at best and, inevitably, work-related.

By this time, I knew myself well enough to know that it would be fatal to allow myself to become similarly isolated. Learning about human illness and having opportunities to help others still held a tremendous attraction for me. My own diagnosis combined with being interested in others' illnesses made me yearn to understand the human body better. I thought about how much I admired Valerie McKnown, my own pediatrician. I remember feeling awed by how she spent one day a week in the small communities of northern New Mexico simply to serve people in need. I also remembered being genuinely fascinated by *Gray's Anatomy*.

In short, my dream of becoming a physician was rekindled. I reverted to my original plan. I would apply for medical school. I took the MCAT (Medical College Admission Test) and began to fill out the necessary voluminous applications.

In the end, the only place that granted me an interview was the medical school of my alma mater, the University of Colorado.

Walking through the dreary hallways of the University of Colorado Medical School in Denver, I once again found myself sitting behind a desk being questioned by an authority figure. This time it was the Dean of Admissions—a woman.

After a few perfunctory remarks, she began to ask questions that took on a distinctly prosecutorial flavor: "What do you plan to do with your degree after you graduate? Do you plan to get married and have children? Do you plan to practice if you do? You know you will be taking up the space that should go to some deserving young man."

Did I tell her having children was out of the question for me? In retrospect, I don't believe I'd even mentioned the fact of my having Turner's on my application. I was still too embarrassed, too certain I was a freak. I was convinced (given the era as well as my own self-damning convictions) that if the admissions committee knew about my diagnosis, they wouldn't even consider me. There was no recourse but to tolerate the dean's accusatory questions and answer them as honestly and intelligently as I could. Today, the dean's questions would be not only tasteless, but also blatantly illegal. Evidently, my interview satisfied her because I was accepted as one of only four women out of ninety students for the 1963 entering freshman class.

I returned to my parents' home in Boulder from Stanford three weeks before medical school was to start.

My parents were delighted by my acceptance into medical school, and Mother wasted no time plotting practical needs.

"We need," she announced, "to find you an apartment."

Soon, she and I were driving to Denver to spend a day prowling for suitable quarters.

The medical school and Colorado General Hospital were near a lovely tree-lined neighborhood that featured several small wooded parks. The first day of our quest gave warning that our search would prove difficult. Both of us felt depressed by what we saw: "The kitchen's too small" or "Look at the hideous purple linoleum." Another apartment came close but was far too dark. I realized that the lack of basic daylight to study (let alone maintain any semblance of morale) would be disastrous. After looking at another, I said, "Ma, it's too far away to walk, and parking near school is said to be terrible." We ate some lunch and resumed our search, with no results. Finally, we headed home empty-handed, tired, and grumpy.

The next day, she declared, "You'll be needing an entirely new look. After all, you are on your way to becoming a professional."

At this, I could only laugh. We both knew it would be years before I could be considered a professional woman, but it was fun to see her find so much vicarious pleasure in my newfound potential.

A week later, she and I once again set out for Denver. This time we hit pay dirt. We found an airy one-bedroom apartment two blocks from school. The large glass-brick window with several glass shelves sold the apartment for me. Rainbows danced over the carpet.

My mother smiled and said, "What a wonderful place to put knickknacks."

When we arrived home to Boulder that night, she and I looked through the house to find special little objets d'art for the shelves: a wooden figure of a man on a donkey from Haiti, several southwestern baskets, and assorted vases. Once I'd moved in, we arranged my record collection on one of the shelves. I loved the patterns and silhouettes that the diffused light made around the objects and across the room as it streamed through the glass bricks.

I placed a bouquet of cosmos from Mother's garden in one of the vases. In another, I placed the roses my father had given me. Soon the apartment was a warm, hospitable place to live and study.

# 24
## Preparation and Preclinical Years

On the first day of school, I walked the two leaf-strewn blocks in the bracing fall air. I was feeling lightheaded with a combination of excitement and dread. My heart was racing. What am I getting myself into?

I entered the doors of the old brick building that housed both the medical school and Colorado General Hospital and fell in with several other lost souls heading to a large lecture hall. In the sea of male faces, I saw a lone woman seated close to the front of the auditorium. I wasted no time heading there and sat down beside her. Sue Gloster wore a strained expression that told me she was just as uneasy and nervous as I. Susan Luck soon joined us. The only other woman, La Dean Spinuzzi, sat several rows behind us with her husband, Ralph. Waiting for the orientation to begin, Sue, Susan, and I began to talk, and I felt myself start to relax a little.

I hated medical school with its punishing course load and insidious putdowns. Nonetheless, I grew to appreciate what it enabled me to do with my life. Medical education was, and to some extent still is, predicated on the theory that adversity is an essential element in the training of physicians. If one could survive four years of hell, then one could face the real world of medicine with all its rigors and demands. Like military boot camp, the purpose of medical school seemed to be to first tear us down and then secondarily mold us, step by step, into an image of what the professors thought a physician should be. This was abundantly evident during the years I was attending. The entire culture was that of a staid, rigid "good old boy" network. Very few of the professors were women, and often the women were as contemptuous and domineering as their male counterparts. During medical school, I had not been aware of my forté—my intuitive, pattern-recognizing approach to patients. And nowhere during my training was this particular strength singled out, admired, or encouraged. It wasn't until much later that I was able to appreciate what a powerful and helpful tool these strengths would prove to be. My intuition eventually permitted me to triage patients swiftly and accurately. It told me when I had time to watch and develop a diagnosis or when a patient was in a crisis and needed immediate attention. For example, if a child came in with meningitis, I would be able to recognize the condition quickly. Noting that she was not responsive, that her cry was shrill and constant, I would know immediately, for example, that she had more than a simple ear infection.

Throughout the first two years of medical school, we four women— La Dean, Sue, Susan, and I—would support and encourage one another. We often met at one of our apartments to study. More frequently than I could count, a point in the evening would arrive where the pressure would boil over, and one of us would declare that she was going to quit.

We took turns being that person.

"I can't take it anymore. I've had enough. I'm going to quit."

"Not now. You've come this far. Just tell yourself you'll hang in for this week. Just this week. Then we'll meet here. We'll get some dinner and talk it over again."

Our collective mantra became something along the lines of "I really want to quit but I don't know what else I would do." We all knew very well that simply because we were women, we drew disproportionate attention from our professors, and it wasn't attention of the desirable kind. Because we provided such easy targets, we often were the brunt of a lot of teasing from our male colleagues.

One day, I arrived in anatomy lab to see my three lab partners, all men, leaning over our cadaver. They appeared to be totally frustrated. Each wore a look of bewilderment and frustration.

"Judy," one said, "we're supposed to find and trace the upper trochlear nerve and can't find it in any of our anatomy books. Maybe you'll have better luck than we did?"

I immediately began paging through every anatomy book we had in the lab. I couldn't locate any reference to the nerve and was about to go to the next level and seek advice from one of the instructors. It was at this point that my partners burst out laughing and confessed that there was no such nerve. They had made up the entire search, including the name of the mysterious missing nerve. Laughing, their eyes lit with mockery, faces flushed with merriment, they seemed to be reveling in their little joke.

To say the least, I was not amused.

# 25
## The Genetics Lecture

Our first year was devoted primarily to anatomy lab and basic science lectures. The seats in the dark lecture hall formed a steep wall surrounding the lectern. As usual, I sat in the second row surrounded by my women colleagues. One day the lecture was focused on genetics. The professor commenced a slide show as he started talking about chromosomes and chromosomal abnormalities. After discussing Down's syndrome, he began to discuss Turner's.

He showed slides of girls with the syndrome. Click. Before our eyes on a ten-foot projection screen, a stark black-and-white full frontal view of a naked teenager with Turner's appeared. On the side of the slide was the imposed image of a ruler, indicating the specimen's height. I could almost feel the pain as his pointer beat ominously on the broad chest with no breasts and widely spaced nipples. The girl had no pubic hair. *Click.* A different view showed her webbed neck. *Click.* A side view revealed her barrel chest.

My hands were shaking so badly, I could no longer take notes.

As the professor talked on and on, my eyes darted first to my colleagues on the left and right of me. They then roved frantically over the faces of the entire class. In each, I read disgust, pity, and discomfort. The amphitheater's silence was broken now and then by someone's nervous laughter. I felt my face redden and then drain, gone pale with shame for my short slightly webbed neck, my short arms and legs, and other telltale defects. Surely all my classmates were stealing glances at me.

I was certain that they now all knew my secret.

The professor ended his presentation proclaiming that girls with Turner's were usually mildly or moderately retarded.

For a moment, I too thought I deserved that assessment.

I wanted to hide under the desk—better yet, to vanish into thin air.

Somehow, I blundered through the first two years of med school. In fact, I'd actually done well enough in my courses to be in the top 10 percent of the class academically. Upon entering my third year of medical school to begin my clinical clerkships, I started to fall apart much like a bale of hay whose twine was tied with the wrong type of knot.

The disintegration started slowly.

In 1965, my father received a Guggenheim Fellowship, and my parents moved to London for a year. As when I was going to Stanford, Mother's comfortable presence was no longer available. She couldn't come down to take me to lunch. I couldn't go home for a day or weekend. Socially, I was isolated from my colleagues. Essentially, the only contact I had with them was in activities surrounding school. It was the first time I couldn't go home to celebrate "Jackie" holidays with her special food and good cheer. My brother, who at the time was going to the University of Colorado, had married his high school sweetheart. We tried to carry on our holiday traditions without Mother. We used her recipes for the turkey and stuffing; we made her pumpkin chiffon pie and her Christmas cake. There were presents under a gaudily decorated tree. In spite of our best efforts to duplicate our family's Thanksgivings and Christmases, they weren't the same without her. Winter descended, and too many times I found myself picking up the phone to call her in London. I longed to seek her advice, complain, or just hear her familiar, reassuring voice.

Each time, I reluctantly hung up before dialing.

Without Mother's presence, I found I had no recourse but to rake up the mess and try to make sense of everything on my own.

# 26
# Tsunami

My spirits soared when my friend Karen decided to come to graduate school in Boulder to pursue a PhD in mathematics.

Karen and I had always kept up with each other's lives, corresponding by letter and talking on the phone. But this would be the first time since the doll-playing days of our Berkeley childhood that my best friend and I would actually live within forty-five minutes of one another. For a time, I floated, smiling through my lonely hours. I was certain that my isolation was about to be broken.

It turned out we were only able to visit each other infrequently. I was buried in writing papers and studying during the weekends, and she was busy learning everything there was to learn about higher mathematics.

Then an unforeseen and unheralded change occurred. Karen's friend, Nell, arrived in Boulder, and she and Karen decided to share an apartment.

Once again, I was "third man out."

I didn't feel the undersea earthquake. I didn't anticipate the water's retreat. I was visiting Karen in her apartment in Boulder one weekend. I didn't have a clue about what was about to transpire. We sat together, relaxed, and talked over coffee at her kitchen table. After a time, she asked if I'd like to see the rest of their one-bedroom apartment.

The tsunami hit with brutal force as she and I stood at the door of the bedroom, which only had one large bed. I gulped, and fought back tears as the realization hit me.

*Oh my god, Karen and Nell are lovers!* The sensation was that of being rolled over and over by the overpowering waves. The sand, which not too long before had been a gentle beach, shredded my skin and tore through my mind.

In the rush and tumble, my memory shot back to the summer of 1962 when I first met Nell.

Karen, Nell, and Susan (another of Karen's friends) joined my cousin Janet and me on a trip to Europe. On that day in Karen's apartment, I remembered the few times that Karen and Nell had shared a double bed during our travels. No one appeared to think twice about it then; it had seemed nothing more significant than an occasional solution to accommodate the fact that the room we had rented didn't have the requisite number of beds. Then it came back to me with instant clarity how uncomfortable, how betrayed I'd felt each time it happened. In those years, it had been utterly beyond the scope of my experience to imagine Karen and Nell's friendship might amount to something more profound.

As I stood in the bedroom of their Boulder apartment, I was clubbed over the head by it, my skull ringing with the understanding of their true relationship.

I could not think of a single word to say. I only stared, mute. Karen, perhaps guessing my shock and confusion, also remained silent. All I knew was I wished I had been sharing the bed with Karen.

My true feelings, at that moment, had plunged underground to be consumed by the volcano's heat. There, like the hot magma of the volcano spewing in the depth of the sea, they would roil for a very long time. The shock waves from that day would reverberate beyond the moment and challenge my ability to assess others. In Karen and Nell's apartment, I found myself not only facing the loss of a lifelong friendship, but also dealing with my own sexual confusion.

After the visit with Karen, I spent the night at my parents', who had recently returned from Britain. Mother and I sat in the living room drinking Courvoisier. I fidgeted and stared at the floor as I told her that I had discovered that Nell and Karen were lovers.

Like many others of her generation, my mother felt that being gay or lesbian was a learned trait, adaptable as a hairstyle or clothing. All she could say to comfort me was "It's all Nell's fault. She's succeeded in seducing Karen. Karen really isn't queer. It's Nell who led her into this."

I said nothing. I felt no such certainty.

# 27
# Clinical Clerkships

The eruption continued as I was faced with ward assignments and dealing with patients. The clerkships commenced during our third year after academic classwork had been completed.

Feeling a little conspicuous, we donned our white jackets, slung stethoscopes over our necks, and in copious pockets stashed various other necessary tools needed to examine our patients. As students, we were often the first people to meet the patient. Our assigned mission: to perform a complete physical and take a voluminous history. After we'd made our way through every step of both of these processes and finished our write-ups, we presented our findings to our resident and attending physician.

I had no clue what was expected of me. At this point, I felt myself at a complete loss. No longer was information spoon-fed. No one in the immediate vicinity seemed particularly eager or able to teach. If I wanted to know something, I had to ferret it out myself. With no prior knowledge or training of unassisted detective work of this sort, I was far from adept at it. Whenever I read about a series of diseases, for instance, it was difficult for me to sort out which of the main signs and symptoms would confirm the diagnosis. This made the going rather muddy and, as a result, painful for me.

Intensifying the pressure was that fact I was intimidated, in those days, by breathing sick human beings. Not able to summon the easy manner, the calm authority needed in coaxing patients to tell me their stories, I felt shy when I had to do a physical, especially on a man. And then there was the fact that I had to face the interns and residents every day in one-on- one conversations. This required a certain amount of self-confidence of which I was sorely lacking. For me, clinical work appeared worlds more difficult than relating pleasantly to the professors as I had in the pre-clinical years. During the first two years, all that had been demanded of us was to complete assignments and do well on the tests. I was familiar with this type of educational ritual. I had had plenty of practice at it. But where once I could have picked my battles, ignoring some professors if I chose, there was simply no turning away from the personalities and the demands of my interns or residents.

My predicament came to a boil one day just after I started my surgical rotation. At 5:30 a.m., the hall lights in the surgery ward gave off a strange, unearthly glare. Under them, like an apparition in a bad dream, my resident loomed. He was a short, heavyset young man with thick unruly brown hair. We stood outside the patient's room where our voices echoed through the hall as we discussed the results of his surgery and his progress. The resident handed me the patient's chart. His words came out like a growl. "Write the IV orders for this patient."

The chart's steel-gray cover seemed to freeze in my hands. My hands laboriously calculated and wrote what resembled hieroglyphics on the blank page. The resident stood too close, staring. I heard his breathing and felt his pure disgust. His mere presence at such close quarters caused my heart to race and for my brain to turn to mush. My scribbles became illegible even to me.

Suddenly, he could no longer wait. He snatched back the chart and thrust it toward one of my male colleagues, bellowing back to me.

"You're totally incompetent. Can't you even write a simple IV order?" Defeated, I turned. It was all I could do to not run away.

Not long thereafter, I encountered another indicator that I was not cut out to be a surgeon. After I'd scrubbed up at the sink outside the operating room, the nurse handed me a sterile gown and placed the sterile gloves on my hands. Taking my place at the operating table with the resident surgeon, intern, and another student, I found that three stools were needed for me to be high enough to help. The surgery was not microsurgery. It was a long, arduous back surgery involving a lot of retracting to hold open the wound. Often a small saw had to be used to cut into the vertebrae. The smell of the cut bone and blood reminded me of dehorning. The stools began to wobble. Suddenly, I heard a muffled voice. The retractor I was holding dimmed.

"She's as white as a sheet. Get her out of the room before she falls into the operating field."

I was escorted out.

Later, I dreamed of owning a pair of magical hydraulic-lift shoes. Maybe then I wouldn't be such a nuisance.

# 28
# The All-Night Vigil

The cavalcade of humiliations marched on during my obstetrics and gynecology rotation.

One night I kept vigil beside a young mother-to-be, watching her sweat, cry out, and work to bring new life into the world. I monitored her progress and taught her how to breathe. I held her hand, reassured her, and sponged her off after each contraction.

Daylight finally lightened the room, and with it, the moment we'd waited and worked for: her infant's silky black hair peeked through. The young mother was wheeled to the delivery room, and I hurriedly donned my surgical cap, sterile gown, and gloves. I placed myself in position. With the help of my resident, I had planned to deliver her baby.

However, my resident, a woman, pushed me aside.

"You aren't going to deliver this baby. I told one of the nurses, Mrs. Sandoval, she could deliver it."

I protested. However, the arrangement had been made.

I could only stand aside, watching as the nurse and the resident helped the head, shoulders, and body of a new human being emerge into the bright lights of the delivery room.

Later, anger blackened my mind and then turned inward.

Yet despite my enduring bitterness and disappointment, I thought back with fondness to the first time I ever saw a calf born. Somehow this erased the pain.

The lights in the barn cast a ghostly light on the cow as she lay on her side in labor. She was breathing hard, but didn't bellow or even seem too upset. Suddenly I saw the calf's small front hooves emerging. The mother seemed to give one big push, and in one wet whoosh, out slid a perfect little animal. Surrounded by blood, feces and other detritus the baby heifer lay for a while as the mother licked it, first cleaning its nose to make sure it could breath. She dried it and stimulated it at the same time. In less than ten minutes, the tiny red-and-white creature stood up, shook herself, and on wobbly legs, proceeded to nuzzle the underside of her mother's belly, searching for her food. The mother gently nudged the calf toward her udder, which the baby found, fastened on, and drew forth its first meal. Totally entranced, I watched every moment of this stunning process—amazed in its apparent simplicity, yet overwhelmed by its complexity. The awe I felt toward the process of birth never waned throughout my entire career.

# 29
# Pediatrics

My two months in pediatrics helped me gain some of the confidence I needed to become a physician. They erased much of the bitter taste of my other rotations. A scene in my examining room during my years of practice was that of a blond-headed one-year-old perched alertly on her mother's lap. The toddler and I would play a game of peek-a-boo. She would smile and laugh. I'd inch closer and offer her my stethoscope. She would be fascinated, grasping and examining the shiny object with its long strap. After she'd thoroughly looked it over, I'd place it around her neck. She'd giggle—a special necklace. Finally, she let me take the instrument back. I warm it with my hands and press it gently to her chest and back, listening to her heart and lungs.

In the beginning, of course, I hadn't developed even one step of this choreography, and I didn't feel so calm, easy, and sure. As a medical student, I wasn't nearly as successful in reassuring a frightened one-year- old as I learned to be later on. It took years to truly own that rhythm, my modus operandi, but no question about it; the seeds were planted when I was a third year medical student on my pediatrics rotation.

Each day some child's smile captivated me, transforming even my darkest, most hectic hours into something alive and fresh. I often arrived home reenergized, eager to read more about pediatrics, and beginning to suspect that I might, in fact, have a shot at become a physician after all.

In stunning contrast to my other rotations, in pediatrics the residents, interns, and attending pediatricians actually taught. What is more, they enjoyed it. It felt as though I had entered a different country from the one I'd been slogging through before—this one with a more humane system of laws. If I was having some difficulty looking in a child's throat or ears, my intern or resident showed me some tricks for managing it better. If I had difficulty in drawing blood, the intern didn't scream and rant but patiently showed me some of the techniques he'd used with frequent success. Rounds didn't only involve checking on particular patients, but we often sat down together in seminars where we discussed one or two more relevant and interesting diseases. Instead of berating us by staging dramatic scenes, our attendings and residents showed us shortcuts in writing orders.

These welcoming habits and attitudes forged a marvelous sense of camaraderie among the house staff and students. The feeling of being part of a team was heightened when Dr. Henry Kempe, the chairman of the department, invited everyone who had just finished the rotation to an afternoon barbecue at his home. I felt genuine awe for Dr. Kempe. He was a gentle but firm taskmaster and an excellent teacher. After my prior dreadful experiences, his kindness and expertize made him something close to saintly in my mind. Spending a lot of time in India, he and his colleagues were successful in their effort to eliminate smallpox there. It was during my time in medical school that smallpox was completely eliminated as one of the scourges of the world.

By the end of the rotation, I had no doubts left, and the certainty filled my whole being with new air and resolve. I knew I would pursue a career in pediatrics. During my fourth year, I began looking at possible venues for my residency. In medical training, the process of finding an internship-residency is a well-defined process. As a senior medical student, one goes through "matching," in which the student puts down their choices of residency in order of preference. The hospitals then list their choices of applicants, also in order of preference, and the student is offered a space in the first match. I no longer remember what my first two choices were, but I was extremely pleased to be matched with my third choice—the department of pediatrics at the University of Wisconsin Hospital in Madison. Once I knew I had a decent internship, I was able to relax somewhat. My final rotations were much less stressful.

For graduation, my father bought me a gardenia to wear on my gown. I spent the entire time during the main graduation ceremony inhaling its scent as deeply as I could, luxuriating in the tangy seductive sweetness of the waxy white flower.

After the main event, my medical school classmates and I walked over to a small amphitheater where we were to receive our diplomas and recite the Hippocratic oath. We floated in a state of suspended disbelief, stunned by the reality. We had made it! We were physicians. When I walked up to get my diploma, my grin never stopped. The only slight disappointment for me was that that my diploma wasn't in Latin. For some reason, I felt that the diploma would have more impact and elegance if it had been.

All the trials and tribulations of medical school disappeared that night when my parents' house became the site of a celebration of my valiant success.

Milly Danielson and Mother had spent two days preparing a combination of Southwestern and Chinese food. A flutist friend, Serge Paul- Emile, who was one of my father's graduate students, organized a small musical group and provided music for the party. My father joined in with his flute.

Val, my own pediatrician, brought me several prized medical instruments, among them bandage scissors and a percussion hammer to test reflexes with. The event was full of laughter, dancing, and delicious food.

In bed that night, as I thought over the celebration of a momentous milestone, it occurred to me that my party had fully equaled any of the best celebrations I'd ever attended—as jubilant and sophisticated as any that my parents, those masters of wild parties, had thrown in Berkeley when I was a child. I mused for a while that things had truly come full circle.

My party and everyone's excitement over my achievement felt like a bona fide initiation into adulthood.

# 30
## Internship: The Making of a Physician

Mother and I climbed into my red Studebaker Lark convertible to drive to Madison, Wisconsin, where I would enter into a new phase of my life's journey. It was early summer, a trifle cloudy and humid. The drive took three days. The scenery was pastoral but monotonous—unrelentingly flat. Mother finally commented, "I would find it stifling to live on the plains." Both of us bemoaned the lack of significant hills.

Our talks about landscape cloaked the real agenda: my fears about commencing my internship. Mother was keenly sensitized to this and was determined to bolster me in every way she could. "Judy, you have survived four years of medical school. How much more difficult can an internship be?"

"Ma, I'll be one of the people that the patient depends on." I paused to look out the car window, almost paralyzed with nervousness. "I'll be the first to write the orders."

Mother, ever my loyal supporter, had her rebuttals all lined up. "Judy, remember you'll have backup. I know you can do it. When you set your mind to it, you have been able conquer huge obstacles." As always, I felt touched by her staunch belief in me even though I was unconvinced by it at the moment.

Once we arrived in Madison, I felt that there might be reason to take heart. I fell in love at once with the look and feel of this small tree-lined university town. By now my mother and I had become the intrepid duo of apartment hunting. Our instincts and methods honed to perfection, we launched into action and this time found a place not too far from the hospital.

When we embraced good-bye, tears filled my eyes. Mother flew home to Boulder, and I was on my own.

On the twenty-third of June 1967—the first day of my internship— it was raining, gray, and humid. With trepidation I entered the old brick hospital where signs in the dingy hospital-green hallway directed me to a large auditorium. Interns from every department already waited there for a general orientation about benefits, support services, and the like.

At once, I felt tremendous relief to spot the familiar faces of my former medical school classmates, La Dean and Ralph Spinuzzi and Ed McCabe.

I sat down beside them with the confidence and pleasure of all our shared history. I greeted them with a cheerful "Hi, Doc. Can you believe it? We're actually being paid $12,000 a year for being doctors."

When I got up to go to our pediatrics department orientation, I discovered I'd been sitting on my umbrella. Though it still functioned, it was bent unmercifully. Grinning ruefully at my friends, I quipped, "I hope this isn't an omen for the next year." We laughed then, but later the crushed umbrella took on significance. In hindsight, it became a metaphor for the year that lay ahead.

I was assigned to the pediatric hematology-oncology service for my first two months of internship. After making cursory rounds with the resident and another intern assigned to the service, we all congregated in a small bare conference room to wait for the attending, Dr. Patricia Joo, to give us our orientation.

While we sat and chatted together, the resident spoke of her glowingly.

"She's a terrific doctor. Warm, kind, and very bright. You'll be amazed." And this pre-briefing proved to be totally accurate. When Dr. Joo entered the room, the very atmosphere suddenly felt lighter and softer. Patty was, it turned out, only a few years older than I. Her smile and her compassionate eyes instantly put me at ease. Even dressed in her white lab coat, she seemed approachable and kind.

The next day, my alarm went off at 5:30 a.m. Welcome to the world of an intern. An overarching fatigue that would dominate the working day rhythm for the next four years was being established.

Three days later, I was on call. I have no idea if I slept a wink that first night. Working nights with no sleep made handling every new patient, every IV, every phone call in the middle of the night for a new order or a problem with a patient felt like climbing Mount Everest wearing a sixty-pound pack. The days fared somewhat better. Patty never screamed or insulted me. Instead, if I had a question or didn't know something, she simply assumed I could learn—that all I needed was to be taught. Temporarily, my self- confidence soared. My fund of information grew exponentially. Patty believed in having a multidisciplinary team of nurses, a social worker, as well as physicians. At least once a week the team met to discuss each patient. We worked with their psychological and social problems as well as their medical treatment. I was able to offer insights into some of the patients and their families. The others on the team acknowledged and praised my input. At the end of the two months, Patty told me how well I was doing, especially praising me on how well I was able to relate to my patients and their parents.

Patty facilitated an incredibly rich period of learning for me.

My next two rotations were in internal medicine, two months at the Madison VA and two months in the inpatient student health service. I don't remember any of the attendings at the VA or in student health, but during these rotations I met Rod Layton, who would serve as my resident for both.

Like Patty, Rod respected my brain and was more than willing to teach. We worked extremely well as a team. Thank goodness for this because it was with Rod that I would experience three of the most harrowing incidents of my internship. One, a man at the VA had a ruptured aortic aneurysm—a widening and thinning of the body's main artery. In this case the thinned wall had torn, and the patient bled to death. Also at the VA was a three-hundred-pound man with Guillain-Barré—a progressive but usually temporary neurological disorder that can lead to respiratory arrest and death unless the patient is placed on a respirator or, as in this case, in an iron lung. This patient did suffer a respiratory and cardiac arrest while in the iron lung and died. Lastly, when we were on the student health ward, we luckily were able to treat an eighteen-year-old student with meningococcal meningitis. Finally, by degrees, both positive and negative, I felt I was becoming a physician.

Nonetheless, I still felt very clumsy whenever I had to start an IV, perform a spinal tap, or do some other procedure. Often I needed to call on my resident or fellow intern to complete the task. Though I knew that I had correctly assessed the patient, I was many times unable to effectively impart my knowledge to my colleagues or attendings. My perceived problems were magnified when I compared my skills (or lack thereof) with those of my fellow interns or residents. I was certain they knew everything and were as dexterous in performing procedures as fine watchmakers.

The final humiliation came in the spring during my rotation on pediatrics at Madison General Hospital. The attending there was an uptight, dogmatic young man by the name of Gordon Tuffli. No matter how I tried, he was never satisfied. Whenever he looked at me with his cold, judgmental eyes, I was reminded of my father when he was angry. Except Tuffli's eyes carried none of the life, playfulness, and intensity that had pulled me toward my father for years. When I presented a patient, Dr. Tuffli continuously interrupted me. Even when he did not speak, his face never stopped sending its contemptuous message. I often arrived home after a hard day at work and burst into tears.

In spite of this, I was utterly unprepared when, in April 1968, two months before my internship was to end, the chairman of the department, C. C. Lobeck, called me into his office.

Once again I faced the ever-present desk and, opposite it, the executioner's chair. Dr. Lobeck, a nattily dressed man with a bow tie, motioned me to the chair across the desk from him. The desk became a dark foreboding chasm. I felt very small. My body seemed terribly misshapen. Even though I had no idea why he called me in, I felt like a person accused of some heinous crime.

"Judy, I'm afraid I can't offer you a residency next year."

The statement hit me like a wrecking ball, and I was plummeted into a canyon. Struggling to maintain composure against waves of tears, my voice echoed deep from within the black abyss.

"But why?"

"Dr. Tuffli feels that you're not ready for residency."

"What did I do wrong?"

"He talked about one patient who had Adrenal Genital syndrome that you didn't get a full history on. You didn't ask the parents if the child ate an excessive amount of salt, which is one of the symptoms of this syndrome. He also says your presentations are not well organized, and you didn't seem to have an adequate fund of knowledge."

"He never talked to me about any of these problems. Have other attend-ings complained?"

"No one else gave me any specifics, but some have said you lack confi-dence and sometimes judgment."

My heart skipped some beats. My voice was someone else's as I strove for logic and clarity.

"At this point, what do you expect me to do? It's too late for me to apply for any other residency. Why didn't someone talk to me sooner? It seems to me to be grossly unfair."

His unyielding voice stung as he said, "I'm sorry, but I really don't know what you'll be able to find for next year."

The interview ended with no offer of help or compassion. Walking out of his office choking on the sobs that were trying to leap from my throat, the rest of the day seemed surreal, muffled. Anxiety and fear cloaked the air. Shame made it impossible for me to even look at or speak to my colleagues. After sev-eral days, the initial shock and pain abated enough for me think of a possible solution.

I spoke to Patty. After telling her about my conversation with Dr. Lobeck, I plunged. "Patty, I know this is a very unusual request. But would you consider my doing a hematology-oncology fellowship with you next year?"

"What an interesting idea. I'd love to have you. I'll talk to Dr. Lobeck about the possibility. It's worth a try."

Patty was successful in convincing Dr. Lobeck that I could spend the fol-lowing year with her.

# 31
# Pediatric Hematology-Oncology Fellowship

My year with Patty felt like successfully fording a river. Most of the time, the rocks Patty provided allowed me to slowly but safely wend myself to the other side. This process set a pattern and built a foundation— the foothold of my future success as a practicing pediatrician. As with any river crossing, I frequently slipped off the boulder's solid foundation and was caught up in the whirlpools of my past and my depression. Each time, Patty was there to rescue me. She was a born teacher—patient, kind, and encouraging. She seemed to trust my judgment implicitly. She knew I would ask for advice whenever I needed it to.

When Patty asked me to join her on her trips to the meetings of Children's Cancer Group-A, I was thrilled. The Children's Cancer Group was a consortium of pediatric oncologists from all over the United States. Clinicians from the participating hospitals met to discuss the results of clinical trials they had been performing. Not only were these meetings educational, but they also helped me take myself more seriously. I began to feel as if I were truly a physician and was learning to become an oncologist. I looked forward to the plane rides and the hotel stays, during which Patty and I discussed both deep and unimportant topics alike. Patty is one of the first women who confided in me in a way that I sensed she did with few others. We talked about her family and her husband's, Paul's singing. We also had fun socializing with the other participants.

One such trek was to Park City, Utah. At the reception, Patty and I were drinking manhattans, and I was feeling quite giddy after one.

"Patty, we've got to be careful how much we drink. We are at a very high altitude."

Neither of us heeded my advice. The next morning we were faced with horrendous hangovers. Somehow, we mustered enough strength to attend the meetings, and despite the shape we were in, I think both of us actually contributed something.

During that year, I became the primary physician for a small group of patients. I was the one who initially evaluated and talked to them and their families. With Patty's help, I planned their therapy. Success in my relating to my patients unlocked and gave structure to my impulse to give and heal. I was not afraid to become involved with them or their families. They all gave me the gift of their trust and their strength.

There were four patients in particular whom I will never forget. They taught me what it meant to be a physician.

# 32
## "Anyway, There Are Always Wigs"

Linda was sixteen and in remission when the local PBS station interviewed both of us. The interview was done in the studio of the television station.

All the lights, cameras, and crew running around positioning us to get the best shot initially intimidated me. Linda seemed unfazed by all the attention. A radiant young woman with lively eyes, in the interview she showed a marvelous mixture of pluck and realism. When asked how she felt about losing her hair, she replied calmly, "I hated losing it, but I would much rather lose my hair than my life. Anyway, there are always wigs."

At the time I first met her, Linda was a tall good-looking fourteen- year-old with a buoyant mane of long thick brown hair and a vivid smile that seemed to light up her pale face. She had just been diagnosed as having ALL (acute lymphocytic leukemia). She and her parents—a stolid, kindly, but deeply unnerved middle-aged couple—sat together with me at the institutional gray table in the small conference room. The paint on the walls was peeling which added to the feeling of doom in the room. I asked Linda why she had come to Madison.

"Because I have leukemia."

Having her mention the name of her disease relieved me. Many parents demanded that their child never know the name of their disease. They were certain the mere mention of the diagnosis would cause him or her to lose all hope. However, in my experience when children don't know the basic facts, it proves very difficult to explain to them what is going on and what to expect.

I told Linda and her parents that leukemia was a disease of the bone marrow. "The marrow is the soft part of the bone you notice when the bone is cut. It is where all the blood cells are made." I drew cartoon pictures of the normal marrow with its white cells, red cells, and platelets. "The white cells help fight infection, the red cells carry the oxygen, and the platelets help the blood clot so you won't bleed. In leukemia, the marrow is taken over by useless malignant cells called blasts. Because of this, you may have infections, bleeding, or become anemic which will cause you to feel tired and weak."

I was watching their faces; they still seemed to be listening. I continued. "The drugs we use help rid the marrow of all its leukemic cells, allowing the normal cells to come back."

I then wrote down the names of the drugs and began to talk about their side effects.

"I know you won't remember half of what I'm saying. Don't worry. In no time at all, we'll be speaking the common language of leukemia."

Linda looked at me and asked, "How long will I have to stay in the hospital?"

At the time, most patients stayed in the hospital until they entered their first remission. I answered, "At least a month."

Both she and her parents were somewhat shaken. Her mother asked, "Will we be able to stay with her?"

Shortly before our meeting the hospital had provided foldout chairs in the patients' rooms so parents could stay with their child.

"It's not elegant living, but yes, one of you can stay."

Their relief was tangible.

Linda and her parents asked many questions. Toward the end of our session, Linda quietly voiced their collective terror. "Do all people with leukemia die?"

"No. Each person is different. The drugs we are using now have a much better chance of working than those we had before." I paused. "Until we have evidence to the contrary, I'm going to assume you will go into remission, and that it will last."

Linda did respond to treatment and returned home and to school. But our hopes were shattered when her leukemia recurred, and we were never able to get her into another prolonged remission.

One day in the clinic after she had just suffered another relapse she told me, "You know, Dr. Oppenheimer, I can always tell when the news is going to be bad."

"How?"

"If it's bad news, you always start with 'Well, young lady…'"

We both laughed, though I felt a small needle pierce my heart. The phrase was a habit I've never been able to break, and her bravery had mustered sufficient wit to joke about it.

The disease progressed, and she spent more and more time in the hospital, often with recurrent headaches as the leukemia spread to her brain and spinal cord. She also was hospitalized several times for serious infections. By the time she was sixteen, we essentially had run out of effective treatment for her.

I was sitting by her bedside when she looked at me in a new way. With a strong, clear voice, she said, "Dr. Oppenheimer, I don't want anything else done for me—even blood transfusions."

I swallowed.

She went on. "I just can't see getting any more treatments, feeling better for only two or three weeks, and then needing to return to the hospital." She, her parents, and I had several long discussions and decided to acquiesce to her wishes. Her parents' faces, which already showed so much sorrow, turned gray as we spoke.

Her father, his voice halting, said softly, "Of course we don't want her to die, but we can't stand to see her suffer. We think her decision is the correct one."

Patty was also supportive of her decision. Shortly afterward, with Patty on vacation, I happened to mention our decision to the other hematologist on the staff.

He was furious and would not hear of it.

"Of course, we need to give her blood."

As we entered her room, without fanfare, the attending strode over to her bedside.

"You're anemic and must have blood."

Linda's pale face became even paler. Her eyes cast downward, her breathing accelerated. I knew she was anxious, afraid her wishes would not be respected. After rounds, I stepped back into her room.

"How did Dr. — make you feel?"

"He scared me."

"Don't worry. Our pact still holds. You aren't going to get blood."

She relaxed then and smiled gratefully.

In 1970, no hospice care or similar community resources were yet available to help patients die at home. The end of Linda's life had to be one of prolonged hospitalization.

Whenever I had time, I sat by her bed and merely held her hand, sometimes saying nothing or quietly talking to her parents. The silences were like the pauses in music—they truly added to the meaning and poignancy of our time together. One day, I sat at her bedside holding her hand, not talking. I must have had tears in my eyes. Linda looked over at me and smiled.

"It's going to be okay, Dr. Oppenheimer."

Soon after, Linda died.

# 33
## The Birthday Fish

At nine o'clock on the night of my birthday, I had returned to the hospital to check on Linda.

I opened the door to the ward to be greeted at once by a crowd of eager faces. Gathered together like a group of Christmas carolers, there were nurses and house staff. Led by Jenny, a vivacious, curious six-year- old being treated for Wilm's tumor (malignant tumor of the kidney), the group fired up an exuberant chorus of "Happy Birthday." I listened with amazement and moist eyes. Jenny then commanded me to close my eyes. She led me down the hall to the tub room.

I opened my eyes to see the largest ugliest catfish I'd ever beheld in my life swimming in the ordinary sized porcelain bathtub.

Jenny had just returned from a weekend on her uncle's farm where she apparently had caught the fish. Somehow she cajoled her parents into letting her bring her treasure to me as a present. After laughing and hugging her, I tried to mask my silent worry. *What on earth am I going to do with a live catfish?* I knew that if we kept it in the tub overnight, the head nurse would either have a heart attack or make life unbearable. She was a stickler for cleanliness and rules.

We placed the unattractive fish into a large plastic wastebasket filled with water. I fervently hoped the fish would live until morning when Jenny and I could take it to Lake Mendotta to release it. The fish did not cooperate, perishing during the night.

The next day Jenny and I were sitting outside in the warm spring air when Jenny began sobbing.

"If I hadn't caught him, he'd still be alive. I killed him!"

I hugged her.

"Jenny what you did was thoughtful and kind. You didn't know he was going to die. If he had lived, you and I could have let him go in the lake."

She looked at me; tears coated her cheek.

"Am I going to die like the fish?"

I gave my voice all the warmth and firm authority I could.

"I hope not for a long, long time. Your tumor seems to have gone away. You're doing very well. "

She sniffled, calming a little. "Could it come back?"

I kept my eyes on hers.

"Yes, it could, but I don't think it will. If it does, we have other medicines."

Our conversation lasted an hour or more.

Happily, the last time I heard from Jen, she was a cheerful, healthy eighteen-year-old who had just graduated from high school and was on her way to college.

# 34
# Wolfman

Richard was five when I first met him. He was a vibrant, impish little boy with thick brown hair. Like Linda, he had ALL.

For two years Richard had raged against his leukemia. Starting IVs or doing procedures on him became a several-step ordeal. It began with trying to sooth and cajole him, letting him have as much control as possible. Even so, it often involved having several people hold him still. Seven years old, bald, face bloated with prednisone, he lay in his hospital bed, angry and sullen. His mother sat at his bedside, drained; her forehead creased and her shoulders tight.

In the playroom, we kept a number of hand puppets. Maybe, I thought, casting about one day for inspiration, they could reach his heart. I seized a green one with a red mouth and yellow eyes. As I sat on his bed, my puppet spoke.

"Hi, Richard. I'm Greenfrog."

He shouted, "I'm not Richard! I'm Wolfman."

"Glad to know you, Wolfman. How are you?"

He growled and grabbed Greenfrog. Greenfrog tumbled onto the bed.

"Aha! I murdered you."

I queried, "What does murder mean?"

"That someone kills you, and you're dead."

"What does dead mean?"

"That you can't hear, smell, or see anymore."

I took a chance and said, "For how long?"

"Forever!"

So I found more puppets. Wolfman yanked, twisted, and karate- chopped. Within an hour, seven Greenfrogs were eliminated. I held the last puppet on my hand when I said, "I'm not sure I can trust you anymore, Wolfman."

He turned to his mom. "Tell Greenfrog she can trust me." His mom turned and smiled as she vouched for Wolfman.

"You can trust Wolfman." I did. I was instantly killed. Wolfman smiled, triumphant. Unfortunately, Richard didn't triumph over his leukemia and died several weeks later.

# 35
## No Time for Hope

I'd known Peter, or more correctly, his family, for only a few brief hours. Peter's father had brought his ten-year-old son to the ER at three or four o'clock in the morning with a fever of 104 that the family could not control. The ER physician diagnosed leukemia complicated by a severe infection. By the time I saw Peter, he was desperately ill.

He responded only to touch. His breathing was labored. The doctors in the ER had already started antibiotics and blood. As gently as possible, I explained to his father how seriously ill his son was—that he might die soon. The father's face was drawn and expressed shock and disbelief.

"Do you think that I have time to go home so I can break the news to my wife in person?"

"I'm not sure, but I hope so. Maybe the blood and antibiotics will help. I still think you should go home to tell your wife."

Peter's father left. Peter died shortly thereafter.

Pacing the hall, waiting for his parents to return, I had no idea how I was going to help them. Parents who have been made aware of their child's diagnosis well in advance of their child's death are at least somewhat prepared for the worst. Peter's illness and death had swooped through utterly unexpectedly, as sudden and final as the fire after a lightning strike. After what seemed like hours, his parents returned. Holding hands and silently weeping, they rushed through the double doors of the ward. With sweaty hands and a somewhat shaky voice, I intercepted them before they could get to Peter's room.

As I embraced them, I could barely keep my composure.

I looked directly at them and said the words. "I'm sorry. Peter died a few minutes after his father left."

Silence. Their faces were frozen in horror.

"Do you want to see him?"

Both parents nodded yes. We filed into his room and stood silently. They walked together over to their son, held his hand, and kissed him. Noiselessly, I slipped out the door to leave them alone with their grief. Sometime later, after they had finished saying good-bye to their son, I led them into the small conference room to talk. Here was one situation where I had few words at the ready. For a moment the three of us sat in stunned silence.

Finally, I plunged in. Barely able to keep my voice from breaking, I asked, "Do you know what leukemia is?"

Both slowly shook their heads. "Not really." Once again I took my pencil and begin my usual scribbles explaining about white cells, red cells, and platelets.

I couldn't read their faces.

After a time, Peter's father said, "We had no idea how sick Peter was. Yesterday he was playing and seemed fine to us. Would it have made a difference if we had noticed sooner?"

This was tough. Peter had the type of ALL that was difficult to treat, and the likelihood of him going into remission even if we had the time to start chemotherapy was slim. I didn't want to dwell on this nor did I want them to feel guilty.

I said, "We might have been able to treat his infection a little better, but ultimately, it probably wouldn't have made a difference."

Peter's mother voiced different concerns.

"We have two other kids, a boy, four, and a girl, seven. What are we going to tell them?"

She was shaking and wiping tears from her eyes. I handed her a box of tissue.

"Do they ask questions, or are they quiet?"

"Oh, the four-year-old is always talking and asking questions. His sister tends to be quieter."

I relaxed. Perhaps there was something I could offer after all.

"I suspect that their first reaction will be not to let you out of their sight. They may alternate being extremely angry with you and being extraordinarily clingy. They may play roughly with their toys. They probably will cry. The seven-year-old may tell you that sometimes she was so mad at Peter she wished he were dead—that she caused his death."

They listened, trying to assimilate. Peter's mother murmured, "Anything else?"

"It probably won't be easy to get them to bed for quite a while. They may have bad dreams or even nightmares. I wouldn't be surprised if they insisted on sleeping with you. That's okay."

Dad asked, "How should we act around them? Should we talk about Peter?"

"Don't hide your own grief. The kids will see that it is acceptable to be sad or even mad. All of you need to help each other remember Peter. Keep him real."

I left the conference room depleted and shaken. I wasn't sure they had absorbed a word I said.

They went home to face their grief alone. Several months later, they sent me a wonderful letter thanking me. They wrote that both of the kids had indeed asked if they could catch leukemia and if they had caused Peter's illness. The parents were prepared and were able to reassure them.

I look back in awe on these patients and all those I saw later in my practice. In addition to being inspired and moved by their supreme courage in the face of the incomprehensible, I realized afresh each time how desperately important it was for me to have open, honest conversations with them and their parents. I can see how my own bottomless yearning— to have had someone to do the same for me when I was diagnosed with Turner's—played a profound part in my willingness to discuss difficult issues with patients and their families. In this sense, it is a singular gift my own condition wound up giving me: the gift of not being afraid and of understanding that it's often the unknown and unspoken that exacerbates confusion, fear, and anger.

Reflecting on how I survived the obvious heartache of pediatric oncology, I've come to believe it was in part because I was helping make horrific situations a little more bearable. Patients gave me a gift of their warmth, trust, and strength. I was devastated whenever a patient died, not necessarily because I had failed to cure him or her, but because another human was suddenly gone from my life.

How did I deal with this ever-present grief? By investing in a new patient, a new family, and helping them navigate the crisis in their life.

# 36
## Small Triumphs

I managed several small triumphs on the social front during that time. Foremost among them was a deepening friendship with Patty and her husband, Paul Heiser. I finally scraped together the nerve to ask them over to my place for my shrimp curry dinner.

To my delight, we had a wonderful evening. All of us were relaxed and cheerful. We began telling one another about our lives. This first dinner confirmed what I had long suspected: Patty and I were on the same wavelength in terms of attitudes and beliefs about politics, cultural affairs, and any number of other contemporary events.

This kind of connection offered a relief that was nearly indescribable. The bond with the Heisers strengthened and helped sustain me during my years in Madison. They invited me to their home for dinner. From time to time we attended concerts, lectures, or gallery openings together. Once we spent an entire evening simply rearranging my art. Most of my art were prints: Van Gogh's, Picasso's, Renoir's, and one Bruegel. Patty and I would stand back to direct and approve of the placement of the prints while Paul carefully measured and hammered in the hangers. When we were finished, we stood back to admire our work and toasted each other with glasses of wine. With fifteen or twenty perfectly hung prints, my apartment looked like a mini gallery.

By the end of the four years, I was able to call Patty whenever I felt exceptionally scared or distressed. She often invited me over. Although some small part of me still suspected she was only inviting me because she felt sorry for me, I always felt better afterward.

I also spent many afternoons and evenings with Rod Layton and his wife, Pat.

The Laytons were wonderfully easy to be around. They were a kind, witty couple who were casual and caring. Their house was filled with the happy chaos of two young sons. Effortlessly, they made me feel completely comfortable talking to them about some of my personal trials as well as the politics of the day. The Laytons lived in a close-knit neighborhood, and I was often included in their block parties.

They gave me, in short, a sense of community.

Going to visit them gave a welcome respite from the rigors of the day. We railed together against LBJ and the war in Vietnam. We too began telling each other our life stories. Rod and Pat were able to break through some of my depressive fog so that once again I grew interested in politics.

In 1968, the Vietnam War was raging. Many of my fellow residents had to cut their residencies short because they were being drafted into the Medical Corps. Others were able to get a deferment only if they committed themselves to the military for two years after completing their residencies. In Madison, university students carrying placards marched in huge numbers down State Street chanting civil rights and antiwar slogans.

"Hell no, we won't go!" "No more war."

"Get our troops out of Vietnam."

The atmosphere felt charged and compressed. Police bore down in military formations using tear gas. Students were arrested. The quiet city of Madison had morphed into a mini war zone.

Yet despite my outrage over the war, I'd been so exhausted, so pressed for time, and so depressed that I kept myself on the sidelines.

One evening in the thick of the campus disruption and rioting, Rod convinced me to go with him to help at a makeshift first aid station. We drove to the periphery of the campus of the University of Wisconsin to a one-story warehouse-like building. Outside, tear gas filled the air. Once inside, my eyes acclimated to the dim light, and I became aware of the people milling around. Rod and I began to work. The students straggled in, coughing, eyes burning. Some had severe breathing difficulties, their asthma being triggered by the tear gas. As we washed out their red stinging eyes, treated the wheezing, and sewed up a few lacerations, the scene became more and more unreal. The lights were kept dim for fear that the campus police would raid our building. We spoke in whispers. No one had walkie-talkies or other means of communicating with the outside world. Rumors ran rampant. Students came in from the outside reporting massive arrests and told us that the police had tossed tear gas into one of the dorms. I remember feeling surrounded by the enemy, bereft of any verifiable information. I was in a combat zone; anything could happen. Suppose we were dragged off to jail? I strove not to let the feeling of helplessness and fear overwhelm me. At last, things calmed down a bit. Rod and I left the building late at night and headed to his car and home. Several police cars were patrolling the area. With racing hearts and dry mouths, we walked to Rod's car, trying to act as nonchalant as possible. Rod quickly unlocked the car doors, and we drove away. The cops didn't follow us. We were free from the combat zone. I was proud of Rod and myself. Even though we didn't bear the brunt of the chaos, we did put ourselves in some danger. If we had been arrested, it is unlikely that either of us would have been able to finish our residency. During medical school, I had had a chance to go to the Selma-to-Birmingham civil rights march; however, when I asked the dean whether I would be able to come back if I should be arrested, he told me that I probably wouldn't be able to. I didn't go and, even to this day, I'm sad that I didn't. Helping in the first aid station somewhat assuaged my guilt.

# 37
# The Phone

In spite of visiting often with the Heisers and Laytons and my congenial relationship with my colleagues, at heart, I still felt like a freak. My old mantra of "They only associate with me because I am an Oppenheimer and they feel sorry for me" reared its ugly head often.

I remember sitting in the nurses' station when I overheard two colleagues standing in the hall talking, apparently making plans for their families to go on a picnic to Lake Mendotta. Brightly, animatedly, they agreed on how well their kids played together and complimented each other's spouse's cooking. As they chatted about what each family would bring, I turned and walked away. Once again, I would spend the weekend alone. At home, like a schoolgirl, I kept waiting for the phone to ring, hoping someone might invite me over to dinner. I spent my nights in front of the television, existing essentially on crackers and cheese. At times I felt desperate enough to walk over to the phone, pick up the receiver, and start to dial anybody just to hear a human voice. Halfway through my dialing, I'd quickly hang up. I'd return to my couch and TV or simply give up and go to bed.

I couldn't even call my mother. I didn't want to burden her with my miserable reality. Whenever she called, I would revert to my best rendition of a successfully socialized young woman, hoping she could not discern in my singsong "Everything is fine" bravado the hollowness in my voice.

A new milestone in my parents' lives was taking place just then. They had moved, during this period, from Boulder to Sausalito, California. During his Guggenheim Fellowship spent in Europe, my father had grown excited about the idea of establishing a science museum that would serve as both an educational and recreational resource. My mother and he decided they wanted to return to the Bay Area. Once settled in San Francisco, he cajoled the city into leasing him space in the old Palace of Fine Arts, a huge ornate building designed by Bernard Maybeck for the 1915 San Francisco World Fair. The building had just been renovated and stood empty.

Within a year, the *Exploratorium*—a unique museum of science and perception stressing their relationship to the arts—was created and opened to the public.

# 38
## Second Year of Residency

By my third year in Madison, I was once again a general pediatric resident. For a while, the attending staff seemed to view me in a more respectful light. No longer the struggling intern they had given up on, I had transformed into a capable young physician, able to learn and be trained. During my residency, I continued to follow my oncology patients from my previous year of fellowship.

Because the University of Wisconsin, like most university hospitals, was a referral center, many patients had other chronic or fatal diseases. I took care of children with congenital heart disease, kidney disease, and saddest of all, severe neurological disorders. When I was an oncology fellow, I was part of a team the members of which worked together to care for the oncology patients. Interns, residents, oncology fellows and attendings, a nurse practitioner, a social worker, and nurses from the ward were all involved in coordinating the patients' medical, social, and other needs. This experience proved invaluable. I would take the team-building skills with me. So when I became a resident, I was able to get the neurologists, the cardiologists, and others to at least partially agree to the importance of coordinated care.

My presentations were more organized, and I began to learn how to read about diseases, distinguishing the important, relevant material from that which didn't help in making a diagnosis. I saw some of the attendings actually began to perceive that I was able to recognize a truly ill child and that I could now ask for help when I was uncertain about the next course of action.

Despite my successes and in spite of Patty's continued support and friendship, fatigue again took its toll. Because of my perceived ineptness in doing procedures such as drawing blood and starting IVs, I often felt my treatments were needlessly torturing my young patients. I felt my lack of knowledge also put them at risk. I didn't seem to be generating reports to referring physicians fast enough. I didn't talk to anyone about my doubts— my demons. My depression once again deepened. I plunged into a state of self-loathing and lethargy.

I obsessed continually about having Turner's. One day, our geneticist, an extremely tall gangly man who we all thought had a genetic abnormality himself (probably Marfan's, an inherited connective tissue disease) was conducting rounds. He was discussing various syndromes and their unusual fingerprint patterns. Many chromosomal abnormalities have distinctive fingerprint patterns, such as absent or unusually formed arches or malformed whorls or lines through the fingerprints. He turned to me, took my hand, and called the other house staff and students over.

"Judy has Turner's syndrome. Look carefully at the pattern of her fingerprints. The absence of whorls and the closely spaced arches are classic for Turner's."

I stood mute, awash in self-conscious horror. I began to hyperventilate and to become dizzy. My heart was racing. Incredulous, I was both furious and mortified. What kind of human being, what kind of doctor, behaves this way? I momentarily thought of withdrawing my hand and announcing to him coolly in front of the others, "Doctor, the group has long suspected you have Marfan's. I'm sure you're familiar with it. With your tall stature, your hyper mobile joints, you seem to exhibit all the textbook manifestations." Of course I didn't.

To this day, I shudder to think about how insensitive he was. He never asked my permission to be "outed." He had no idea whether or not I had shared my secret with my colleagues. I had not.

Despite of the fact that I spent my fourth and last year in Madison with Patty again doing pediatric hematology-oncology, her support was not enough. When I thought about what I was going to do with the rest of my life, I panicked. I asked Patty if I might be able to join the clinical faculty. She agreed to talk to Dr. Lobeck, but this time she was not successful in obtaining a position for me. I felt—illogically and with paranoid overtones— that even Patty didn't want me to stay. In any case, I suddenly had no place to go.

The last spring in Madison was one of weekend afternoons standing under awnings in people's grassy backyards or in public parks holding cold bottles of beer or tinkling cocktails, swimming, and barbecuing "brats" and hamburgers. We reminisced about the four years we'd spent together and were about to complete. My colleagues chatted about their plans for the following year. One or two of them were staying in Madison to enter into private practice with various groups. Others were either going into private practices elsewhere or on to fellowships. Several had signed up for the Barry Plan, a plan that allowed residents to complete their residency but stipulated that they spend two years in the Medical Corps after their residency's completion.

And even though I had worked closely with all of them, in large parties like these, I couldn't help feeling like an outsider. I envied what I perceived to be their maturity, their confidence, and their ability. Did they notice my moist eyes, my sad face? It's doubtful. I certainly never dared confess my deepest thoughts to any of them. They only saw my facade— my thin attempt at appearing to be confident and mature. They saw the beginning of the persona of Dr. Judy, the confident cheerful physician. They did not see the scared, lonely, self-critical young woman—the other Judy.

Today, I scuba dive and love the freedom, the colors, and the quiet of the underwater world. However, my first dive occurred in 1971, in Madison, Wisconsin. It was not into clear warm tropical waters but rather the murky depths of my psyche.

Soon the weight of the despair was great enough to overcome the buoyancy of the small victories. Slowly, irrevocably, I sank to the bottom.

# 39
## The Deepest Dive

Outside it was a bleak, overcast early spring day during my last year in Madison. Snow still lay on the ground, old and dirty, not white. The world had no color, no brightness.

Inside my small one-bedroom apartment, I sat alone.

The phone was quiet. The television might have been blaring a football game, or maybe I was listening to the music from my stereo or maybe experiencing nothing but silence and emptiness. It didn't matter.

All I could think about was how no one ever called and how I was unable to make friends. Stewing over the little errors I made—the IV I hadn't been able to start, the times on rounds when I couldn't answer a question the attending asked—convinced me that I was a terrible doctor, a menace to my patients, and I would never be able to get a job.

These thoughts and others spiraled in a never-ending cacophony of voices pounding, pounding ever louder, and inhabiting my entire being. I was alone and frightened. The deep velvet curtain of despair descended. Behind this curtain, there was no light, no air, and no hope. I sat in the corner of a stage with my knees drawn up, head between them, trying to return to the womb, to float in life's first ocean. The only water was that of my tears. They were never enough.

Like an apparition, I rose and went to the kitchen, numbly picked up a paring knife, and returned to my corner, to my makeshift womb. Shaking, sobbing, I began slowly, methodically, to saw at my wrist. Mesmerized by the motion, the total lack of pain or fear, I kept sawing. Blood appeared. It was not gushing. No vein or artery had been severed. Instead, only a long red line appeared. Although no anesthetic had been administered, the gash was completely numb. It oozed bright red beads that fell onto the carpet. The shaking and sobbing suddenly ceased. I stopped my sawing mid-stroke, cleansed the wound, and slept.

The next day everything seemed shrouded in fog. Patty—my mentor, friend, and confidant—noticed my silence, my bandaged wrist. "Judy, what's the matter? You seem so distracted, so down."

Patty's kindness tipped whatever was left of my shields. I burst out sobbing and told her a small portion of what had happened the day before—how hopeless life seemed. She wanted to call my parents, but I pleaded with her not to. Instead, she called a therapist and demanded I go to see him immediately. At that instant, a nascent hope emerged. Someone cares! Reluctantly, I walked toward the therapist's office, looking over my shoulder each step of the way for anyone who might spy on me. I couldn't bear the thought of any of my colleagues learning I was seeing a shrink.

I entered a well-lit, simple, but clean office with little more decoration than the therapist's framed diploma on the wall and two comfortable-looking chairs. The therapist, a pleasant-looking medium-height man, shook my hand and invited me to sit in one of the chairs. After many tissues, I began to try to describe to the therapist something of my pain. In doing so, some of the pressure lifted. He listened carefully, and toward the end of the session, he looked authoritatively into my eyes.

"Judy, if I am going to work with you, I want you to make a contract with me that you won't try to take your life again."

This took me aback.

"How can I do that? I feel so desperate. How can I promise you?" He was firm, calm, and adamant.

"If you are going to work with me, you'll need to."

With no recourse, I agreed to his terms. But the entire time, some demonic, secret voice was quietly murmuring, reassuring me: *You can still kill yourself any time. It really doesn't matter if you break the contract.*

# 40
# Houston

The worst of my depression lifted, and I was once again able to function at some acceptable level. With Patty's help, I was able to obtain an oncology fellowship at M. D. Anderson Hospital and Tumor Institute in Houston, Texas.

Mother flew to Madison from San Francisco to help me drive to Houston. We headed south in my yellow Plymouth Barracuda convertible. For some reason, we decided that we would only stop at Holiday Inns. Maybe it because they represented some sort of cautious, bottom-line standard, and we wouldn't have to hunt for acceptable lodging each night. However, after the third such stop, we began to laugh at ourselves for not being more adventuresome. Each Holiday Inn had the same plastic nondescript décor and the same bland menu.

Together, my mother and I lamented the fact that the only job I found was in the south. I had never before set foot in the American south, and from the first day I arrived in Houston, I was not encouraged by what I saw. I was exposed to its not-so-subtle undercurrent of racism.

We first arrived in Houston, our car was absorbed, inadvertently, into the cortege of a funeral procession. Mother became more and more frustrated and followed the procession off the freeway thinking it was the exit she needed to take to get to M. D. Anderson. Instead, it led to a slum that was obviously the black ghetto. Most of the houses we saw were in terrible need of paint and repair. The yards were mere patches of sandy dirt. On the main thoroughfare loomed lines of large dingy concrete apartment buildings. A few houses appeared to be abandoned and gaped at us with broken windows. Defunct cars sat in the front lawns, windowless and rusting. Garbage was scattered everywhere. Worse by far than the dilapidated buildings were children in rags and no shoes. They had no place to play but the streets.

I was angry and aghast by what we were seeing, but Mother went straight into a rage.

"This damned country. How can they let such poverty exist? I hope that you don't end up spending your life in the south. It would depress me every time I came to see you."

After my parents' deaths, I was going through some of the letters my mother wrote to my father while he was working in Oak Ridge, Tennessee. Apparently, there was a possibility that he might stay there for an extended length of time, and he wanted us to move there from Berkeley.

> Dear One,
>
> Don't know what to think, what to say about a thing. You have probably now received the letter I wrote on Sun. after your call in which I tried to explain some of my reasons for not being completely at ease in my mind. I have told them to you over and over, and you no doubt are sick and tired of hearing them. Christ, why couldn't it be Arizona—any place but there below the M-D line [Mason-Dixon line]. God, Frank, I want to be with you, but I'm all mixed up. I just hate the south. Oh Christ, I don't know. I could weep. Mostly in frustration because I am in such a stew about it and because if I do come there, I know how much against my will it will be and because I'm afraid something would happen to me in a joint like that. I can develop absolutely no sense of humor about the place at all. I don't mean that anything physical would happen to me but more of a split between us. I might build up a resentment, which had nothing to do with you but which might be applied to you as an outlet.

Over the year, I, too, began to loathe the stark contrast between the super-rich occupants who lived in huge nouveau riche homes and shopped at Neiman Marcus and those condemned to live in the wretched ghettos I had first encountered when I arrived in Houston.

I had been in Houston for only three months when I became unusually tired and achy. Depleted of energy for even the most mundane tasks, I felt as if a Mack truck had hit me. In spite of my fatigue and the feeling my brain wasn't fully engaged, each morning I dutifully dragged myself from bed and went to work. One morning while we were sitting in the conference room discussing the patients and the day's work, one of my colleagues peered at me intently, frowning.

"Judy, you look extremely jaundiced."

Blood work revealed I had very abnormal liver function tests. I had contracted hepatitis B from one of my patients. Thus began one of the most surreal years of my life. I traveled to my parents' home in Sausalito at Thanksgiving and stayed there until after New Year's. I spent most of my time resting or sleeping. Mother became my caretaker and companion. My father spent most of his time at the Exploratorium.

When I returned to Houston, my liver functions were still very abnormal, and I was admitted to the hospital. One day a nurse came into my room to prepare me for a liver biopsy. She had me lie on my left side. Silently, the gastroenterologist numbed a spot between my ribs. The biopsy needle, as large as my small finger, was shoved through my side. Suddenly, I felt the force equal to being kicked by a horse as the knife was released. It almost knocked me off the bed and onto the floor.

To add to my gloom, I had chosen to read William Shirer's *The Rise and Fall of the Third Reich* and reread *War and Peace*.

The biopsy confirmed the diagnosis of chronic persistent hepatitis. Hepatitis is a viral infection of the liver that usually abates within six to eight weeks. In the chronic form, the virus persists and, in some cases, continues to destroy the liver, leading to liver failure and cirrhosis (an irreversible massive scarring of the liver). If this happens, the liver can no longer produce the necessary proteins to do many vital functions, including clotting of the blood. It can no longer filter many of the toxins that the body produces or ingests. It can lead to brain damage and heart or kidney failure.

I was petrified.

I had visions of my liver being destroyed, of my getting sicker and sicker. The irony wasn't lost on me; less than a year before, I had made my suicide attempt and had chosen not to die. This time I might not have such a choice.

I returned to my apartment where, day after day, monotony ruled. Since I had been in Houston for only three months when I caught hepatitis, I had few acquaintances. No one came to visit. For hours upon days, I lay zombie-like on the couch in my apartment. The television blared on and on, but the fog in my brain muted the sound. Often only flashes of light from the screen penetrated my consciousness. I began to have what at first seemed to be hallucinations. I heard rapping at the door and a ghostly voice (my mother's?) saying, "Judy." I would stir, haul myself up, and walk to the door.

No one was there. I was sure I was losing it, falling apart psychically. At the time, I was certain that the mighty hepatitis virus seemed to have damaged my brain.

Sitting in my apartment alone and frightened, I felt that I had effectively ceased to exist; that I had died. On rare occasions someone from work called, only to ask me when I planned to return. No one offered to go to the grocery store or bring me food. I must have mustered enough strength to do it myself, but I don't remember doing so. Being on prednisone made me ravenous. For breakfast I ate two or three bowls of granola and two or three pieces of toast and still wasn't full. I gained a great deal of weight and experienced wild fluctuations in mood. At times giddiness overtook me, only to be followed rapidly by extreme depression.

I look back on this year and realize that perhaps the strangest thing about it was that I didn't simply resign my fellowship and go home to get the badly needed rest and be cared for by my mother. To this day, I'm not sure why I didn't. It's possible that I was desperate to show everyone, especially my parents and myself that I could survive on my own—that I was now fully and authentically a grown-up. I also didn't want to admit to my parents how terribly sick I was, that I had an illness that could become fatal.

Another factor that must have entered in was how uncomfortable I felt being around my father for any length of time. I couldn't stand his hovering or his wringing his hands melodramatically whenever I was sick. Today I realize that these gestures were signs of his love, but at the time, they made me feel smothered. I also still cringed whenever my parents would argue. Altogether, the atmosphere in Sausalito was not conducive to healing.

After six months, I returned to work. I was still tired and unable to think as clearly as I would have liked. Somehow—and this is still a mystery—I completed my fellowship and began looking for a real job as a clinical pediatric oncologist.

To my relief, I found a position at the City of Hope National Medical Center in Duarte, California. Duarte is a small middle-class city situated in the megalopolis of the Los Angeles area near Pasadena.

As I prepared to leave Houston, I sighed with indescribable relief. The past year had turned into a year in hell. It was a year in which work was demeaning and difficult. Not only was I on call every third night, but I also lost my respect for Dr. Jordan Wilbur, who was the head of the department. During the first portion of a child's illness, he was hopeful and articulate whenever he talked to the parents. But by the time patients were at the end of their lives, he seemed to resist talking to the patients or their families. He wasn't able to give them the emotional support they needed. Instead, he would put them on respirators even when we had no treatment left for them. To me this only prolonged their and their families' agony.

It was also a year of enduring the area's heat and humidity, made worse by the pollution and stench of the oil refineries. It was a year of being sick and lonely—so lonely I felt that I was an object rather than part of the human race.

A year in which I am sure even my stainless steel began to rust.

# 41
## The City of Hope

Arriving in LA, my fortunes seemed to get a boost. Robert Rosen, the director of pediatric oncology at the City of Hope, was as unlike Jordan Wilbur, my boss in Houston, as anyone could be.

As a small wiry man with dark brown hair, he didn't tower over me. His voice was soft and reasoned as it reassured and soothed. His manner struck me as very kind and gentle. I sensed that he cared a great deal about his patients. The first night in town, I was invited to dinner at his home. He and his wife spoke warmly with me. Both suggested places where I might look for an apartment. In no time, I found a two-bedroom apartment in Arcadia, a town just north of Duarte.

For a while, Bob Rosen seemed to live up to my original assessment: the image of a caring doctor and a helpful colleague. I was a full-fledged staff member and no longer needed to do the nitty-gritty tasks of patient care. There were fellows available to do most of the day-to-day work. I began developing my own practice. I loved the fact that my role was that of a consultant. Unfortunately, my appraisal of Dr. Rosen began to erode. I still admired his interactions with the parents and patients but found him extremely stubborn when opportunities to use new therapies arose. He was still treating his patients as he did fifteen or twenty years before, when he first became a pediatric oncologist. He apparently was determined to stick by these archaic therapies. In short, he resisted and distrusted change, even when it promised better results.

One day Dr. Rosen, the other physicians, and I were gathered around a long table in our conference room. I was the only woman in the room. A new patient with leukemia had just been admitted, and we were discussing the best treatment options. I advocated using one of the multiple-drug therapies that I had used in Wisconsin and at M. D. Anderson.

I said to the group, "I think we should use Children's Cancer Group A's protocol of prednisone, 6-MP, methotrexate, and vincristine. These have more than doubled the remission rate."

Dr. Rosen's features assumed an expression I'd begun to recognize.

"It's too toxic. We'll use 6-MP and prednisone."

I began citing more statistics, comparing the relative toxicities of each regimen. My lips and tongue moved in vain. His face was set and suggested that none of my remarks had registered. It was as if the words I spoke evaporated into the stratosphere.

The feeling transported me at once back to an incident on the ranch. My brother and I were sitting at our large oak dining table listening to our parents talking to one another, ignoring us. "Pa," I tried to interrupt. "I noticed that Hiwan [one of our bulls] was limping today. You should look at him. I think that he may have a sticker in one of his hooves that should be removed. Maybe his foot should be soaked in Epsom salts."

Neither parent looked up but continued to argue about something that I have long since forgotten. Two days later, my father stomped into the house declaring that the bull was limping, his foot was swollen and red. When I pointed out that I had mentioned it to him previously, he became angry and snapped at me and told me that I should have kept mentioning it to him. Hiwan did indeed have a thorn in his front hoof. My father removed it and soaked the foot in Epsom salts and gave him a shot of penicillin. Hiwan recovered nicely.

In a manner I'd adopted when dealing with my father, I stopped trying to talk to Dr. Rosen. Silence too (I knew from long experience) carries a potent message and wields it own kind of energy. Each time we had a staff meeting, the tension mounted until it became nearly unbearable. I began to feel that Bob Rosen was thwarting my suggestions only because they were mine.

Soon, both Dr. Rosen and I realized the situation was untenable, and I was asked to leave.

I scoured pediatric journals seeking a new position in pediatric oncology. Very few seemed available, and the ads were inevitably similar.

Wanted: Person trained in pediatric oncology with experience in setting up new program. Must have experience in basic research and grant writing as well as patient care.

Position available: Director of well- established four-man pediatric oncology department at a Midwestern university. Must be able to develop department into a leading basic research center.

As I read through the ads, I felt the familiar heavy discouragement settling on my shoulders.

I knew I was a clinician and that my forte was interacting with patients and their families. None of the positions appeared to want a clinical pediatric oncologist. Although I had done clinical research, I never had done nor was I interested in doing basic research. Starting a new department was beyond the scope of my imagination.

One position seemed like a possibility. The department of pediatrics at Vanderbilt in Nashville, Tennessee, was looking for an additional clinical oncologist. Once I'd contacted them, they wanted to interview me. I flew to Tennessee with no clue what I would find there. I had spent the year in Houston, and had listened to my mother deride the entire concept of the south. How could I think about living in another southern city When I arrived in Nashville though, its beauty partially seduced me.

I was charmed by many of the neighborhoods I passed through. The streets were lined with large shade trees and unique stately houses with well-kept yards.

Arriving at the hospital, the staff graciously greeted me. They then gave me a tour of the hospital. The pediatric wards were welcoming and colorful. Some of the walls displayed enchanting murals. Those children who could were freely walking the halls or playing in a spacious playroom. The wards had beds so that parents could stay overnight. I don't remember much about my interview except that I was nervous and felt my answers were inadequate or incomplete. I was not offered the job.

After a period of panic, I decided I was going to have to find a job as a general pediatrician. Initially I felt terrified about my chances of locating such a job. My mind kept playing its doomsday voice over and over, instructing me precisely how and why I wouldn't be able to master general pediatrics.

*How can you even think of doing general pediatrics? For four years you have concentrated on pediatric oncology. Will two years of general pediatric residency be enough for you to do a good job as a run-of-the mill pediatrician?*

# 42
# Do You Know the Way to San José?

I was frightened as I drove the 350 miles from the City of Hope to my parents' home in Sausalito.

I had visions of never being able to find a job as a pediatrician or, if I did, being fired for incompetence. Still, relief overcame me knowing that I was making my way to my parents' home. After a year and a half, I still had not completely recovered from the nightmare of my hepatitis and was weak and tired and looked forward to my mother fixing all the meals, doing my laundry, and pampering me in innumerable ways.

It took me from July to September to get mobilized enough to start my job search. Once I began, I'd found that I was genuinely excited about the prospect of doing general pediatrics. I was ready for a break in the constant grieving that I had experienced as a pediatric oncologist—the endless heartbreak of telling the parents bad news, witnessing the pain that the treatments invariably caused, the death of a young person so full of promise.

One of the first places I applied to was Kaiser. However, before receiving their answer, I noticed an ad for a job as third pediatrician in a small group in San José, California.

I mailed my résumé at once.

A week later, Mother answered the phone. She turned to me and smiled. "It's for you. It's someone calling from the clinic you applied to."

I took the receiver, drawing my breath.

"This is Dr. Oppenheimer."

At the other end of the line I heard a woman's pleasant voice that was spiced with a Scottish accent.

"Dr. Oppenheimer, I'm Jeanne, the office manager for Alexian Medical Group. The doctors have received your résumé and want to set up an appointment to meet with you. When are you available?"

My heart began to pound. I wanted to shout, "Now! Today!" Instead, I used my most professional not-too-desperate voice. "Whenever it is convenient for the doctors."

"How about ten o'clock next Wednesday morning?"

Despite the fact that I was capable of driving myself to the interview, I needed my mother's support and encouragement. Cupping my hand over the receiver, I whispered to her.

"Can you drive me to San José next Wednesday?" Grinning with the relish of a co-conspirator, she nodded. I took my hand off the receiver. "That will be great."

After I hung up, I cringed as the realization hit that here I was, a thirty-three-year-old woman who had just asked her mother to drive her to a job interview. Christ, Judy, when will you ever grow up?

While we drove down I-280 to the interview, I nonchalantly pointed out the beauty of Crystal Springs Reservoir and the rolling hills where the cattle stood grazing. To further distract me, Mother insisted that we start to make our Christmas lists: a Steuben glass figure for our friend, Martha; a wool shirt for Michael; and some games for Michael's eight-year-old son, Mark.

The list making served as a diversion, and for a time, I was able to relax. But I began to panic when we took the wrong exit off the freeway and were forced to navigate surface streets. I was sure I would be late. Not an auspicious way to begin.

We arrived at Alexian Brothers Hospital with fifteen minutes to spare. As I left the car, Mother said, "You'll do fine, Judy. Relax." I took in the first of many deep breaths.

When I entered the hospital, I noticed gurneys filled with patients lined up along the hallways from the overflow of a too-busy emergency room. It seemed to be total chaos.

Dr. Seigel, the director of the small medical group, was a pathologist. His office was accessed from the main laboratory. The small lab waiting room was hot and crammed with patients. It was hectic. I approached the harassed young woman who was manning the desk.

"I'm Dr. Oppenheimer. I have an appointment with Dr. Siegel."

She made a quick phone call, and five minutes later, a pleasant woman appeared. She smiled. "Dr. Oppenheimer, I'm Jeanne."

I fell in love with her Scottish brogue.

"Welcome. Dr. Siegel is waiting for you."

We went through a side door into the inner sanctum of the pathology department. Dr. Siegel, a tall debonair gentleman with a bow tie, stood to greet me. Smiling, he motioned for me to seat myself in the chair across the desk from him. It was a déjà vu experience. It seemed to me as if the last eight years had been spent sitting across a desk or table facing some looming male authority figure.

He began. "What made you decide to give up pediatric oncology?"

I had my narrative ready.

"My boss at the City of Hope and I couldn't communicate. When I began looking for another job as a pediatric oncologist, none of the openings seemed to fit my talents as a clinician."

We spoke along these lines a short time, and then he led me on a tour of the hospital. The hospital was clean and pleasant but extremely busy. The pediatric ward was filled with sick kids receiving IVs. Dr. Seigal then introduced me to the two pediatricians in the group, Fred Gerber and Herb Schwartz.

Fred, a short, stocky man in his mid-thirties, was the titular head of pediatrics. Herb was in his late fifties, early sixties. He was gray haired, short, and wiry. He projected an air of quiet confidence—hewn, no doubt, by years of solo pediatric practice.

Fred also sported a bow tie and had a cocky manner that immediately alerted me to be on guard. He asked confrontive questions such as "How would you begin to work up a child with a fever?" and "What are the signs and symptoms of meningitis? Of appendicitis?" Whenever I hesitated or frankly admitted I didn't immediately know the answer to some of these challenges, he frowned. He told me that he had just finished his residency, and at the end of his interrogation, he appeared to puff up as he said, "Well, I can see I have a lot more experience than you."

Herb, on the other hand, immediately put me at ease. When I didn't have an instant answer to one of his questions, I simply told him, "I'm not sure, but I'm very willing to learn. Being a pediatric oncologist did prepare me for almost any emergency."

Finally, trembling slightly, I rejoined Mother in the car. With practiced radar, she searched my face. "How did it go?"

I hesitated and sat staring out the window, trying to decide myself how the interview had gone. Finally able to answer in some form, I turned to her. "All right, I guess. Fred Gerber strikes me as a little Napoleon."

She paid no attention to my concerns. She was terribly excited about the prospect of my getting the job—even more so than I.

"I hope you get this job. I watched the people come and go and saw such marvelous diversity." She paused, lit a cigarette, and exhaled. "They seemed to come from all walks of life."

"Dr. Schwartz talked about that. He also said that at the present, East San José has only five pediatricians. It is a terribly underserved area."

A week later, Fred called to offer me the position. I was to start after New Years Day, 1974. I was relieved. The search and my uncertainty were over.

I hung up the phone and yelled to Mother, "I got the job!" She smiled and exclaimed, "Wonderful." Only the faintest undercurrent of that ancient fear— that I wouldn't be capable enough—shadowed my excitement. I tried to shake it off. That night, my parents and I had a mini celebration. Dinner consisted of my favorite meal: salad, sourdough French bread, and fresh Dungeness crab, which my father had picked up from Fisherman's Wharf on his way home.

When the table was laden and the wine poured, my father raised his glass toward me, his face alight with pleasure.

"To Judy's new job."

At once my mother lifted hers.

"To Judy!"

I raised mine. Glasses chimed.

# 43
## The Golden Stiletto

After my contract with Alexian Medical Group was signed, Mother, her friend Martha, and I made a visit to San José to hunt, yet again, for an apartment.

We marveled at the fact that so close to the city proper, large productive orchards and open farm fields still existed. East San José had not yet begun to be developed and was still a quasi farm community with a few remaining scattered small farms and broad fields of flowers and greenhouses. It was also the Latino neighborhood, with only a few small shopping centers and bars lining its main streets of Alum Rock Avenue and McKee Road. Young Hispanic mothers pushed their kids in strollers. We drove into the hills where we saw large well-kept Spanish-style houses and unique custom homes with large yards.

A vision struck me.

"Someday I'd like to live in this area," I said.

We stopped at a development of newly constructed town houses. They had large rooms and were light and airy. However, none of them were for rent, only for sale.

The three of us were all discouraged as we sat down for lunch.

I complained, "I can't believe there aren't more apartments close to the hospital. We'll have to look farther away, and I really don't want to commute."

Mother thought a moment.

"Maybe we should stop thinking about renting and consider buying one of those town houses we saw. They were pretty nice, and you would even be able to plant a small garden in the backyard."

Martha was enthusiastic. "I think it's a great idea."

I was taken by surprise. Owning my own home hadn't registered as even a blip in my consciousness. All I could think of was that I wasn't old enough to have my own house.

By the end of lunch, I'd talked myself into it. Buying was the right way to go. I'd already managed to save enough for the down payment. The monthly payments and taxes were even cheaper than it would have been to rent. Walking or biking to work would be good exercise. Best of all, across from my town house was a working farm where the farmer worked the dark fertile soil. Watching his tractor and breathing the scent of the moist dirt evoked pleasant memories of my life on the ranch.

I signed all the necessary papers, wrote a check for my "earnest" money, and was on my way to owning my first home: a three-bedroom town house. Two days before my job was to begin, I drove from Sausalito to my new home. Listening to Mozart and watching the scenery flow past I was filled with a great sense of freedom and exhilaration. At my parents' home, I'd inevitably lapsed into a combined state of boredom and discomfort. Though Mother's tender care was heartfelt and welcome, guilt crept in as I continued my lifelong behavior of sitting like a lump, never helping her cook, clean, or do other mundane tasks. My unease was sharpened by my parents' ceaseless arguments that, it seemed, had become a fixture of their lives. During these episodes, I slunk into another part of the house, silently always siding with Mother.

Most pediatricians started out with four years of general pediatric training. I had obtained only two. On my way to work that first day, I was filled with apprehension very much like stage fright. I drilled myself on questions such as the following: When are immunizations given? When do babies start on solid baby food? When do you start giving babies fluoride? Will my patients like me?

Arriving at the office, I relaxed. Kathy, my nurse, and Linda, my receptionist, welcomed me with smiles and enthusiasm. My waiting room was a mini United Nations. There were young mothers with their newborns or professional women with their six- or seven-year-olds. They came dressed in hand-me-down clothing or the latest in middle class attire. Dark-haired, brown-eyed kids sat or played with blond, blue-eyed ones. My schedule was leisurely enough that I had time to play and goof off with the kids.

Often the exam room was filled with giggles or laughter. I loved it.

Things seemed, in fact, to be going wonderfully. I relished making hospital rounds with Herb. He was a kind and gentle teacher. Many occasions found me slipping across the hall to his office to gather advice on a particular problem. For example, when I wasn't sure of whether a child's rash was rubella or merely a viral rash, he came to look at it and then chatted with me about easy ways to distinguish between the two.

My initial reaction of Fred being a little Napoleon was correct. I did all I could to avoid him and rarely asked him for advice. When I did, he often frowned and shouted at me. Over time he began to grind me down. Without consulting me, Fred began making minor additions to the orders I had written for my hospitalized patients; he changed the frequency of vital signs or revised my diet orders. However, he never voiced any concerns about my overall care.

Ultimately, we locked horns. Things came to a head over what seemed, at first, to be a relatively insignificant issue. The temporary furniture in my exam rooms, flimsy and cheap, proved to be a menace. A couple of times a pregnant mother found herself on the floor because her chair had slid from under her. I discussed my concerns with Fred. He seemed to listen and agreed to let me have a hand in choosing new furniture. I was relieved. One afternoon I returned from seeing a patient in the ER to find that my office had indeed been fitted out with new furniture, and I had had no part in its selection. I began a slow burn when I saw the new chairs; they were exactly the same as those I had before.

Enraged and not too diplomatic, I confronted him. His face wore an expression of impatience and distaste.

I had only been at the clinic for six weeks when Fred went on vacation. At the end of one workday soon after Fred had left, I was summoned to Herb's office. I didn't know what to expect. Instead of his usual friendly welcoming face, he wore one that was glum and stern. My apprehension increased as I noticed Herb sitting stiffly behind his desk. He pointed to a chair.

*For God's sake, here it goes again.*

"Judy, I'm afraid that it's not working out between us. We have to let you go."

"What? Why?"

"Fred was upset by the way you handled a newborn with jaundice. His bilirubin was 10, and you let him go home." (Bilirubin is a substance in the blood that measures the level of jaundice.) Jaundice, or yellow skin and eyes, is common in newborns because their livers haven't started to function at full capacity. If the bilirubin is high (above 12 or 14), the treatment is phototherapy where the infant is placed under a special light. This helps convert the bilirubin into substances that the body can get rid of without depending on the liver. If the bilirubin rises above 20, it can cause brain damage, and more aggressive treatment is needed.

"Ten isn't high, and I sent him home with orders to return the next day for a repeat bilirubin."

"That wasn't good enough."

Whose verdict, I wondered, was that? Fred's or Herb's?

Silence. I felt numb.

Finally I asked, "When is my last day?"

"You can pack up your belongings tonight. There is no need for you to come to work tomorrow."

That night I made my way home stupefied. Dragging myself upstairs to my bedroom, tears blurred the view of the farmer still hard at work in his field. I ranted and raved to no one and pounded the pillows.

I simply couldn't understand what I had done that was so terrible. I knew—could see and feel—I had a good rapport with my young patients and their parents. I had the clear impression that most of my colleagues respected me. Yet somehow I'd been fired once again. Was my competence truly that low? Could I be as bad a physician as Fred and Herb implied? The prospect of looking for a new job, of selling myself all over again, crushed me. I felt as if I were forced to do somersaults into infinity. At that point, I could not conceive of finding enough energy to pursue such a bleak venture.

I was also certain Herb and Fred would not give me a fair evaluation.

The group didn't plan to honor my contract that said that they had to give me three months' notice or three months' salary. When I realized this, I called Jeanne, the group's office manager, who had become a friend and ally. Both of us suspected one of reasons for my being fired was because many of Fred's long-standing patients had preferred coming to me.

Jeanne directed me to one of the most feared and prestigious law firms in San José. A letter from the lawyer was all it took for the group to give me most of the money that was owed.

Grief overcame me. I loved having my own patients and getting to know their parents. I knew I would miss the daily challenges of my patients as well as the fun that they provided. Every day they'd drawn me out of my shell, made me a better doctor. I had had gathered more acquaintances and colleagues than I had ever had before. I felt buried. I couldn't move and leave my first house.

Then slowly—from the dark and the sadness, the inertia and chaos—a tiny sprout of a thought emerged. *What about starting YOUR own practice?*

This tiny sprout began to grow. There was no eureka moment, no lightning flash. I was still stung by the latest challenge to my competence. In addition, I didn't know the first thing about the business of medicine. I only assumed that, as with all I'd managed this far, I could learn.

Still today I am amazed about how politically savvy I actually proved to be as I went about collecting all the information I would need to start my practice.

First, I set off to talk to the ER physicians. They all felt that I was a good pediatrician. Each felt very comfortable having me consult. Next, I spoke with the nurses in the ER, nursery, and pediatrics. All concurred with the ER doctor's assessment and encouraged me to set up my own practice. I met with all the obstetricians and talked to other pediatricians. The ER physicians and obstetricians were happy to begin referring patients to me. The pediatricians not only approved of my care but also said, "There are more than enough patients. We actually need more pediatricians in the area." The project seemed, from the start, to drive itself. With Jeanne's help, I began in earnest to set up my practice.

She gave me the name of an accountant. For legal work I used the lawyer suggested to me by Barbara Floyd, wife of one of the obstetricians. My old office staff, Linda and Kathy, were elated by the prospect and eager to work for me. I talked to a group of four pediatricians who agreed to share weekend call with me. This meant that I only had to be available to take phone calls and visit the hospitalized patients one out of five weekends.

The next few weeks were a whirlwind of activity. Barbara Floyd, who ran her husband's successful obstetrical practice, instantly took me under her wing. She became a solid friend and advisor. Over the years she taught me most of what I needed to know about the business of running a successful medical office. I borrowed money from my father and found office space in a building owned by one of the obstetricians.

Jeanne, Linda, Kathy, and I made lists of the equipment and supplies I needed. We went on a shopping spree.

I was like a kid in a candy store. Colors! I chose orange, blue, and yellow for the surfaces of my exam tables. I bought otoscopes, ophthalmoscopes, and a microscope. Also I purchased a desk and credenza and waiting room furniture. I learned about the suppliers of the vaccines I would need.

Soon, the infrastructure of my practice was in place. All I needed were patients! We sent my ex-patients cards announcing the opening of my new office. Six weeks after leaving the group, I saw my first patients in my new venue. Soon I was seeing sixty newborns a month, more than half of all the newborns delivered at Alexian Brothers Hospital. I received almost all the referrals from the ER, the nursery, and pediatrics.

The public health nurses began to refer families to me. Medi-Cal (California's version of Medicaid) had just started, and many children in the community had never seen a physician except when they were very ill. My practice grew so rapidly that after six months, I was seeing forty to sixty patients a day and had to temporarily limit my new-patient appointments.

Every single time I saw Herb and Fred in the hospital or at meetings, I offered them my most open pleasant face. Each time, they looked the other way.

Fred soon left practice to work at a pharmaceutical company. I felt my success was revenge enough. I called it my golden stiletto. Over the ensuing years, Herb and I actually overcame our unhappy history and developed mutual respect and friendship for each other. Sometime before his death we were having lunch together when he stopped eating, looked me in the eye, and said, "You know, Judy, letting you go like we did was a great mistake." I only smiled.

# 44
# The Bubble

My practice thrived.

I became one of the pediatricians to go to. I felt honored as my colleagues brought their children to see me. As my practice matured, so did I.

Because so many of my patients were poor and had not had access to decent preventive or acute care previously, I felt as if I was doing almost as much good as Val, my own pediatrician, did when she made her circuit of clinics in northern New Mexico.

My emotional investment in the work deepened along with my knowledge of the science. Over the years I began to love observing the uniformity and inevitability of human development. Henry would roll over at four months, crawl by seven months, walk by a year, and start talking when he was eighteen months. With some minor differences, Jim, La Shawn, Maria, José, Eddie, and Manuela all did the same. I had a lot of fun interacting with middle schoolers like thirteen-year-old Ernesto and twelve-year-old Sue. I can also admit that I was happy I didn't need to live full-time with their ebullience and craziness. Adolescents like seventeen-year-old Pam needed to talk about birth control; many teenagers wanted to share the difficulties they were having with their parents.

With time and practice, my knowledge and confidence increased. Intuitively, I recognized when immediate action was needed or when more diagnostic steps were necessary. Handling real medical emergencies no longer generated panic. I remained somewhat shaky in dealing with major trauma but always had the physicians in the ER to help. In fact, they often had begun to stabilize the patient before I arrived on the scene.

I was no longer ashamed when I didn't know the answer to a patient's problem and needed to consult surgeons and specialists. My surgical colleagues,

Ken Watanabe and Hugh Walsh, gave me the expertise and confidence I needed in diagnosing surgical emergencies. Their teaching made me more confident in detecting hernias and other surgical conditions such as appendicitis.

The pediatric cardiologist from the county hospital, Phil Benaron, patiently and expertly took me through the subtleties of diagnosing baby boy Garcia and other newborns with heart disease. I learned to get advice from the subspecialists from Santa Clara Valley Medical Center, Stanford, or UCSF. For the first time the confident, competent Dr. Judy began to emerge not just as a façade but also as a reality—someone who fully and joyfully inhabited her profession.

In addition to my growing feeling of competence, I enjoyed the ritual of going to work and interacting with the children and their families. The years flew by, and patients I had first seen as young adolescents began to bring their children to me. Young adults who had been my patients often surprised me by dropping by to say hello, to tell me about college or work. I treasured following each one of them through their various stages of development.

And in an unexpected way, I became part of the "in" crowd. The medical staff at Alexian was young. Several times a year, we made an excuse to have a huge bash. Often held in the lobby of one of the office buildings or at one of my friend's homes, these parties involved a lot of drinking, talking, and dancing. I participated in the dancing, but as the effect of the alcohol waned, I still felt very foolish and awkward. Nevertheless, the sense of being included, liked, and admired overcame my self-chastisement. I began to form some solid friend-ships, particularly with the Floyds and the Diamonds. Tom Diamond was an ophthalmologist, and his wife, Marilyn, worked in my office as my nurse when I was in between new personnel or when my office nurse was sick. Barbara Floyd became my business guru. She also taught me how to ski. Learning to ski caused me to once again come face-to-face with my physical limitations. I remember one time when I was first learning and kept falling in the un-groomed snow. She bellowed, "Damn it, Judy, turn." I shouted back, "Damn it, Barbara, I'm trying." At the time I had only frustration and self-recrimination, but today we laugh about my klutziness.

I went to friends' homes for dinner and, in turn, invited them over to mine. Yet in spite of these successful social contacts, old ghosts die hard. Whenever I was alone, I regressed to the fearful and self-denigrating young woman I still somehow secretly believed myself to be. It was still the case that I rarely picked up the receiver to initiate contact. Work became my savior, my all-consuming raison d'être. During weekend and the nights, I was on call and too busy to dwell on my unhappiness. I felt I was living in a bubble, both professionally and personally.

Surely it would be only a matter of time before it burst.

# 45
## The Last Holidays

Throughout the busy and fruitful years of establishing my own practice, my mother continued to be my main source of solace and companionship.

In 1975, I sold my town house and bought a large one-story custom- built house situated on one-and-three-quarter acres in the East Foothills of San José.

We began visiting model homes just to laugh at the décor and criticize the construction or the layouts. We laughed at what we decided were attempts to make the rooms look larger, by using mirrors, for example. Mother focused on ornate lampshades. Just before she died, she told me of dreams in which she designed the most outlandish ones. Her dreams designing lampshades morphed into ones where she designed hats that rivaled those featured in the musical Beach Blanket Babylon, a long-running show spoofing modern culture and known for its towering theme-driven hats.

Mother loved my new house, and she and I spent uncountable weekends gardening and swimming in the pool I had installed. True to form, she cooked, helped me clean, and even helped me with my washing.

In 1976 when I was thirty-six, things changed dramatically.

I was just finishing up with my last patient when my father called to tell me Mother had suffered a heart attack. When I arrived in the ICU at Ralph K. Davies Medical Center in San Francisco, the curtains of her cubicle were drawn. Behind them was a flurry of activity, many personnel moving swiftly. I saw the edge of the crash cart through one of the openings. The crash cart was a large cart containing drawers of drugs, IV tubing, needles, and other things needed for dealing with emergencies. It also had the defibrillator to deal with abnormal heart rhythms. No one had time to say a word to us about what was going on. I felt terrified.

As we sat in the waiting room, my father's forehead was furrowed, his blue eyes liquid with tears. I too sat weeping silently. Finally, I regained some of my composure, turned to my father, and gulped. "She just can't die. She's too neat a lady."

He merely blinked, smiled wanly, and nodded.

After what seemed an eternity of waiting, her physician came out looking solemn. He explained that her blood pressure had dropped precipitously, but they were able to stabilize her.

She did survive, but her strength never returned.

Before her heart attack, Mother had had a mastectomy in 1972 for breast cancer. Sometime later, she found a lump in her other breast. The second lump was biopsied and proved to be benign. Her response had been, "Take the damned thing [breast] off. I don't want to spend the rest of my life having to worry about being nitpicked every time I find another lump." She had her second breast removed. She refused reconstructive surgery or prostheses and spent the rest of her life as a breastless woman wearing caftans and other loose-fitting clothes.

When she was diagnosed with metastatic cancer in 1978, everyone assumed her breast cancer had spread. For one-and-a-half years, she underwent chemotherapy and various courses of radiotherapy. Despite the cancer's spread to her brain, she remained alert until her death. She simply became weaker and weaker, and much of her time was spent in bed.

I drove to my parents' house the Thanksgiving before she died. Michael was unable to come. Mother was weak but alert and feeling slightly giddy from the Decadron she was taking to prevent her brain from swelling. I was to be the sous-chef and she, the master chef who would give instructions from her bedroom. Since duck was one of my father's favorite meals, she had decided we were going to have duck instead of turkey for Thanksgiving dinner. The problem was, I had never cooked duck before. I spent Thanksgiving morning walking back and forth to my parents' bright bedroom where she was propped up in bed reading Agatha Christie.

Anxious and unsure myself, I asked many questions, such as "Do you cook the rice for the stuffing before placing it in the duck?"

With a twinkle in her eye, she smiled. "Yes, but don't cook it completely."

Things seemed to be going well. The duck baked fragrantly in the oven; the pumpkin pies were cooked. However, I had no comprehension of how long duck took to cook and had baked the pies before the duck was even started. We waited and waited, starving, but the duck was still not done.

Finally, in desperation, my father set up a table in front of the living room fire where my mother could lie on the couch. There, the three of us ate pumpkin pie and our traditional family holiday cake for a first course. By then the duck was done, and our dessert was duck with all the trimmings.

Early the next morning, I woke up just as daylight was breaking. Outside, the neighborhood was shrouded in fog billowing over the hills. I heard murmurs from my parents' bedroom. Just as I was taking a photograph of the dreamlike scene out of the window, I heard my mother say, "I'm so afraid you won't love me anymore."

Silence. My father spoke no words. I wept.

Did my father hug her and kiss her? Or did he merely walk to the bathroom? Was she referring to the fact that she was so sick and weak or to my father's previous womanizing? I will never know.

I had planned to return to San José that day, but Mother insisted I stay. She wanted my help in catalog shopping for Christmas presents. That gray winter's day, we sat on her bed in the midst of catalogues from I. Magnin, Gump's, FAO Schwarz, and other wonderful stores. Mother, high on her Decadron, would see something she liked and have me put it on the order sheet.

Often she said, "I don't know exactly whom I am getting this for, but it's so neat let's order it anyway." I recorded the item. We spent the day talking, laughing, and relaxing.

The following day, I returned home, but the merriment and excitement did not abate. About a week after the orders were sent, UPS began delivering packages to my parents' home. Mother called every day to report what had arrived. Christmas was to be held that year at my house. My cousin Peter and his family came from Santa Fe to spend the holidays with us. My parents arrived with their car stuffed with presents. Mother and I sorted them and made decisions about who was to get which present. Under the tree, a huge circle of packages formed.

Peter's kids and my nephew, Mark, were overwhelmed. So was I. Any object Mother hadn't assigned to anyone else became mine—an Imari plate, a ginger jar, candleholders, and other treasures from Gump's.

Shortly before she died, Mother told my father of three things she wanted before she died: a trip to Hawaii, a Mercedes, and the set of china she had seen in a San Francisco antique store that was exactly the same as the one her parents had when she was a child. She didn't get the trip to Hawaii or the Mercedes, but my father returned to the antique store to get the dishes. The set she had seen was gone. However, my father found a set of Limoge china almost identical to the original set. Mother was ecstatic and told me that after she died, this china was to be mine, and we named it the Legacy.

I was sitting on the raised fireplace hearth in my living room while Mother rested on the couch. And apropos of nothing and everything, my anxiety boiled over.

"Ma," I blurted, "you just can't die before Pa. I can't deal with him alone."

She only smiled tiredly.

# 46
## The Perfect Storm

I was still dealing with the certainty that my mother would die soon when in January of 1980, I had a hysterectomy for a pelvic mass.

At first, my gynecologist (Bob Floyd) and I thought the worst—that one of the cells in the area that normally would have been my ovaries had become malignant. I remember both he and Barbara trying, with all their power, to reassure me. Bob observed calmly, "I don't think it's an ovarian malignancy. Women with XO Turner's essentially don't have enough ovarian tissue for it to become malignant."

I asked, "What else could it be?"

At the time neither Bob nor I had an answer. I traveled home from Bob's office that night stunned and alone. Even Blanca, my German shepherd, was unable to cheer me up. Mother was struggling with her own cancer, and I didn't want to burden her with my fears. I knew my father would emote and feel guilty. I knew I would have to help him cope instead of having him support me.

Despite my reluctance, I knew I had to tell my parents about the mass and what was about to happen. I did call to tell them. They both did all they could to respond reassuringly and lovingly.

I was admitted to the hospital the evening before surgery. Women who were scheduled for a hysterectomy met with the nurses as a group to voice their fears and to be told what to expect both in terms of the surgery itself and its emotional impact. I was not invited. After all, I was an MD, and was assumed to know everything about the surgery. While the others met, I stayed in my room, frightened and overwhelmed.

Surgery took four hours but was a success. The mass was not a tumor but instead was a walled-off appendiceal abscess. Sometime in the past, apparently without my knowing, I'd had appendicitis, and my appendix had ruptured. My body responded by forming thick layers of scar tissue and infection to form a chronic abscess. My friend Marilyn Diamond, an RN, stayed with me for most of the afternoon after surgery—my own personal nurse. She sponged my clammy face and made sure I received my pain medications. Because of her nurturing, the immediate post-op period was a gentle dream instead of a painful nightmare.

The five days I spent in the hospital went by rapidly. Throughout most of my hospital stay, my spirits held. The pain had moderated, and colleagues and friends visited. My room was filled with flowers. On the day I was to go home, however, the weight of depression and fear descended on me as heavy as lead. No one had warned me this was a frequent occurrence for women after a hysterectomy. Many times their depression was due to the enormous hormonal shifts that occur after surgery; at other times it was because a symbol of their womanhood had been removed, and they felt less valuable. In my case, though, since I had known for years my ovaries could never produce an egg and that my uterus could never bear a child, I couldn't understand my depression.

The first week I was home from the hospital, my parents came down for two days. After that visit, Mother was too weak to return. I went to see her in Sausalito for what was to be the last time.

Three weeks after surgery, I flew to Bellingham, Washington, to visit Michael. It was good having a break and being with my brother. His very physical presence, tall and thin, was reassuring. We talked about Mother's illness, and just being able to share seemed to lessen the burden. We drove to Vancouver, BC, where we spent time at the harbor and had dinner in Chinatown.

The night before I was to return to San José, our father called to tell us Mother was going to have surgery the next day to drain fluid from around her heart. He gave her the phone, and I spoke briefly with her. She sounded tired but otherwise appeared to be her usual self. After the phone conversation with our parents, Michael asked, "How dangerous is this procedure?"

"Quite dangerous. Ma could easily die during it. Why don't you come home with me? I'm tired, Michael, and not sure I can deal with Pa's emotions by myself."

As he thought about my plea, Michael's face was full of anxiety and pain, his blue eyes moist. He finally said, "Deedle (his nickname for me), I really can't come now."

Although he didn't explicitly express it, I knew he meant he couldn't face our mother's illness or impending death and that he too could not cope with our father. I tried to understand, to be sympathetic about his reluctance to join me, but I couldn't help but feel disturbed and hurt that he didn't accept my plea.

As I flew home on February 13, 1980, the plane's engines droned on and on. Other passengers were engrossed in reading or conversation. I was alone. About thirty minutes from San José, while flying at thirty thousand feet above the earth, I thought about my mother and her suffering. I knew she would die soon. I had a premonition that I would never see her alive again.

I buried my head in my hands and let the tears pour. Exhaustion and grief overcame me.

Just as I put the key in the door to my house, the phone began to ring. Even before I picked it up, I knew.

My father simply said, "It's all over."

I began to cry.

Mother had died during the procedure. I knew in my heart she had died the moment the tears were streaming down my face on the plane. I needed no explanation, no theory of divine intervention or insight.

She was sixty-eight years old.

My friend Marilyn Diamond, who had driven me home from the airport, gave me a passionate hug that wrapped around me like a soft cashmere blanket. She then drove me to St. Mary's Hospital in San Francisco where Mother had died. During the trip, I sobbed and laughed in turn, reminiscing to Marilyn about my mother.

My father was waiting for me in her hospital room. Her cleaned-up body was lying under crisp white sheets. Her face looked smooth, peaceful. My father kept opening and shutting Mother's eyelids. Was he trying to convince himself that she was indeed dead? We cried together. Taking her wedding ring from her finger he handed it to me. I handed it back, feeling that he should keep this memento for himself. He then placed it on his little finger, where it remained until he died.

It was four weeks after my surgery.

Michael flew down that evening. As he emerged from the Jet way, he looked much older than his thirty-six years. He walked hunched over. His face was ghostly, and there were remnants of tears on his cheeks. I hugged him. I longed desperately to have his support in the burden of dealing with our father, but he was, ultimately, unavailable. Even at the time, I realized how difficult it was for him. Recently he told me that one of his life regrets was that he didn't spend more time with Mother and that he didn't come down to be with her as he did when our father was dying.

During the week that followed in Sausalito, my father came to me for hugs and consolation. He never seemed to go to Michael for support. Although Michael and he did have conversations, they were often terse and took on a more intellectual hue. He seemed to not acknowledge his son's pain. As the week progressed, their conversations became less frequent. I often saw Michael sitting at the table in the corner of our parents' living room. As he looked out the window at the San Francisco skyline, his eyes held tears. At other times they radiated a sadness that pierced me. Though I understood how much my brother was suffering, I couldn't ignore my father's neediness; he and I often talked softly to one another. On one such occasion, I saw my brother standing not ten feet away. His downcast eyes had tears as well as a spark of anger. I glared at my father, suddenly very angry with him and with myself for letting him once again manipulate me to exclude Michael. I desperately wanted our father to talk to his son. I went over to my brother to comfort him but was unable to make him feel any more welcome or included. It was too late.

The three of us spent the dark rainy week trapped inside a shadowy house listening to the rain and our own tears. Silence filled every corner. We had no rituals to relieve the pain. I'm not sure we even looked at any photographs of Mother. I, like my brother, tried to avoid any deep conversation with my father. My mind was filled with vivid memories: the time Mother and I went for a one-week vacation in Mazatlan, where we laughed a lot and played in the surf;

the trip to Cripple Creek, Colorado, with Martha and Karen, where we saw an old-fashioned melodrama. I recalled her caustic wit and her dogged yet often unspoken love and support for me. I ended up trying to be the support for both my brother and father.

Friends called to ask if they could bring food or to invite us to their homes for dinner. I desperately needed the human contact, compassion, and companionship of reminiscing that such excursions would have provided. My father adamantly refused every one of their offers. Thus I was forced, during that time, to suppress my own grief.

I returned home to San José mentally and physically exhausted. Five weeks after my hysterectomy, one week after Mother's death, I tried to go back to work.

Marilyn gave me hugs and invited me to dinner. Otherwise, life carried on seemingly without change. When I told my colleagues that my father had set up a memorial fund in my mother's name at the Exploratorium, no one asked for more information.

Thus, the doctor who formerly considered herself to be Superwoman often dissolved into a tearful, ineffectual blob. I would stand over a bassinet trying to examine a newborn and suddenly find myself shaking and, in spite of my resolve not to, beginning to weep.

I took another week off. Returning to work the second time, I was at least able to concentrate on my patients at an acceptable level.

The short days of winter descended, and the rains came, and I slumped into another world: my old abyss—the dark, silent world devoid of activity or human contact. Through the large windows of my bedroom, I saw the sparkling lights of San José. My dog Blanca would snuggle up to me. Though the scene looked peaceful, every night I looked at the other side of my bed wishing someone were there to take me in their arms and tell me everything would be all right. Sometimes I tried to hug myself, but this too was a failure.

Although I had dealt a lot with grieving and death and dying, I was not prepared for the moment when awaking just after Mother's death I realized that I could not remember her voice.

It was several months after her death before I could again capture it in my mind and hear it once more in my dreams.

# 47
## Trip to the Southwest

In 1980, six months after Mother died, my father, Mark-Michael's thirteen-year-old son from his first marriage-and I flew to Albuquerque, New Mexico, to attend the first Oppenheimer lecture in Los Alamos. As we drove through the desert between Albuquerque and Santa Fe, my father began reminiscing about their summers at Perro Caliente. In Santa Fe we stayed at the La Fonda. Once settled in our hotel room, we visited my cousin Peter, who lived in Santa Fe. The next day we all drove up to Perro Caliente. Once we arrived, my father insisted Peter take a photo of me crouched on the same hill, striking the same pose as that of my mother in a photo taken when they vacationed there in the 1930s. At first I protested. It made me queasy, feeling somehow like a traitor to her memory. To me, this request was a symbol of my father's cloying sentimentality, a weird web to be ensnared in. Finally relenting, I let Peter take the picture. The photo is, thankfully, unique. The pose and the atmosphere is nothing like that seen in the long-ago image of my mother.

As we drove up the familiar route up to Los Alamos, I was transported back to 1945 when I was five years old.

In 1944, my father spent most of his time in Oak Ridge, Tennessee, where he was one of the lead scientists involved in developing a method to separate uranium 238 from the fissionable isotope uranium 235, which was to be used in the atomic bomb. This involved building and calibrating a special centrifuge. In December 1944, his work in Oak Ridge was completed, and he moved to Los Alamos during the first week of January 1945 where his expertise was needed for the final stages of the construction of the bomb. Mother, Michael, our dog Richard, and I had been able to join him a few weeks later.

We drove from Berkeley in our DeSoto convertible. My mother's friend Martha had come along to keep her company. Because of Martha, I had to sit in the backseat with Michael and Richard. Michael, who was two at the time, had begun vomiting and having diarrhea just as we left Bakersfield. The backseat smelled of vomit.

Indeed, the trip had proved long and difficult. My mother was naturally preoccupied with Michael. We were all hot, smelly, and grumpy by the time we made the required stop in Santa Fe to see Dorothy McKibben at her office nestled off one of the courtyards in the Governor's Palace, an old 1700s adobe.

Dorothy was a statuesque lady with unruly gray hair. Her desk was always was immaculate. Neat lines of memos (the precursor to post-it notes) were aligned in graceful overlapping formations at one corner. Not only had Dorothy become a family friend, but she also provided the sole interface between the top secret Los Alamos Manhattan Project and the public. Single-handedly, she found housing for the scientists in Los Alamos. She was also the person who issued the passes to enter the secret city. She presented Mother with a bunch of papers and a card with her picture, and we left to continue our journey.

We made our way along the winding dirt road to Los Alamos and were eventually stopped at a small shack by guards dressed in army drab. With angry faces, they leaned through the car window. I noticed they wore big guns along their sides. Terrified and mute, I pointed to the guns and turned to my mother for reassurance, but she was too busy answering their questions and showing them all sorts of papers to pay any attention to me.

Once we'd passed through the gate, I could breathe again.

We crawled along dusty streets. All I could see were small shabby houses and Quonset huts. No stores, trees, or parks softened what seemed to be a makeshift community.

We finally stopped at a one-story house surrounded only by golden- red sand. I spotted my father standing at the door and ran to him. Grinning, he gave me a huge hug and swung me between his legs. We stepped inside to inspect the small house. There was an L-shaped living room, a small kitchen, and three small bedrooms. The walls were bare. I didn't care. After the long year that my father was in Oak Ridge, we could feel like a family again.

After our visit to Santa Fe and Los Alamos, we drove through Taos, New Mexico and on to Alamosa, Colorado, where we picked up our family friend, Milly Danielson. The Oppenheimers and the Danielsons had shared a long and warm history. They had met on the first day that my parents had moved from the ranch to Boulder and thereafter spent a great deal of time together. Milly's first husband, Phil, died suddenly in 1968 at the age of forty-two. After that, Mother and Milly took several vacations together, and when my parents moved to Sausalito, Milly often visited. She had been one of my mother's best friends and confidants.

We stayed in a motel where we occupied two adjoining rooms. Milly and I slept in one room, Mark and my father in the other. Late at night I heard my father sobbing.

Suddenly he appeared kneeling at my bedside still sobbing.

"Oh, how I wish Jackie was on this trip with us. I miss her so much! I remember so many things we did together: all the horseback riding through the mountains and the desert, the ranch . . ."

Realizing this was first time he had been in the southwest without Mother and that memories were flooding his dreams and daytime thoughts, I tried to talk to him. When I found none of my words were able to calm him, I reached out to pat his arm. Instantly, an old queasiness and confusion flared up within me. I drew my hand back as if my father was on fire. Part of me wanted to support him, the other part felt alarmed, on guard, unable to trust him. I questioned the sincerity of his emoting. I thought again of his betrayals of Mother's trust, of how he could be such a bastard to her when she was alive.

Finally I said to him, "I know how much you miss her. I miss her too, but let's talk about it in the morning. We should be quiet, or we will wake Milly and Mark."

Then he tried to get into the bed with me.

"Pa, stop it! You can't get into bed with me! Go back to your bed." When he persisted, I began to panic. He was kneeling, and I pushed his chest from the side of the bed. He wouldn't stop, and I used all my strength to pry his arms from my mattress and then push him into his room. Ultimately, I convinced him to get into his bed. I sat by his bed for a while, and once he appeared calmer,

I returned to my bed, exhausted.

The rest of the night, my mind was a kaleidoscope of tangled visions and dreams. In one, my father had become a monster who was chasing me. I had to float to escape and became lost in a labyrinth of a hospital where no one acknowledged my existence. No one tried to help.

All night I wondered what would have happened if I had not been able to keep him from my bed. Could I have freed myself? At the time I was too frightened to be angry. What did I do to bring on his behavior? At first, I labored to justify his actions. I first told myself he was sleepwalking and then tried to convince myself he was looking for Milly's bed.

I awoke in the morning shaken, softly weeping. Immediately, I began to form another layer to my emotional cocoon. My father and I never discussed the episode. I never told him how aghast and frightened I'd been.

When I returned home from this trip, I again found myself unable to function well at work. But I persevered.

A month or so after returning to work, I began to comprehend how angry, depressed, and desperate I was. The moment of truth occurred during a drive home following a visit to my father's in Sausalito. A casual glance at the speedometer showed that I was doing 90 mph, and my foot was still on the accelerator. Only some unconscious impulse intervened to cause me to release the pressure before the car careened out of control. Once again, sadness and self-loathing dominated my thoughts. Life at home now held the pent-up anguish of a primal scream fully worthy of Munch's painting resounding throughout my empty house and yard. During the day, tears weren't always welling up, but at night I cried myself to sleep, bedeviled by dark, sinister dreams where monsters chased me. Nothing in my dreams came easily. I was always at wit's end, struggling to navigate mazes, float down stairwells, always only a dwindling step ahead of the demons in angry pursuit. I had to jump from floor to floor. I ran along steel girders to escape, but no help was ever in sight.

Following the moment of becoming aware of the fact that I was speeding in a life-threatening way, I made a monumental resolution. I would dig to the bottom of this depression and start the healing that was so long overdue.

My friend Dodi Benaron recommended a Jungian psychologist, Tom Parker. After a few weeks, Tom wisely sensed I was not able to really open up with him. He referred me to his wife, Harriet, who was also a therapist. With Harriet, I did indeed feel much more at ease, and gradually, I began to slowly unpack my lifetime burdens.

We began to talk about my anger toward my father. Just talking about this somehow took the edge away. With her help, I realized that becoming a physician had allowed me to use my feminine creative side as I'd never been able to use it in my personal life.

I told Harriet about the time near the end of my mother's life when she came down to stay for three days. She was tired and weak, and I'd tried to make her comfortable, yet I'd began to feel I was failing her miserably. One day the time for lunch had come and gone, and I was continuing to putter around. Suddenly, I heard her angry voice coming from her bedroom.

"Damn it, Judy, I'm starving. Where in the hell is lunch?"

Horrified, I felt immobilized by guilt. What was wrong with me? How could I be such a terrible daughter? After talking to Harriet, my self-recrimination began to dissipate. She helped me see that my pattern of letting Mother do everything for me when we were alone was not entirely my doing. Mother had also liked and needed it in a way. In fact, she probably preferred it that way. Consciously or not, we'd both gained from this design, this particular pattern of emotional support.

For the first time in my life I kept a journal. My writing helped me voice my feelings without fear of recriminations. Often, just writing my thoughts down made them less scary, less powerful.

I also began to behave more self-protectively in dealing with my father.

After our trip to New Mexico and Colorado, my father and Milly began seeing each other frequently. My father visited her in Boulder, and she made a few trips to Sausalito. There was obviously a great deal of shared history between them, and no one was surprised when they were married in 1982. At first, I thought their marriage was a great idea. I was extremely fond of Milly, and I hoped she could help my father with his loneliness and grief so I'd no longer have to function as his major emotional support.

I was mistaken. He still insisted on using me as his confidant, often to the exclusion of Milly.

Sometime during the first year of their marriage, my father telephoned me. "I'm coming down alone to talk and to bring you some of Jackie's things."

I had neither the energy nor desire to provide an audience for my father, to give him the rapt attention and emotional buttressing I knew he would require. This time, I held my ground.

I spoke calmly and quietly. "You can come only if Milly comes with you."

His voice rose; I could hear his anger and disappointment when he said, "I'll have to think about it." He hung up abruptly.

He called me shortly after to tell me that he and Milly were coming together. By the time they arrived, both my father and I had calmed down a bit. I felt a wonderful sense of empowerment.

I had taken my stand and won.

At around the same time, I ventured out to San José State University to enroll in a photography course. Soon thereafter, I took my first creative writing course with a professor named Gabriele Rico. She was exactly the kind of mentor I needed to awaken my long-dormant creative energies. She was nonjudgmental, thoughtful, and kind. I thrived in her class and actually made some progress in poetry writing. I loved the feeling that went with learning to sculpt words into powerful statements.

I continued to see Harriet for five years, stopping only because she and Tom moved out of the area. By the time they left, I had just begun to unravel my self-spun cocoons. My dreams now often had real people in them. Instead of having to float away from danger by myself, someone in the dream would appear to offer help. These sessions stood me upright once again, not only helping me survive, diminishing sleepless nights, and increasing my energy, but giving me that courage to own myself and my story.

But the greatest gift of all was that my sessions with Harriet gave me the courage to form a family by adoption.

# 48
# The Adoption

As I drove home after a session with Harriet I was excited. Harriet and I had, this time, been discussing adoption. During the conversation, she'd played the devil's advocate: "Why not?"

By the time I arrived home, I must have looked like a madwoman, simultaneously smiling and weeping. For the first time, my dream of adopting a child seemed real and within my grasp.

I wept because I no longer felt that being a mother would be a selfish act, an act designed merely to ensure that someone would love me unconditionally.

I smiled because, for the first time in my life, I realized I did have something to give—my values, my warmth, my humanity. By evening I decided to pursue this dream.

From the time I was fifteen when I was diagnosed with Turner's, I had known the only way I could become a mother was through adoption. I had flirted with the possibility several times before, but never followed through on my impulse. Now I was overcome with joy and certitude. It had been a long time since I'd felt such a terrific sense of mission and passion.

I sank my bulldog perseverance into making my dream become reality. The next few weeks, I flung myself at the necessary steps, whirling around my home and city with nonstop phone calls and visits. I called adoption agencies. I attended their orientations. I talked to my friends. All the women rejoiced.

"Wonderful!" they exclaimed. "You'll be a great mother!" Or, like Harriet, they simply grinned said, "Why not?" The only person I couldn't bring myself to tell was my father.

Because I was to be a single parent, the standard adoption agencies wouldn't even consider me for adoption of an infant. I could have adopted an older child, a hard-to-place child, or a foreign child, but my heart was set on a newborn. As a pediatrician, I had seen so many foster kids who had been moved from place to place and had been abused. Even if they had had warm, caring foster parents, by six months of age, they often had been in two or more homes. I knew I didn't have the wherewithal to face the challenge of undoing all the harm that had already been done; I wanted to make my own mistakes, not to inherit someone else's.

I talked to my colleagues who were obstetricians and emergency room doctors about my desire to adopt. A friend and mother of one of my patients, who already had adopted one child and was in the process of adopting another, gave me the name of her attorney, Mark Gradstein. Mark and his wife, Bonnie, a social worker, were well versed in the ins and outs of independent adoption. At the time, independent adoptions were not common, but I pushed forward.

When I was first ushered into Mark Gradstein's office, he was on the phone with adoptive parents whose birth mother had just given birth to a baby girl. He placed the receiver against his shoulder and turned to me.

"What do you know about Turner's syndrome?"

My face probably turned as white as alabaster.

"That's why I am here. I have Turner's. I can't have kids."

The little girl who had just been born was suspected of having Turner's. Apparently, she had several aspects of Turner's: slightly webbed neck, low-set ears, and proportionally short extremities. The adoptive parents were under-going the anguish of deciding whether to begin the adoption process. If this couple was unwilling to accept this newborn baby girl, I could adopt her.

My mind raced as I thought about karma. If the baby did have Turner's and became my daughter, I would be able to help her with her identity, her struggles.

At his invitation I took the phone from Mark and spoke calmly to the potential adoptive parents about the realities of Turner's, its various manifesta-tions, and what support a child with Turner's might need.

Throughout a previously planned trip to China, while I was out of range of communication with Mark and Bonnie, I kept hoping—hoping the couple hadn't adopted her. When I returned for the news, I learned that the little girl did not, after all, have Turner's, and the couple had in fact adopted her. But at that moment in Mark's office, I felt eerily sure that synchronicity did exist.

In mid-October, one of the obstetricians told me about a young couple who already had one child and didn't want a second. They were considering placing the baby up for adoption. The birth mother had been instructed to call me. She never did. Convinced that she had changed her mind, I gave up on this lead.

Then, early on the morning of December 17, 1982, the obstetrician called me at home. "I have a lady who just delivered a baby girl. I'm assigning the baby to you."

"Frazier, you didn't have to call me at home. I'm not on call. Either Amara or Rayna [the two women pediatricians I shared call with] will admit her for me. I'll see her in the morning."

"Judy, you misunderstand me. She's the lady I told you about some time ago. She still plans to place her baby up for adoption."

After he hung up, I did a little dance and shouted to the empty house, "Oh my god, I'm really going to be a mother!"

I called Mark and then rushed down to be with my petite, red-haired, blue-eyed daughter, Gabriele Jacquenette Oppenheimer.

Barbara Floyd raced to the nursery to be with me. We headed out for a celebratory lunch and then spent the rest of the afternoon on a shopping spree buying diapers, bottles, formula, and a myriad of other assorted necessities for caring for a new baby. I rushed around in a kind of delirium, so much so that during our spree, I left several bags full of new merchandise on the checkout counter. Barbara had to retrieve them. In fact when we returned to the car after lunch, I realized I had left my purse behind. Barbara looked at me with one brow raised.

"I hope you don't forget Gabriele sometime like you forgot your purse and packages today." We both laughed.

I borrowed a bassinet, crib, and other furniture from friends. I was ready to bring Gabriele home.

When I returned home from shopping, I called my father.

"Hi, Pa, you're a grandfather!" I heard him gasp. "What?"

"I have a little girl I'm going to adopt. Her name is Gabriele Jacquenette."

To my amazement, he did not miss a beat, never questioned my decision, or asked why I hadn't told him of my plans before. Instead, his voice flowed, warm and animated through the phone.

"What a wonderful surprise Christmas gift! I love her name." He continued, "When will she be home?" "Probably tomorrow."

"Milly and I will be right down. See you tomorrow."

That night, I attended a party and could not help making some conversational mischief, inwardly gloating as d nonchalantly remarked, "I just became a mother of a little girl today." Talk about showstopper! Whoever I'd address would stare at me, utterly baffled. "But you look so rested." Only then would I confess, "Oh, I didn't give birth to her. I am adopting her." And everyone laughed. That night and for weeks afterward, everyone told me I had a grin that never left.

Gabriele came home when she was two days old. My father held her and played with her. He watched as I held her. "I love watching you when you are holding Gabriele." He added, "You seem so happy, so relaxed."

I was relieved and thrilled to feel my father was looking at me now with different eyes. He seemed to be accepting me in my new role.

Gabriele was a cuddly baby, easy to quiet by letting her sleep on my chest. I spent many hours just holding or watching her. I resented being on call or having to go to meetings. I wanted to spend every minute I could with my newborn daughter.

Sitting with other mothers in Gabriele's pediatrician's office, I was able, for the first time in my life, to enter a world I thought I would never enter. People would ask, "Does being a pediatrician make you a better parent?"

"No," I would answer. "Being a parent makes me a better pediatrician."

Like any other new parent, I worried Gabriele was not gaining enough weight, that she spit up too much. I wondered about her development.

I adapted to the sleepless nights, the rite of passage thrust upon all parents of a newborn. Yet for me, it felt like a gift. I found a kind of magical quality about quiet hours spent in the middle of the night with Gabriele. I loved the way her hands searched my face and massaged my breasts.

I often recounted this newfound magic to the harried mothers who came into the office with their newborns. It felt wonderful to be able to counsel them from immediate, powerful experience. "Enjoy the quiet of the early morning times with your baby. Nap during the day whenever your baby is sleeping. Housecleaning and other chores can wait."

I should have had some inkling that this euphoria was too good to last. The birth parents, it turned out, were young and Mormon. Although I knew how strange it was for a Mormon couple to be giving their baby up for adoption, I'd assumed they had dealt with the grandparents and the church.

They had not.

Gabriele was six weeks old. I was playing the piano while Gabriele slept in her bassinet by a blazing fire. The phone rang.

"Judy, this is Mark. I am making the kind of phone call I hate most." He paused, and I could hear something fatal in his silence.

Not really wanting to know, I none-the-less had to ask what was transpiring. "Mark, what is it?"

Another pause.

"Gabriele's birth parents want her back."

"Oh my god. Why?"

Mark told me the couple had told their parents the baby had died. Gabriele's birth grandfather had become suspicious, and when the social worker that was involved in Gabriele's adoption called asking to speak to the father, the grandfather pretended to be his son. The social worker told him they needed to find a time to get together and talk.

Once the grandparents knew the baby had been placed for adoption, they demanded that their son and daughter-in-law get her back.

Stunned and shaking, I murmured, "Isn't there anything we can do?"

"Not really. Until the papers are signed, you have no legal rights." The rest of the evening was a blur. I called friends, who rushed to the house. My father talked to Mark and me. Mark and I talked to the birth mother. I poured out my heart as I told her how much in love with Gabriele I was, how much it hurt to lose her. I had hoped that by hearing my voice, my passion for the baby, both she and the grandparents would relent, that a miracle would happen.

I spent the last portion of the evening alternating being on the phone and holding Gabriele. I was crying and crying, wanting to bang my head, to make this nightmare disappear. I whimpered about how unfair life was.

Gabriele and I spent much of the night on the living room couch, basking in the warmth of a blazing fire. As she slept on my chest, I tried desperately to cope. All I could do was try to memorize her. I reveled in her warmth, her baby smell, and her cuddliness for one last time. I fervently hoped the birth parents and the grandparents would think once more about their decision, that in the morning I would get a call from Mark saying the birth parents had decided it would be best for Gabriele if she stayed with me. Around two or three in the morning, she and I moved into my bed where she continued to rest warmly and quietly on my chest. My mind stormed and lulled, lulled and stormed. After sobbing, the circular thinking again started. I would cry and then drift off into a restless sleep.

I wondered how I was going to survive without Gabriele. I felt at that point that my entire life consisted of broken promises. I was sure I would never find the warmth, the sensuality I'd allowed myself to feel when Gabriele was in my arms.

I longed to fight for her, but Mark had already told me I had no real legal recourse. All hope disappeared.

The next morning, I actually dragged my exhausted body to work. I made it to the nursery to examine my newborns. I looked at each tiny being, stupefied. How could it be fair that these new moms would experience the wonders and difficulties of raising a child and I wouldn't?

I had an almost uncontrollable impulse to shout—not a calm, gentle shout but one that would reverberate from the walls like the explosion of the first atomic bomb at the Trinity site.

I came home to spend my last afternoon with Gabriele. That night, Barbara took her down to Bob's office and handed her back to her birth parents.

From time to time, over the years, I have thought about what a different life Gabrielle would have had if she had been my daughter. I can only hope that the love she received during the first six weeks of her life made a positive difference to her.

In the aftermath, the house was my tomb. There was no way I could face spending the night in the huge dark place that so recently had been a nest, a sanctuary of joy and hope. I spent the night with my friends Dodi and Phil Benaron, getting their emotional support and a bit of rest.

The next morning, everyone was telling me how I should go to the beach, escape to Hawaii.

"I don't want quiet," I murmured. "I need to go somewhere where there is a lot of noise and life and motion, like New York."

My office staff Jeanne D'Arcy and my nurse, Vickie King arranged for the three of us to fly to New York. We boarded the red-eye that same night. I spent three packed, recuperative days there. We stayed in a hotel on Fifty-Sixth Street right in the middle of downtown Manhattan. We arrived at the hotel early in the morning. Jeanne and Vickie left me to go explore the surroundings. I was exhausted and I slept hard in spite of the thunder of a wrecking ball demolishing the building next door.

Periodically, I would wake, realize where I was, and would pound the pillow as I drifted in and out of remembrances of Gabriele. Eventually, I'd sleep.

We went to museums, saw *The Fantastics,* talked, and shopped. In the midst of the urban hubbub, tears kept reappearing. At some point, I was able to tell myself, *Thank God it was only six weeks and not six months.*

When I returned, facing the newborn nursery still closed my throat, but for that matter in the office, any baby between newborn and four months caused me to fight back the tears. Harriet was on vacation. The pain was too great to allow me to talk about my deepest feelings to anyone, even with my best friends.

Gradually, the searing branding iron of pain lifted so that I once again allowed myself to take the risk and go through a process that had the potential of being so emotionally suicidal.

I was able to revise my letter to potential birth parents. I told everyone I was going to try to adopt one more time.

This go-around, I managed my expectations with strict care, deliberately keeping them much smaller. Emotions were relegated to the back burner. Hoping to minimize the emotional perils, I vowed to be more straightforward in trying to find out how serious the mother was about adopting. I was determined to minimize the risk.

Mark gave me the name of a teenager who was due to deliver the end of April or beginning of May. After talking both to Mark and the mother of the pregnant teenager, we all agreed I would become the adoptive mother. I was scheduled to meet this young woman when, suddenly and rapidly, things changed.

On the morning of February 16, 1983, I was in an exam room with a patient when my nurse knocked on the door.

"Dr. Livingston from the ER is on the phone for you."

I went into my consulting room assuming Larry had a sick patient that needed to be admitted or he wanted a consult on. I lifted the phone.

"Yes, Larry, what to you have for me?"

"I have a lady who just walked into the ER in labor. She wants to give the baby up for adoption. Do you want to come to see her?"

In spite of my resolve not to become too excited, my heart was hammering as I replied, "Let me finish with this one patient, and I'll be right over."

I went on automatic pilot as I examined my patient, and after what felt like infinity, I rushed to the ER.

I walked into the ER cubicle to see a scared young woman in active labor. I felt like a ghoul or vulture as I told her, gently and soothingly, that I wanted to adopt her baby. Briefly, I outlined the story about Gabriele and explained that I could not go through such an experience again.

She reassured me she had no thoughts about changing her mind. I asked her some questions about prenatal care (she had had none), about drugs and alcohol (she denied both). My intuition told me this twenty-six-year-old woman was trustworthy and that her baby would be okay.

I called Bob Floyd to ask him to deliver her baby.

I was in Bob's office with Barb when at 8:03 p.m., Bob phoned to say he had just delivered a baby boy.

Even though I had chosen a name for a boy—Neal Andrew—I was somewhat subdued. I had envisioned a daughter. I knew I had another chance—the young lady who was to deliver in April or May.

Even though I visualized the birth of a girl, after seeing this lanky, blond baby boy, I felt ecstatic. He was alive! He sucked in his lower chin as he looked all around, seeming to take everything in.

When she saw his long, thin fingers, Barb said, "He's going to be a basket-ball player."

I countered, "No, he's going to be a concert pianist."

In spite of my excitement, I had to spend the night soul-searching to get used to the fact I was going to be the mother of a son and not a daughter. I kept telling myself a baby in hand is worth two or three not yet born. Maybe a son would be better than a daughter. I wouldn't have any expectations of what our relationship should be. With a daughter, there would always be my relationship with my mother to deal with.

And what about the agreement I made to the young woman who Mark had found for me?

Neal came home with me when he was two days old. His birth mother drove away in the same dusty pickup she used to drive herself to the hospital. For the first two weeks, I took Neal with me to my office where he held court in my consultation room for a series of adoring fans.

This time the experience was calm, real, and grounded.

Neal's birth mother signed the adoption papers within ten days. At six months of age, Neal legally became my son.

I was a mother again. This time for keeps.

For me, being Neal's mom filled a huge void. From the time he was an infant, every free moment I owned was spent with him. Suddenly I had someone to care for, someone who depended on me. I continued to be thrilled to be able to talk with other mothers at the pediatrician's office. People often approached and started talking to me simply because of the fact that I had a child with me. Just being able to nurture erased many of my self-perceptions of inadequacy. I was now a woman and a mother. No longer was I as isolated.

Neal's first nanny was a young woman from Mexico. She talked to him freely in Spanish, which in a way became his first language. He also took Spanish in school and as a consequence he is now quite fluent in the language. Initially, I remember I felt somewhat concerned when he still wasn't talking a lot at eighteen months, but once he started, he never was silent again.

It was hard leaving Neal during the day with his nanny, but the evenings and weekends were ours. Watching him develop his own personality forced me to learn interpersonal skills I had never actively had to summon before. I had to learn to listen to him, accept him, and accommodate to him. I found that I was able to do this intuitively.

From birth, Neal has been a strong "I can do it myself" child. As an infant, whenever he cried or was fussy, I tried to comfort him by picking him up and holding him close to my chest. I soon learned that this usually didn't work. Instead, I would have to lay him down, and he would slowly calm himself. This need to be alone to calm himself down became even more apparent when he was two. We had just returned from Sausalito after my father's death. He was having a terrible afternoon with one temper tantrum after another. Finally, I simply had him go into his room telling him he couldn't come out until he calmed down. It took two or three trips back to his room before he was able to face the day again.

Three weeks later, I was trying to change his diaper, and he was hysterical. At last he looked up at me and on his own said, "Neal calm down. Go to room." We went into his room together, and he immediately calmed down. His diaper was changed peacefully.

Slowly, I began to accept that I was able to communicate with another human being in an intimate, caring manner. I could be the adult in the situation. My confidence of being a mother soared. I enjoyed letting my maternal feelings rush to the surface. Neal was a blond-haired charismatic kid. His ability to connect with others slowly began to rub off on me. I enjoyed talking to the strangers who were captivated by him. I became less shy when opportunities arose for initiating conversations.

As he became older, almost every weekend I wasn't on call, Neal and I took off. We went to Monterey where we road our bikes, went to the Monterey Bay Aquarium, or just walked around sightseeing. At other times we drove to San Francisco were we stayed in a hotel close to Union Square. We spent our time joyfully sampling from the smorgasbord of activities near us there: visiting FAO Schwarz, the Academy of Sciences, the zoo, or the Exploratorium.

Neal and I spent hours in our pool paddling, floating, racing, or inventing new water games. He was a true water baby. By the time he was eight months old, he was swimming the width of the pool underwater. I remember feeling awe as I watched him bob up and down as he kicked across the pool.

Plenty of deep conversations happened between us. In fact, I wasn't quite prepared for how early they'd begin. When he was about two-and- a-half, he had gone to friends while I attended a staff meeting. The family was composed of a mother and father and three children. That night when he came home, he announced with ringing determination, "When I meet my dad, I'm going to kill him."

I was stunned. I had expected this anger when he was a teenager but not at two years old. I asked him why. Of course, he couldn't articulate it, but I could deduce. He had witnessed the conventional nuclear family structure. Over the next week or so, I noticed his play included a father figure, whose voice (provided by Neal) sounded authoritative.

One night, shortly after this pronouncement about killing his father, he came to my bed at three in the morning.

"Mom, some kids have dads. I don't."

Quietly, I agreed. Then I asked him how he felt.

"Happy." He explained that he thought a father would be mean.

At last I said, "I'd like to have a partner and for you to have a dad, but, honey, we just don't."

He smiled as he looked at me and said, "Don't worry, Mom. That's the way the cookie crumbles."

We never lacked for exciting adventures together, vacationing in the Bahamas and St. John, USVI, where he learned to snorkel. We spent time in England and on the ranch in Colorado. From kindergarten through sixth grade, Neal participated in his school's performances, first as Peter Pan in his kindergarten play and then in the dance programs. At ten he started ballet at the San José Dance Theater. I marveled at his physical grace and stage presence as he danced the kopek dance in the Nutcracker.

Naturally, we also never lacked for challenges, difficulties, and crossroads forcing us to grow and adjust. At five he entered kindergarten at Harker, a private school in San José. The first year, he had a wonderful teacher, Jeanne Davey. Although I had read to him many nights, it never became a bedtime routine. Therefore, I was totally amazed when after eight days in kindergarten, he sat down to read me one of his books. He was well on the way of decoding our written language. I came home one evening to find Neal on the couch in my bedroom reading. He showed me what he was reading. It was a script for a play. "Mom, guess what? Mrs. Davey is going to do *Peter Pan* with all the kindergarten kids."

I hugged him. "Wow, that sounds neat." He smiled slyly as he looked at me. "Guess who's going to be Peter."

I made my face a portrait of puzzlement and curiosity and opened my mouth to begin guessing any number of wildly inappropriate names. Within seconds, he could contain himself no longer.

"Me!"

In spite of his love of kindergarten and his kindergarten teacher, Mrs. Davey, by third grade, he told me that he hated school. Thinking it was a phase, I didn't take him too seriously. But by sixth grade, Neal had developed a serious school phobia. Regularly he would wake up on Monday morning announcing he felt "yucky."

On occasion he would throw up. Once, he actually passed out. He developed a pattern in which he would hibernate under his blanket all day. I began to realize that if he announced that he was sick on Monday, he would be unable to function for at least an entire week. During sixth grade, he missed thirteen weeks of school.

All my training as a pediatrician was no help. The common advice of the time was to drag the child with a school phobia to school, come hell or high water. There was no way this tactic worked with my son. I really wanted to try to understand how Neal was feeling and I learned more about school phobia and childhood depression than I had during all my years of practice. I began to develop enormous compassion for the parents and patients with school phobia.

It helped somewhat when in seventh grade he sarted Menlo School. However, it wasn't until he began attending our small public high school that the healing became complete. In high school, Neal fully blossomed. He tried out for and won the position of school mascot. In his senior year, he was elected student body president.

To this day, I am uncertain of all the causes of his school phobia. Certainly, the environment at the private school had been terribly wrong for him. Although Neal is very bright and he could have excelled, the competitive atmosphere totally turned him off.

To make matters worse, there was a group of his classmates that were teasing him because of his dancing.

I realize now that I also made a grave mistake when he was ten or eleven. I replaced Mila, his Filipina nanny who had been with him since he was two, with a series of male au pairs from the Netherlands. At the time, I felt strongly that he needed some male influence. This proved to be a disaster. But more importantly, I had misjudged Neal's love for Mila. Although I didn't realize it at the time, Mila gave Neal something I couldn't—the sense of being a part of an extended family. Mila often took him with her to visit her daughter. There he was automatically and casually treated like family, playing with her two grandsons and going on excursions and parties with them. The intensity of his bond with Mila and her family didn't fully hit me until her death in 2002. When I told Neal that Mila had died, he burst into tears. And when we went to her funeral, there at one side of the altar was a picture of my son and Mila. Tears came to my eyes. No wonder my son had been depressed when she left.

I owe part of learning to be comfortable with my body and my physical limitations to my son. He was the one who convinced me to try to scuba dive. We had taken several vacations to the Caribbean where he learned to snorkel. Every time we went snorkeling, Neal would ask the dive shop if he could take scuba lessons. The answer was always no that he had to be at least twelve. The summer after he did turn twelve, Neal asked once again to take scuba lessons and implored me to take them with him. It wasn't a difficult sell. I have always loved the water, and at some point years earlier had started taking lessons. However, I never completed the course work. This time I had some trouble with diving in open water, but once I found the correct combination of equipment and received the gentle instruction from my dive friend Roger, I began to flourish.

I was hooked.

On land and on the dive boats, I was still my usual klutzy self, but once I was in the water, my body did almost everything I asked it do. I soared with the current, somersaulted over the reefs, and swam through coral arches filled with sea fans. I loved the quiet, the coral formations, and the colorful sea life.

Until recently Neal and I took many dive vacations together. One of our favorites was celebrating Christmas in Cozumel, Mexico.

Today Neal is a tall well-adjusted young adult whom I see frequently. He is always available to fix my computer, to be with me if I am sick or in the hospital, or to keep me company.

# 49
## Death of a Father

Just before Christmas 1983, my father had one of the lobes of his cancerous right lung removed. I arrived late that night with Neal, who, at the time, was almost a year old. A security guard allowed me to go up to the ICU. Milly, my brother, his wife Jean, and their eight-month-old daughter Kate were waiting in a small room adjacent to the ICU. I handed Neal to Milly and went in to see my father.

My father lay in his ICU cubicle. Puff-puff went the ventilator, stroking in and out, causing his chest to rise and fall. This time, clean oxygenated air—not air filled with tar, nicotine, and other carcinogens— was being delivered to his lungs.

Seeing my father on the respirator, scared and unable to communicate, softened any latent anger I'd carried toward him. I hugged him and tried to reassure him that tomorrow would be better. We communicated by writing, a laborious and sometimes frustrating task. Even while on the respirator, my father was soon his old self, asking detailed questions about the operation and what the next steps would be. At these times, I told him firmly to ask his own doctor.

When he arrived home from the hospital, he found he was able to play a small wooden African flute I'd given him for Christmas. Soon he had graduated to playing his regular flute. He even accepted the fact his playing was not as clear and crisp as before. He reveled in the fact that he could play at all.

Both my parents were cigarette smokers. Both of them died of lung cancer. My mother smoked two packs a day; my father, five packs. "I can stop smoking whenever I want" was his customary retort throughout the years when I bugged him about his habit.

I had grown to hate my parents' smoking. At the end of one of the days in high school, I opened my locker to find it full of acrid, foul-smelling smoke.

One of my father's cigarette ashes had landed on my winter coat as we had been driving to school. It had smoldered all day, and a large hole was burnt through the coat where the ember had landed. Luckily, the coat must have had fire retardant. No flames leaped to engulf the hall.

I hated the cigarette ashes that appeared in the soup, the eggs, or any other food when my father cooked. He merely laughed at my disgust. The stale dirty stench of ashtrays permeated the house. Both parents tried to keep the ashtrays clean, but it was hard to keep up with 140 butts per day. I dreaded returning to my own home after a visit to my parents' home. Opening my suitcase after such visits, the reek of stale cigarette smoke floated, like a sinister genie, throughout my bedroom.

Everything had to be washed or sent to the cleaners.

Seven years before he died, my father managed to stop his five- pack-a-day habit. Astonishingly, he achieved it "cold turkey."

But by that time, it was too late.

My father died at home on February 3, 1985.

In December 1984, my brother, his wife, and eighteen-month-old daughter came to Sausalito from their home in Bellingham, Washington, to be with our father and Milly.

My father, though ailing, was still working. Every day, he and Michael would drive across the Golden Gate Bridge from Sausalito en route to the Exploratorium.

Although he was on morphine, my father insisted on doing the driving. Michael began to quake, certain he was taking his life in his hands every time they crossed the bridge, and after much hinting and cajoling, Michael finally convinced him that he should be the chauffeur. My father insisted on dragging himself to work every day until the middle of January, when he was too weak to move from the house.

After all we'd experienced with my mother's death, I felt relieved to have Michael around—more grateful still that he and his father were spending precious time together.

My brother called me one evening. His voice was filled with alarm and fright. "Deedle, Pa is having difficulty breathing and is not too alert. I think he might die very soon, maybe even tonight."

I raced to Sausalito to find my father barely responding. His breathing was labored and irregular. Michael, Milly, and Jean were at his bedside, monitoring every breath. I was worried but didn't sense he was going to die immediately. Before we went to bed, he was talking to us in short, clipped sentences. I canceled my appointments for the next few days.

I had rushed up to Sausalito, leaving two-year-old Neal in the care of his babysitter. Two days later, Barbara Floyd brought him to me.

We settled in for two weeks of one of the most intense, emotionally draining times of my life.

Even though there were four adults in attendance, my father needed almost constant care. On occasion he sometimes was very aware and coherent but progressively became less so. He required frequent pain medication and bathing. The first week I was there, we started having visiting nurses and hospice care. Since I was probably the only one who had witnessed a person die, everyone seemed to turn to me for advice and support.

At times Michael, Jean, and Kate would escape, going to the park or visiting old friends. Milly went on walks and had lunch with her friends. Neal and I were the ones who remained home. I spent a great deal of my time staring out the window, watching the rain, and checking frequently on my father, making sure he was comfortable and that he received his pain medication in a timely fashion. I puttered around the house, trying to keep Neal occupied. I hugged my young son and took comfort in his being with me, but of course he too felt the tension and was not easy to deal with. Two is rarely an easy age to deal with in the best of cases, and he seemed to choose this setting to be his two-year-old worst.

After one particularly hectic and lonely day, Michael noticed my clenched fists, my misty eyes, and my silence. "Deedle, what's wrong?"

My anger and hurt were so great, I was afraid to speak.

"Nothing."

Michael looked gently and knowingly into my face.

"Something is bothering you. I can tell." I finally broke down and began to sob.

"No one has once bothered to ask me if I needed a break. I can't even go outside with Neal."

Michael put his hands on my shoulders.

"Deedle, I'm so sorry. We'll fix that."

And he did his best, trying to prompt me at various intervals to bundle up and get outside, insisting he'd take over the management of our nonstop vigil. This allowed Neal and me to go to a small park near the house where he played on the swings and slides. I went on short walks and even made time to go to Saratoga to see Harriet.

The most memorable times during this period were gatherings we began to call soirées. Large crowds from the Exploratorium would arrive in the afternoon. We would sit around a fire and often telling stories about our father. Most of the time, other subjects crept in: politics, the Exploratorium, or current events. If my father was alert, people slipped one by one into his room to say hello, never staying long. Those winter afternoons by the fire with friends made these dense times a little calmer.

Unfortunately, not all visitors were so welcome.

Before my father became terminally ill, he had begun an affair with a woman he had met in New York. She and her husband had come to San Francisco to be in a play that was given at the Exploratorium.

On his deathbed he actually made several clandestine phone calls to this lady. He invited her to come to San Francisco to visit. Sure enough, she arrived in San Francisco and telephoned us.

Michael, Milly, and I were at first determined she was not going to step foot in the house.

We did not prevail.

When he told us he had in fact made arrangements for her to come to Sausalito, I was furious. Milly was unable to talk to him without an edge of anger in her words. As she went through the routines with him, she became stiff and distant.

I couldn't bear it. I went to his room and confronted him.

"You know, Pa, you're a real bastard. Can't you see how much you're hurting Milly? It's completely beyond me to understand how you could be so cruel."

Except for the telltale gleam of stubbornness in his eyes, my father regarded me calmly.

"Judy, I really need to see her. You have to let her come."

Defeated, I said nothing more to him.

I had an appointment with Harriet that same day, and my drive down to Saratoga was one of pounding the steering wheel and screaming. It still stunned me that my father could not only flat-out ignore the feelings of those who'd loved and cared for him for a life time, but that he could unconsciously turn the knife in the wounds he inflicted.

I told myself I would be relieved when he died.

The pressure was released when I arrived at Harriet's. We had talked for about an hour when Harriet noticed Tom (her husband and colleague) watering outside. She called him in, and the three of us spent another hour talking.

It was emergency therapy, and it helped.

Making my way to Sausalito, I felt restored to a clearer comprehension of the whole tableau, and as a result, I was much more able to cope with the situation. As I drove along Interstate 280, I realized my father, all his life, essentially had a love/hate relationship with women; that due to his egotism, he was only able to relate to them in terms of what they could do for him. His quest for power always had sexual overtones. I suddenly realized what a trap this had always presented for me. If I confronted him, I thought I risked losing his love or being seduced by him. In my mind these were my choices. No wonder I didn't want to grow up.

When I arrived back in Sausalito, one of the soirées was in full swing. Feeling much calmer, I joined the others in diverse conversations.

The day the woman arrived, Michael, Jean, and Kate were out. With our blessings, Milly purposely had disappeared. Neal and I were the only ones left in the house.

I wanted to grab Neal, lock the door, and run. Instead, I was in the kitchen giving him lunch. He was tired and cranky, and I tried to distract him while finding something he would deign to eat. He had just thrown his peanut butter sandwich on the floor when the doorbell rang.

There she stood, a tall stocky woman with straight dark hair and coarse features. She tried to make eye contact, but I gazed downward. I merely motioned for her to enter. She strode down the hall and disappeared into my father's room, where she stayed for almost an hour. From time to time I was tempted to barge in, to yell, and wreak havoc in midst of their tête-à-tête.

Instead I fussed in the kitchen, muttering under my breath, "At least the bastard won't be able to have sex with her."

I thought about Milly and how he had hurt her. I longed to have been able to tell him with words of authority and finality that his lover couldn't come. In retrospect, I now realize that it wouldn't have been appropriate for me to do so. In fact, it would have been cruel. If seeing her lessened his suffering, maybe the woman's visit wasn't the worst thing that could happen. Milly, Michael, and I were resilient adults. We would live on and could deal with our anger and hurt afterward. My father would not.

When her time with him had concluded, she reappeared in the kitchen where I was stewing and trying not to scream.

She spoke to me in a pleading voice.

"Judy, I'm really not the ogre you think I am. I'd like to get to know you better."

I wanted to shout, "How dare you even think that's possible. Get out of here."

I couldn't let myself be so bitchy. I escorted her to the door.

She left and disappeared from our lives. I blocked her identity so thoroughly from my thoughts that I couldn't even remember her name until my brother reminded me: Honora.

Not long after her visit, our father died peacefully in his sleep. The family stood by his bedside. We embraced each other, and a few tears flowed. The anger I had toward my father fomented inside of me.

"Well, at least the bastard won't be around to hurt anyone anymore." A great sense of freedom filled my heart. I wouldn't have to deal with him again.

Or so I thought.

It would soon become evident that the period following his death would feel very different from the time following Mother's. The evening after he died, friends came over bringing wonderful food and conversation.

We sat around the round oak table talking, drinking straight tequila with salt and lime, and reminiscing. For several evenings after, people brought food or invited us to their homes. This time we gladly accepted.

It was unnerving when the press started calling on the day of his death. It was then that I realized that my father was part of an elite group of people whose deaths caught the attention of the media. In the midst of all the emotion and activity, I tried to be kind and helpful but not too open about all the feelings that were raging through my mind. I couldn't say too much to them or Pandora's box would burst, and I'd reveal things it was better for the media and public not to know. I didn't dare to intimate how difficult it had been to grow up the child of this complex Renaissance man.

Our family was flooded with letters and phone calls from around the world. For me the most touching phone call was from E, our housekeeper and friend from Minneapolis days. We talked about her son and grandchildren. I reminded her of the time she babysat with us while my parents were at the HUAC hearings, how in the heat of the Minneapolis summer, she and Mother, dieting and high on Dexedrine, steamed off wallpaper and carried my father's huge maple desk up two flights of stairs. E told me about a time when I started to walk down the steep path going to the Mississippi, and she had to run after me.

The Sausalito house was filled with the sense of deep transition. But this time, it felt apt and timely. Returning home, I once again entered the world of medicine.

# 50
# Return to San José

Early in my career, I had begun to speak out about how I felt the hospital could be improved. I spoke of how we needed to upgrade the equipment in the nursery and how we needed to devise programs to enhance the knowledge of our nurses. These pronouncements earned the respect of my colleagues, and I was elected chairman of the Pediatrics department several times. In 1987, I was elected secretary-treasurer of the medical staff; and in 1989, I became the first woman chief of staff at Alexian Brothers Hospital. It so happened in accepting the position I was also the first woman chief of staff of any hospital in Santa Clara County. Although this was a wonderful honor, the job proved challenging. Not only did I have to care for my patients and business but had to summon all my expertise working with the CEO to improve care, including monitoring the professional performance of other physicians on the staff. One such situation was that of an ENT physician who had not responded correctly to a child with an acute life-threatening throat condition, epiglottitis. The ER physician had already stabilized the child and put a tube down his throat so he could breathe. This was the standard of care at the time. The ENT physician was called to take the patient into the OR where, under more controlled conditions a larger tube could be inserted. However, instead of re-intubating the child, he decided to do an unnecessary procedure—a tracheostomy where an incision is actually made into the trachea and a metal tube is inserted into the incision. In the process, the surgeon punctured the child's lung. The little boy did survive, but he was in the hospital for a prolonged period. Other colleagues and I were disappointed when an independent observer felt that this was a one- time episode and that a disciplinary hearing would not be fruitful. Even though we all knew that this was merely the worst of many transgressions, we decided not to pursue the case any further.

My private practice was still doing well, but by the middle of the 1980s, overhead began to soar. Instead of the DPT vaccine costing $0.15/ dose as it had when I first started, the price had soared to $15/dose. I needed to become a much more astute businesswoman if I was to survive financially. I hated having to worry about money. I just wanted to see patients and not be concerned about whether they were paying me or not. I began to resent having to spend time on call and not being available for my son. Switching hats constantly between mother, physician, and businesswoman was exhausting.

I continued in private practice until January 1990, when I sold my practice to San José Medical Group. I hadn't realized what a difference it made in my mood when I was released from the pressures of private practice. I stayed with that group as an employee until April 1991, when I became director of pediatrics at East Valley Clinic, one of the satellite clinics of the county hospital, Santa Clara Valley Medical Center.

Most of our patients at the clinic were poor and Hispanic. I loved the fact that I was able to help children and parents who had nowhere else to go for their medical care. Not being on call or being responsible for the finances of the clinic let me practice medicine and be a mother at the same time. My life became fuller and much less stressful.

In addition to seeing patients, I taught third or fourth year medical students from Stanford who rotated through our clinic. My teaching was hands-on and clinical, not didactic. I found it exciting to see a student being converted by my love of pediatrics. I recall the day a student came out of the exam room looking frazzled and upset.

"I couldn't really do a decent exam," he lamented. "The little girl cried all through it."

I went into the room with the student to examine the two-year-old. She was soon laughing and being very cooperative. When we left the room, the student looked at me in wonder.

"How did you get her to be so quiet?"

I smiled. "It's taken years of practice. But the first thing I do is not to invade the kid's territory too quickly. I often stop at the door and start talking to the parent before I even approach the child. Why don't you try first putting the stethoscope on the mom's chest? Let the kid play with or feel your stethoscope or otoscope. Play games with them."

The student came out smiling with relief after examining his next patient.

"I tried some of you suggestions, and they seemed to help."

Satisfactions like these added up, and I felt richer for them. In September 1998, after being at the clinic for seven and a half years, I retired.

# Oppenheimer Family Gallery

## Section C

Neal with parrot in Hawai'i

Pensive Neal in Europe (age 13)

Neal and me at his Police Academy Graduation

Neal and his Nutcracker family

Neal going on twilight dive

# 52
# The Healing

In spite of being a confident mother and having a far less stressful job, the prospect of retirement unnerved and frightened me. The old issues of being alone, of not having much of a life outside of work, began to resurface. In addition, Neal was becoming an adolescent, and I realized I was going to have to let him become his own person—that for both of our sakes, he couldn't and certainly shouldn't become my only source of companionship.

Thus my depression resurfaced and deepened. In 1995, I recognized that another mentor/therapist was in order. I found a supportive, compassionate woman therapist whom I saw for twelve years.

In 1982, my friend Dodi and I were traveling in China. One day while we were in Guangzhou square, a vast public space featuring three large Buddhas and a pagoda. The square was teeming with Chinese visitors and a few Western tourists. The crowds and noise overwhelmed us. Hot, tired, and somewhat irritable, we climbed the pagoda together, which offered some relief as it lifted us from the crush of the crowd. Leaving the pagoda, I noticed a thin wall of bamboo mats. Dodi and I walked quietly behind the wall to find we were in a small Buddhist shrine. Suddenly, the outside world vanished. The air around us was thick with the scent and smoke of incense. At once, we both felt a serenity that sustained us for the remainder of the two-week trip. At the front of the shrine stood a well-weathered wooden Buddha surrounded by candles and incense. The candles' small flames lit his torso and folded hands. Small groups of saffron-robed monks worshiped at the altar. Other small groups and individuals flowed up the aisle to light the incense and deposit their offerings. As I stood at the front of the shrine, I sensed a powerful presence—not of God or Buddha, but of my own spiritual core. I was able to accept its mystery. For a moment, I had broken free from my parents' harsh scolding that would have mocked such peacefulness. I marveled that such a place could exist, separated from the chaos of the square only by thin bamboo mats.

When my mother died, we had no rituals, no memorials. I yearned for some acknowledgment of her strength, wit, intelligence, and contribution to the Exploratorium. She had started the gift store at the Exploratorium, and as head of the graphics department, she'd played an important role in the aesthetics of the place and its overall look and feel. But no one had ever mentioned how she had been my father's rudder, his lifelong helpmate. I was filled, in the wake of her death, with a vacuum, a lack of closure. In short, I never allowed myself to finish grieving for her.

One February close to the seventeenth anniversary of my mother's death, I talked to the savvy, intuitive woman who was my therapist about how February, like so many elements of my life, held a number of striking contrasts. It was in February that I witnessed the deaths of my parents, five years apart. February was when I experienced the wonder and joy of the birth of my son, Neal.

My therapist, on hearing this, gave me some homework. I was to find pictures of my mother when she was young and when she was old. I was to bring a votive candle. She and I would have a quiet memorial service, a celebration of my mother's life.

The pictures were easy. The candle and the idea of a ceremony were so foreign to me, I felt embarrassed. In fact, it was Mother's voice I heard in my mind, echoing: *This is ridiculous!*

My mentor sensed my reluctance. I'm sure she knew I would have trouble forcing myself to buy the candle, so she supplied it herself. She entered the room carrying a tray holding two aperitif glasses, water, salt, pomegranate juice, strawberries, and almonds.

We sat with the two pictures of my mother—one when she was in her twenties, the other when she was in her sixties—placed next to the candle that was to light our way. We drank salt and water for the tears not yet shed. We washed them away with pure water. We drank pomegranate juice, a symbol of Persephone's burden and release. We ate the strawberries and almonds—the end of Demeter's rage.

I told stories about the women in my family: my mother, my grandmother, and my great-grandmother.

The combination of symbols of Judaism and Greek myth, of actions based on them, and the clear memories of the women who came before me, felt wonderfully liberating.

After the ceremony, I went home and set up a small altar in my bedroom—a rose, the pictures of my mother, and the candle. I went to sleep that night listening to Mozart's *Eine Kleine Nachtmusik*. The images of Mother lit by the warm glow of candlelight gently lulled me to sleep.

Shortly after this celebration of my mother's life, I went on a retreat in the Santa Cruz Mountains where a friend, several of her women friends, and I were celebrating her fiftieth birthday. The setting couldn't have been more beautiful. Deep in the redwoods, there were four yurts that completely blended into the landscape. When I arrived, the rest of the group was off on a hike. Rain had fallen during the night, and it was a crisp spring day. I went walking by myself up a trail and over a wooden bridge spanning a roiling creek to enter a large mountain meadow where deer were grazing. I was transfixed. The beauty, the calmness, overwhelmed me. I sat for half an hour and then headed back to the yurts. After a delicious lunch, we all went to walk a labyrinth of lichen-covered rocks and multicolored seashells built at one end of the meadow. The other women and I silently passed each other as we spiraled inward to the center where those who had passed before had placed special objects: a collage of coins, rocks, a polished agate mirror, a gold watch, and a feather stuck in the dirt. This experience gave me a gentle initiation into the sisterhood of the sacred feminine.

Memories are ephemeral, capricious things. At the time of their inception, of course, my perceptions felt real and, without question, wielded a huge impact on my life. Yet as an adult looking back, I realize increasingly how these thoughts were internal. They were bleak and distorted because of my own fears and anxieties. This distortion of reality became crystal clear when, in 2000, I attended my forty-second high school reunion. I corresponded with one of my former classmates, Marilyn Breedlove Alme, and as the event approached, I became more and more excited. In one of her e-mails, Marilyn mentioned that she considered me to be one of her best friends in high school. As an adolescent, I was utterly unable to accept that someone might consider me a friend, let alone one of their best friends. Now I was anxious to try my newfound self, to learn what the people I grew up with were doing. Little did I realize what a freeing revelation it would be to meet my classmates again, unclouded by the fogs of adolescent angst.

The reunion began with a tour of the new high school. I was greeted like a celebrity. It struck me that of all the people in attendance, my looks had probably changed the least. Everyone recognized me instantly and greeted me with warm embraces. Sixteen of the twenty-seven in my graduating class had managed to attend.

My father had begun teaching all the sciences at Pagosa High two years before he and my mother left the ranch, and most of my classmates had taken classes from him. During my senior year in high school, I too had my father for chemistry.

Listening to my classmates enthusiastically talk about what a wonderful teacher he had been opened all kinds of windows in my own memories. They told tales of how, if there was no eraser, he used his tie to erase the blackboard (he always wore a suit and tie to school). As they told this story, I suddenly remembered him driving us home at the end of the day. Inevitably he smelled of chalk. His suit pants and jacket were punctuated with white, pink, and blue chalk clouds.

We all shuddered as we remembered him letting us play with mercury in chemistry class, but we also recalled how we loved to watch the silver balls roll across the lab desk and coalesce when two balls came into close proximity.

My former classmates also marveled at what a perceptive and intuitive teacher my father had been. If the class seemed puzzled, he would say something like "I get the feeling you aren't understanding what I'm saying."

He'd then try another method to get the idea across. He did the same thing when he tried to help an individual student. With others, he seemed to have the infinite patience he didn't have with Michael or me.

Interestingly, as my classmates showered me with complimentary stories about my father, I was pleasantly aware I was no longer tempted to contradict their assessment of him. Instead, I let myself luxuriate in their enthusiasm and fond memories. I no longer wanted to shout, "You have no idea about what a bastard he really was."

Jean Corrigan remembered my father reading to her from our 1890s edition of Chaucer's *Canterbury Tales* in the original Middle English. When she related this story, I too remembered sitting with him, looking at the woodcuts and the Middle English as he intoned in mellifluous syllables.

> Whan that Aprill, with his shoures soot
> The droghte of March hath perced to the roote
> And bathed every veyne in swich licour,
> Of which vertu engendred is the flour.

Even before I went back to the text to refresh my memory of it, the rhythm, the confidence, and the love with which my father recited this passage was etched in my memory.

I talked to Jean, Marilyn, and Judy and began to appreciate that my adolescence wasn't as sterile as I'd remembered it. Many tales and memories of camaraderie sprang forward. We recalled walking down to Dairy Belle together to have lunch or going to Jakish Drugs for an ice cream soda at a real 1950s soda fountain.

The entire weekend was amazingly rich, reviving contacts with old friends. None of us really were able, in that short period, to begin to know each other deeply as adults, but the discourse was friendly and free. All the adolescent clichés and uncertainties had disappeared.

In August 2005, my brother, his two kids (six-year-old Emma and three-year-old Henry), and I drove from Albuquerque to the Blanco Basin. I had arranged a reunion of all our old friends from Camp Oppenheimer.

Karen and Eric Essene, Susie, Michael and Harold Greenberg, and Janet were all coming. By now we were all in our sixties. Most of our friends were bringing their families. For Michael and me, the prospect was especially poignant because he and I were able to stay in our old house. Our excitement mounted as we drove down the hill into the Basin. Michael's eyes sparkled.

"I don't remember the Basin ever being so green. I'd forgotten how beautiful it is."

I agreed. "I don't think I have seen it so lush either. Here it's the middle of August, and there are still tons of wildflowers. Wish I could grow them at home."

We rounded the corner on Windy Point. I looked down at the end of the meadow and reminisced.

"That's the spot Pa never mowed. I wonder whether the fringed gentians are still there."

We needed no prompting once we'd hopped from our car on arrival. Michael, his kids, and I slowly walked through the meadow to the river before anyone else arrived for the reunion. The journey to the river was somewhat prolonged because Emma and Henry were intent on catching grasshoppers.

The river still rumbled over the rocks and formed crystal clear pools. Like we had years ago, Emma and Henry made sand castles and played in the cold clear water.

Michael looked back at the woodshed and joked, "We should have an exorcism and burn the woodshed down." I knew he was referring to the time I had barricaded myself in the woodshed so I wouldn't have to babysit. I laughed. "That would be fun. I can see us all dancing and chanting as flames released the remaining evil vapors, but I don't think Frank Harvey [the house's present owner] would appreciate it."

If it had been possible years ago, burning down the woodshed might indeed have helped exorcise the ghosts that inhabited it. Now it no longer held the angst and fear it once did. The exorcism was no longer required.

By the time we returned to the cabin, everyone had arrived for the reunion. Quickly the little building became filled with laughter, reminiscences, and rounds and rounds of embraces. Later that evening, Michael and I were at the sink washing dishes. I looked out the window at Square Top Mountain with the late afternoon shadows descending and visualized my herd of white-faced Herefords peacefully grazing in the meadow across the road.

The clank of dishes being placed on the counter brought me back to the present. I'd begun moving them into the sink when Harold Greenberg came up behind my brother and me.

Harold hadn't changed much. His hair was gray, but he still was a version of the slim, crew cut kid he'd been. He looked out the window and smiled.

"I have such fond memories of those summers. Dad and I spent hours digging for worms and going fishing in the Blanco or Fish Creek." He laughed a warm, resonant laugh—one that I forever associate with Harold. "I don't think we were ever too successful."

I laughed also. "You're right. If we had depended on the fish you and your father caught, we'd have starved."

"I guess that's true. I loved riding up Fish Creek and other trails. Remember how you and Paint were always the last whenever we raced?" "Sure do. I hated it when we raced."

We continued talking when another memory came to Harold. This one was not so idyllic.

"Your father certainly could get angry." His face grew thoughtful. "I was getting my horse ready to go on a ride. I must have done something really terrible because Frank came storming out of the house. He was shouting obscenities and pulling his belt off. Luckily, he didn't use it, but I was petrified."

Eric Essene—dapper with his beard, mustache, and gray-and-white laced blond hair—heard Harold's story. Eric interceded.

"Dad and I used to fly-fish. We were usually successful." He continued, "We helped your father shingle the new addition. I learned so much during those summers on the ranch. We were always busy. I learned to drive a tractor here."

His mood changed as he talked about the tractor, recalling one telling memory. "We were haying, and I was raking. Apparently, I did something not to Frank's liking, and he came toward me screaming and threatening physical abuse."

This cascade of stories continued as Susie said, "I hated the way Frank treated your dog Richard. He was always punishing him. One time he hit him over the back with a crowbar." As Susie related this, I realized that this wasn't the only incident in which my father abused Richard. I remember that each time he tortured my dog I'd been speechless and helpless.

Michael and I looked at each other. We both knew we had been victims of the grenades of anger our father lobbed at us without warning. We knew others were victims of his outrages also, but we had never actually heard them talk about their experiences. When we heard these stories, I know we both felt vindicated.

We weren't crazy after all.

What caused my father's uncontrollable tirades? I'll never know, but can speculate. My parents, particularly my father, were being strangled by external events beyond their control. Longing to return to work as a physicist, he was powerless against the intrusion of the FBI when they came to the ranch, trying to turn neighbors into informants and enemies. I remembered how his voice became animated and confident whenever he talked to his physicist friends. I remembered his eyes becoming wistful as he read their letters in which they described their work. He was impotent when it came to breaking the fear present during this period, the fear that prevented him from finding a job in a profession he loved. I flashed back to all the times he commented bitterly that he was "wasting" his life.

It is not surprising that at times his controls completely snapped, and he became an irrational, angry beast.

I also believe his propensity for anger and melancholy was present even as an adolescent.

Robert and he corresponded frequently during my father's adolescence and young adulthood. Robert was eight years older than my father and was always full of brotherly, slightly paternalistic advice. One of Robert's responses to one of his seventeen-year-old brother's letters triggered in me a realization that my father was struggling with his demons even as an adolescent.

Faculty Club
University of California
Oct. 14, 1929

Dear Frank,

What you write about your feeling for horses is very curious. I cannot think that your sehnsucht [yearning] for them is either very abnormal or at all terrible really. I can't think that it would be terrible of me to say— and it is occasionally true—that I need physics more than friends, and the two assertions seem analogous. As for your abuse of horses, that you must know yourself. If the tendency to browbeat them is real you are right in saying that the desire should be watched and disciplined. But it is not easy. At least it is not easy for me to be quite free of the desire to browbeat somebody or something; and perhaps it is because, in your relations with other people, you do, and infinitely commendably, in my opinion, so little browbeating; that it should frighten you so to discover in yourself too the traces of that beastliness.[3]

I remembered a conversation I had with my father not too long before he died. He looked at me with sad eyes and said, "I must have been a terrible child."

I stared at him in surprise. "Why do you say that?"

"When I was three, the nanny who had also taken care of Robert when he was young left. I must have driven her off."

I was astounded. I couldn't believe that this seventy-two-year-old man was still harboring the magical thinking guilt that is usually reserved for three-year-olds. My heart went out to him, but at the time, I was at a loss as to how to respond.

I told my brother of this conversation. He proceeded to tell me a strange story our father had told him.

"I was walking behind Robert at Perro Caliente. We were fencing, and I carried an axe. It was all I could do not to cleave Robert's head with it."

I began to appreciate what a complex man my father was and what powerful interactions he had with students and my friends.

For many years, the once special ritual of my father's gift of wildflowers had become a hollow even queasy exercise. The flowers which at first were like a bright rainbow faded, the petals dropped, and the water turned into smelly primordial ooze.

Slowly, I was coming to understand that I could no longer trust my inner compass to tell me what was real or merely imagined when it came to my relationship with my father. Some years after my father's death, I sat in my room reading *Robert Oppenheimer: Letters and Recollections* by Alice Kimball Smith and Charles Weiner and came across this passage from page 126.

---

[3] Alice Kimball Smith and Charles Weiner, *Robert Oppenheimer: Letters and Recollections*, 135.

> Birthdays in the Oppenheimer family could no lon-
> ger be celebrated with flower-strewn chairs as at Bay
> Shore [the family's house on Long Island].

Reading the description of these "flower-strewn" childhood birthdays, I was overwhelmed and filled with sadness and humility. Were these wildflowers my father picked a warm, vibrant ritual, a symbol of parental love, or the cloying sentimentality and entrapment that I had so long believed them to be? After years of reflection and therapy, I realize they were probably a symbol of both.

My father was a playful man, a man who often took uncharted roads. That was a literal as well as a figurative habit. He would frequently turn onto a small dirt road just to see where it went.

The trip he, my nephew Mark, and I took to the southwest in 1980 had been no exception. On the way from Albuquerque to Santa Fe, my father insisted on opening the windows of the car even though it was stifling hot. He insisted he had to smell the sage and piñon. Soon he took a small road where we stopped, emerging from the car to crunch along the red desert sand to overlook a multilayered arroyo.

By degrees, I began to appreciate his Renaissance mind. I have become aware and in awe of how adaptable he was.

I am not sure that many people could have put their heart and soul into four consecutive careers. He was a successful physicist. Not only did he contribute to the making of the atomic bomb, but in Minnesota he was one of the first scientists to find that cosmic rays did not just consist of protons from hydrogen and particles from helium but also contained particles emanating from all the other elements.

He adapted to becoming a rancher, gaining the respect of the other ranchers and people in Pagosa Springs. He became known as Doc. Our ranching operation had been as successful as any other, experiencing good and lean years.

He became an innovative high school teacher where he and one of his students discovered some significant findings related to bacteria living in the hot water of Pagosa's hot springs. He had ten years of teaching at the University of Colorado where he spent hours guiding both undergraduate and graduate students. He used his passion for teaching and tinkering to found the most unique and educational of all science museums, the Exploratorium in San Francisco. At the Exploratorium, not only did he make hands-on exhibits for visitors to learn and play with, but he hired high school students to become "explainers." Over time they learned science, some art, and the excitement of teaching.

Each of these vocations might reasonably, alone, have filled an entire life. He embraced them all.

Thinking about my father's gifts smoothed the corners of my anger toward him, allowing me to see him as an interesting multidimensional man.

## Section D

Mother in her twenties

Mother in front of our Picasso in Sausalito

Mother at kitchen table—Sausalito

Me at Great Wall—1980

Me in sterile gown and hat—1970's

Me on 40th birthday

Me at Clinic

Michael on Vancouver beach, 2006

Michael in San Francisco, circa 2009

Me and Margaret O'Brian doll, Minneapolis

Me (2nd from left) dressed as Indian in 3rd grade Thanksgiving pageant

Me in my twenties in college

# 53
## The Awakening

Some years ago, I saw Eve Ensler in *The Vagina Monologues* and emerged from the performance feeling more profoundly connected with my femininity. I remembered how, after my diagnosis of Turner's, my vagina repulsed me as I struggled to insert those yucky, messy suppositories. For years I was not able accept my womanhood. It was someone else's turf, a zone I couldn't allow myself to enter. I was sure my body would never be able to respond sexually, that my hard wiring and my lack of hormones somehow prevented this.

In the *Monologues,* Ensler tells a story about a girl who was born without a vagina. Her father told her, "Don't worry, darlin'. This is going to be just fine. As a matter of fact, it's gonna be great. We're going to get you the best homemade pussy in America."[4] If only (I remember wistfully thinking) my parents could have supported me in this manner. If only they could have made an equivalent statement to help me affirm my womanhood.

I came away from viewing the Monologues no longer so afraid or isolated. I no longer felt like an it but was able to identify as a woman, a sexual human being.

For decades after my diagnosis, I hated to have my photo taken. Each time I looked at the image of myself, it convinced me that I was a grotesque caricature of a little girl or woman.

It has taken years of stubborn perseverance and work, but now when I look at the pictures of me, I see the cute, small girl eating a lollipop sitting beside her dog; the petite girl holding her doll; the smiling alive little girl dressed as an Indian for a Thanksgiving pageant, sitting and clowning in front of the group of her third grade classmates; the portrait of a gentle- looking pretty young

---

[4] Eve Ensler, *The Vagina Monologues* (Villard Books, 1998), 99.

woman in her twenties. I smile, but am also saddened by the fact that for so long the images and related feelings, with the tricks of memory, portrayed this young girl and woman so cruelly, so unfairly.

I rejoice at the change.

For years, my mentor and I danced a gentle waltz around what I believed to be my last cocoon—the repressed, frightening, and verboten— the one of my sexuality and sexual orientation.

Gently, she took me by the hand and helped me navigate this thorny, complicated, and often very painful journey. All the work she and I had done over the nine or so years before led to a huge shift in my inner world that occurred during the spring, summer, and fall of 2003 when I was sixty- three years old. With her help and after seeing *The Vagina Monologues,* I slowly became conscious I was a sensual, sexual woman.

Slowly, I also began to realize that the object of my desires was destined to be another woman. To get to this point, I had to vanquish not only my feelings of being asexual, but also the fear I had of once again being different, of being lesbian.

I began to appreciate that my relationship with my friend, Karen, had in actual fact been that of first love. I remembered her adolescent beauty, her intellect, and sense of humor. I recalled how nourished I'd felt in the lovely ambiance of her playing piano while I sat and read. My love for Karen had been every bit as strong and as comparable as the loves of any of my heterosexual peers. Now, at last, I could rejoice in the fact that even though this love was not acknowledged by either of us, I had indeed loved. Karen and I have reconnected and have had a great time just being friends with no agenda or angst.

In August 2003, I was visiting my brother on Lummi Island, Washington. One day during the visit, he and I were taking a walk in a small wooded park in Bellingham. We were feeling very comfortable and close. I knew I was strong enough to speak the truth to my brother.

I spoke as calmly as could. I was striving for nonchalance, but calm would do.

"Michael, I think—no, I know—that I am lesbian." I added, "You're the first one I've told."

We had been walking side by side. As he stopped and turned, I saw his face break into the warmest smile imaginable. He gave me a ferocious hug. "I'm honored that you have told me."

As we continued on our walk, he spoke thoughtfully. My declaration had been uncannily timely, he told me, because he'd been thinking about me in that context lately—about whom I might love in that way. Putting together the puzzle piece, he, too, had recently come to realize my love for Karen was more than mere friendship.

I felt relieved and proud that we were able to talk gently and honestly as brother, sister, friend.

My heart was filled with love for my brother's gentleness, understanding, compassion, and support. I felt clearer, lighter, and ever so much calmer after talking to him and three other of my friends. In spite of this, I knew that I was not yet ready to come out publicly.

This was all about to change when twenty-three other women and I attended a woman's leadership retreat in the Marin hills.

I knew that they would be focusing on the time in a young woman's life when she was beginning to emerge and differentiate as an individual, distinct from her family. Thus, I drove to the retreat in a raw state of nerves, suspecting that the group would swiftly move toward the topics of sexuality and sexual orientation. I didn't want to come out to the group. I didn't feel ready. Lecturing myself during that agitated drive, I tried to convince myself I was in total control.

All I had to do was keep my mouth shut.

The very first morning, I discovered how wrong I was. On the floor of the large meeting room, the leaders had placed tapes dividing the area into four quadrants. In each quadrant, the leaders had placed signs bearing the names of different group.

We were to place ourselves in the group we most identified with. The first two exercises using these techniques were easy. They had to do with age and whether we were mothers or childless.

Then, the gauntlet was thrown.

We were to divide into four different groups based on our sexual orientation: heterosexual, asexual, bisexual, and lesbian. I swallowed hard. Some women strolled to their appropriate zones and waited, appearing confident and comfortable with their decision. Others walked uncertainly to their quadrant, their faces revealing some anxiety.

I found myself pacing around the periphery of all four groups, but soon began to notice myself moving from the lesbian to the asexual group and back again. My heart pounded, and a delicate film of moisture seemed to cover my face. In actual fact, I had no idea whatsoever, no sense at all, of what would happen or of what I should do. My first impulse was to leave the room, boycott the exercise. I also considered placing myself into the asexual group but knew that would be a cop-out, a regression, partially negating all the hard work I'd done. I knew that my newfound sexuality had to be confronted.

Shaking, my heart racing, I slowly walked over and joined the lesbian group. I had just "outed" myself to twenty-three other women! As I joined my two sister lesbians, a great weight was immediately removed from my shoulders. I felt myself sitting straighter, breathing easier. My protective wrap evaporated. The three of us laughed and chatted calmly, each narrating parts of her story to the others in my group.

This public acknowledgement of my sexual orientation was a monumental, life-altering event, second only to that of being told of my Turner's diagnosis. But this time, instead of sinking into a dark abyss as I had in response to the diagnosis, I rejoiced.

I spent the weekend soaring, freed and dazed, thrilled by the sud- den vast realm of possibilities, by my honesty and my courage. A wide, wide world was opening for me. When the exercise was over, I faced the three leaders of the group.

"Damn you, but thank you!"

All of us beamed.

During the weekend, I also floundered briefly. I fell backward into sadness, frustration, loneliness, and pounding on pillows. Temporarily, I retracted like a turtle, huddling inside my old neurotic pattern of silence, not letting others know what I needed, expecting them to read between the lines and dole out hugs. In time though, with steady encouragement by the group, I was able to speak openly with them and found that having those women witness and accept me felt infinitely more meaningful than facile hugs and small talk.

Returning home exhilarated but exhausted, I raised my arms to the sky and shouted, "Yes!"

Awakening just as the first light appeared, I went into my garden to pick a fragrant perfectly formed yellow rose. I placed it in a slender crystal vase and placed my treasure on the small altar in my bedroom to symbolize my awakening. Lighting a candle, I gently removed my mother's photograph from the arrangement and replaced it with mine.

Then I sat down to write.

*** THE END ***

# ACKNOWLEDGEMENTS

This book has had many incarnations. I would not have been able to have completed it without the loving and gentle critiques of my writing group, The Peerless Poets: Elaine Kahn, Kathie Isaac-Luke, Jean Lin, Nancy Mey- er, Stephanie Pressman, Mary Ann Savage, Ariel Smart, Mary Lou Taylor, Bernis Terhune and Phyllis Williams.

I would also like to honor my brother Michael Oppenheimer, my nephew Mark Nadeau, Jean Emerson, Joan Maser, Pat Jones, Phyllis Theroux, Adair Lara, Joan Frank and Marianne Cogorno for their helpful comments on the early manuscripts.

Finally, I would like to thank my publishing team from Hancock Press: Michael Middleton, William Nelson, Michael Rodriquez and Harold Harper. Without everyone's interest and help my dream would not have become reality.

# APPENDIX

## COPIES OF ACTUAL FBI DOCUMENTS

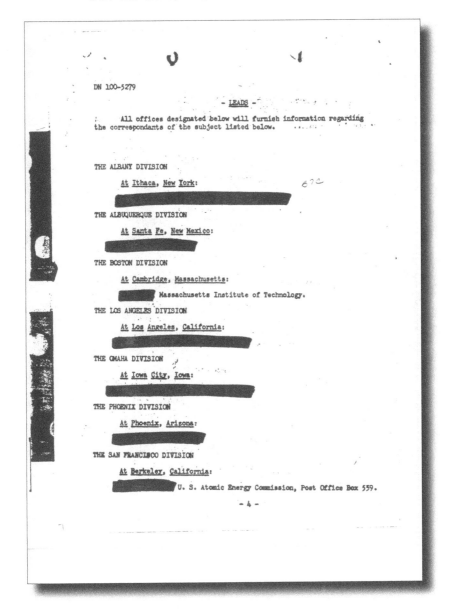

DN 100-5279

- LEADS -

All offices designated below will furnish information regarding
the correspondants of the subject listed below.

THE ALBANY DIVISION

    At Ithaca, New York:

THE ALBUQUERQUE DIVISION

    At Santa Fe, New Mexico:

THE BOSTON DIVISION

    At Cambridge, Massachusetts:

        Massachusetts Institute of Technology.

THE LOS ANGELES DIVISION

    At Los Angeles, California:

THE OMAHA DIVISION

    At Iowa City, Iowa:

THE PHOENIX DIVISION

    At Phoenix, Arizona:

THE SAN FRANCISCO DIVISION

    At Berkeley, California:

        U. S. Atomic Energy Commission, Post Office Box 559.

- 4 -

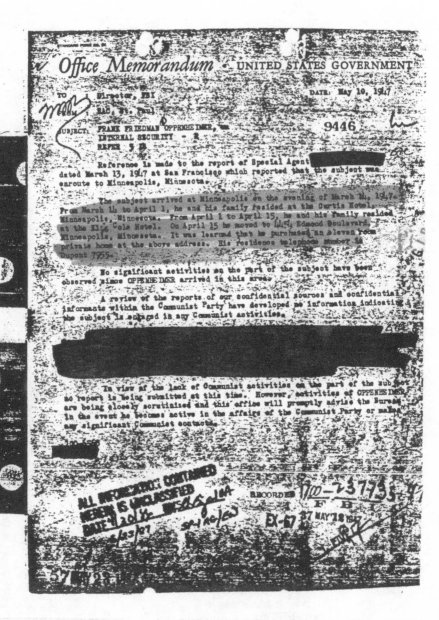

*Office Memorandum* · UNITED STATES GOVERNMENT

TO       : Director, FBI                                    DATE: May 10, 1947
           SAC, St. Paul

SUBJECT  : FRANK FRIEDMAN OPPENHEIMER, was.        9446
           INTERNAL SECURITY - R
           REFER 5 B

Reference is made to the report of Special Agent ████████
dated March 13, 1947 at San Francisco which reported that the subject was
enroute to Minneapolis, Minnesota.

The subject arrived at Minneapolis on the evening of March 14, 1947.
From March 14 to April 1, he and his family resided at the Curtis Hotel,
Minneapolis, Minnesota. From April 1 to April 15 he and his family resided
at the Elks Cole Hotel. On April 15 he moved to 4454 Edmond Boulevard,
Minneapolis, Minnesota. It was learned that he purchased an eleven room
private home at the above address. His residence telephone number is
Dupont 7755.

No significant activities on the part of the subject have been
observed since OPPENHEIMER arrived in this area.

A review of the reports of our confidential sources and confidential
informants within the Communist Party have developed no information indicating
the subject is engaged in any Communist activities.

████████████████████████████████████

In view of the lack of Communist activities on the part of the subject
no report is being submitted at this time. However, activities of OPPENHEIMER
are being closely scrutinized and this office will promptly advise the Bureau
in the event he becomes active in the affairs of the Communist Party or makes
any significant Communist contacts.

ALL INFORMATION CONTAINED
HEREIN IS UNCLASSIFIED
DATE ████ BY ████

RECORDED  100-23775

EX-67   27 MAY 28 1947   F B I

Letter to Director
Re: FRANK FRIEDMAN OPPENHEIMER, wa.

May 24, 1947

recommendation that this office for the time being continue to cover
the activities of OPPENHEIMER by spot surveillance, through our
existing confidential coverage, and by means of informants at the
University of Minnesota who know OPPENHEIMER and who are closely
following his experimental activity in connection with nuclear energy.

It is requested that the Bureau advise whether our coverage
in this case as outlined and recommended in this letter is adequate
under existing circumstances.

Very truly yours,

M. B. RHODES
SPECIAL AGENT IN CHARGE

100-6568 SA

- 2 -

*Office Memorandum* • UNITED STATES GOVERNMENT

TO : The Director

DATE: 3-18-47

FROM : D. M. Ladd

SUBJECT: FRANK FRIEDMAN OPPENHEIMER, was
Frank Folsom
Technical Surveillance

Frank Friedman Oppenheimer has recently moved from Berkeley, California, to Minneapolis, Minnesota, where he will assume his duties as professor at the University of Minnesota. The St. Paul Field Division has by letter requested authority to install technical and microphone coverage at his residence which is presently at Suite 122E, Curtis Hotel, Minneapolis, telephone Atlantic 5144.

There is attached hereto a memorandum to the Attorney General requesting his authority for the installation of a technical surveillance on Oppenheimer at this address and at his permanent residence when it has been established in Minneapolis. It is pointed out in the memorandum to the Attorney General that previous authorization for a technical surveillance on Oppenheimer at his home at Berkeley was authorized as of February 8, 1946.

You will recall that Frank Oppenheimer is the brother of J. Robert Oppenheimer and was one of the key employees at the Radiation Laboratory at Berkeley, California. He was a member of the Communist Party in Los Angeles from 1936 to 1939 and his wife, Jaquennette Yvonne Quann Oppenheimer, was also an active Party member in Los Angeles. Oppenheimer has been in frequent contact with high ranking Communist Party functionaries in California. This contact has continued up until the time of his departure. The St. Paul Field Division advises that circumstances prevent an effective physical surveillance of Oppenheimer at this time, making a microphone surveillance desirable.

I recommend that the St. Paul Field Division be authorized to institute a microphone surveillance at the time they are authorized to institute the technical surveillance on the subject.

Attachment

58 APR 10 1947

RECORDED

1947

Mr. Tolson
Mr. E. A. Tamm
Mr. Clegg
Mr. Glavin
Mr. Ladd
Mr. Nichols
Mr. Rosen
Mr. Tracy
Mr. Carson
Mr. Egan
Mr. Gurnea
Mr. Harbo
Mr. Quinn Tamm
Mr. Nease
Tele. Room
Mr. Jones

**Federal Bureau of Investigation**

**United States Department of Justice**
404 New York Building
St. Paul 1, Minnesota
May 24, 1947

AIR MAIL

STRICTLY CONFIDENTIAL

Director, FBI

Re: FRANK FRIEDMAN OPPENHEIMER, was.
INTERNAL SECURITY - R
ATOMIC ENERGY ACT

Dear Sir:

Reference is made to Bureau teletype to St. Paul dated May 15, 1947 authorizing a technical surveillance _____ on the residence address of the above-captioned, 4454 Edmond Boulevard, Minneapolis, Minnesota, Dupont 7955.

This is to advise that it is not feasible at this time to install instant technical surveillance and monitor same from our consolidated plant _____ as we had originally planned at the time authorization was requested.

_____

For that reason it is believed at this time that instant technical installation should not be made.

There are two alternatives and it is believed that one of them should be pursued: (1) That the technical installation be installed and monitored at a subplant and not at our consolidated plant. This can be done but would involve the tying up of two additional Special Employees and the rental of suitable quarters; (2) That a spot surveillance be maintained on the subject in an effort to ascertain whether he makes any significant Communist contacts.

It would appear that the former alternative is the least desirable since this office has not the personnel available to man this staff at the present time, and further, it is problematical whether suitable quarters could be rented in view of the present critical housing shortage in Minneapolis. For that reason it is my

COPIES DESTROYED

RECORDED
&
INDEXED

LA 100-18721

DETAILS:

In referenced teletype from the Bureau dated January 23, 1946, this office was requested to maintain a surveillance of Mr. FRANK OPPENHEIMER and his wife who were scheduled to arrive in Los Angeles at 1:05 P.M. that date via Western Airlines en route to Mexico City. The above teletype was received at this office subsequent to the arrival of the OPPENHEIMERS who arrived as scheduled and in view of this fact, the OPPENHEIMERS' actual arrival was not observed by Bureau Agents.

[redacted] b7D

[redacted] b7C b7D

A United States Customs search of the luggage and personal effects of the OPPENHEIMERS was conducted with negative results, however, it was noted that the OPPENHEIMER luggage contained the following books:

"Obras Completas de Miguel de Unamuno, Vol. Quatro, author Abel Sanchez, Una Historia Pasion".

"Women and Children First" by Sally Benson.

"A Practical Spanish Grammar", Seymour & Smithers.

"The Student's Dictionary, Spanish-English and English-Spanish."

"Life and Works of Abraham Lincoln, Early Speeches" Centenary Edition.

"Arc of Triumph" by Erich Maria Remarque.

"Neuro-Anatomy" by Ennis.

-2-

Letter to Director
Re: FRANK FRIEDMAN OPPENHEIMER, was.

recommendation that this office for the time being continue to cover
the activities of OPPENHEIMER by spot surveillance, through our
existing confidential coverage, and by means of informants at the
University of Minnesota who know OPPENHEIMER and who are closely
following his experimental activity in connection with nuclear energy.

It is requested that the Bureau advise whether our coverage
in this case as outlined and recommended in this letter is adequate
under existing circumstances.

Very truly yours,

M. B. RHODES
SPECIAL AGENT IN CHARGE

100-6568 SA

- 2 -

**Federal Bureau of Investigation**

**United States Department of Justice**
404 New York Building
St. Paul, Minnesota
May 9, 1947

Director, FBI                                        STRICTLY CONFIDENTIAL

ALL INFORMATION CONTAINED          RE:  FRANK FRIEDMAN OPPENHEIMER, wa
HEREIN IS UNCLASSIFIED                  Frank Folsom
DATE 6/23/87 BY SP-1AG/EW               INTERNAL SECURITY – R
                                                   ATOMIC ENERGY ACT

Dear Sir:

        Attached hereto is Form 142 recommending the installation
of a technical surveillance at the residence of the above captioned,
4454 Edmond Boulevard, Minneapolis, Minnesota, Dupont 7955.

        It will be recalled that the Bureau previously authorized
by teletype dated March 24, 1947, the installation of a telephone
and microphone surveillance on the subject at the Curtis Hotel,
Minneapolis, Minnesota. Instant surveillance was discontinued on
March 31, 1947 when the subject left the Curtis Hotel.

        Since then OPPENHEIMER has purchased a home at 4454 Edmond
Boulevard, Minneapolis, and from all indications, he intends to remain
in Minneapolis for an extended period.

        Authorization to install a technical surveillance on his
home is made at this time.

                                        Very truly yours,

                                        M. B. RHODES
                                        Special Agent in Charge

DECLASSIFIED
ON

Enc. 1

100-237235-50

RECORDED 15 MAY 17 1947

EX-70

DN 100-5279

[redacted]

The Washington Field Office advised that information received from the House Committee on Un-American Activities indicated that the subject was still under subpoena to appear but that it was possible that he would not be called. It was reported that should the House Committee on un-American Activities decide to call OPPENHEIMER, the hearing would not take place until after January 1, 1951.

[redacted], Postmaster, Pagosa Springs, Colorado, furnished the results of a mail cover of subject and the following were noted to have corresponded with OPPENHEIMER:

| | | |
|---|---|---|
| October 15, 1950 | "The Dispatch", an International Longshoreman's and Warehouseman's Union. | |
| November 5, 1950 | [redacted] | Los Angeles, California. |
| November 8, 1950 | [redacted] | Santa Fe, New Mexico. |

(Copies of report, con't)

2 - Omaha
2 - Phoenix
2 - San Francisco (65-4035)
2 - Seattle
3 - Denver

- 2 -

67C

| | |
|---|---|
| November 10, 1950 | ▨▨▨▨ U. S. Atomic Energy Commission, Post Office Box 559, Berkeley, California. |
| November 10, 1950 | ▨▨▨▨ |
| November 11, 1950 | ▨▨▨, California. New Republic, 301 N Street NE, Washington 2, D.C. |
| November 13, 1950 | American Association of University Professors, 1101 Connecticut Avenue NW, Washington 6, D.C. |
| November 13, 1950 | "A Letter from the Wifes", 1586 Crossroads of the World, Hollywood, California. (This is known to be the address of the Committee to Free the Hollywood Ten). |
| November 15, 1950 | Benedict and Benedict, 99 Johns Street, New York 7, New York. |
| November 15, 1950 | Department of Commerce, National Bureau of Standards, Washington 25, D. C. |
| November 15, 1950 | Federation of American Scientists, 1749 L Street NW, Washington, D. C. |
| November 19, 1950 | The Institution of Electrical Engineers, Savoy Place, Victoria Embankment, London, WC2. |
| November 20, 1950 | Yugoslov Information Center, 36 Central Park South, New York 19, New York. |
| November 21, 1950 | ▨▨▨ Phoenix, Arizona |
| November 21, 1950 | ▨▨▨ New York 3, New York. |
| November 26, 1950 | ▨▨▨ Ithaca, New York. |
| November 29, 1950 | ▨▨▨ Massachusetts Institute of Technology, Cambridge, Massachusetts. |
| December 3, 1950 | ▨▨▨ Seattle 5, Washington. |
| December 23, 1950 | ▨▨▨, Iowa City, Iowa. |

-P E N D I N G-

- 3 -